Personality Types

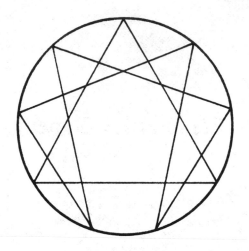

Personality Types

Using the Enneagram
for Self-Discovery

DON RICHARD RISO

Houghton Mifflin Company

Boston

Library of Congress Cataloging-in-Publication Data

Riso, Don Richard.
Personality types.

Bibliography: p.
Includes index.
1. Typology (Psychology) I. Title. II. Title: Enneagram for self-discovery.
BF698.4.R57   1987   155.2'6   87-3651
ISBN 0-395-40575-0
ISBN 0-395-53518-2 (pbk.)

Printed in the United States of America

DOH 18 17 16 15 14 13 12 11 10 9

Artwork by Mark S. Desveaux

Credits appear on pp. 357–358

This book is dedicated to those
who have made it possible.
They know who they are.
They have my love
and deepest gratitude.

I am a man: nothing human is alien to me.

—Terence

Preface

If there is one single overriding theme in my interpretation of the Enneagram, it is the need to acknowledge and understand our inner states so that we can begin to move beyond them. Self-understanding is the prelude to self-transformation, to moving beyond the ego and all that makes up what is called "false personality." Self-transcendence is the gate to every spiritual path, and the Enneagram shows each type (and therefore each of us as individuals) what that gate is, and how to pass through it. We may not ever have the courage actually to do so — but by helping us know that self-transcendence and movement toward higher states of integration is possible, and by providing us with an understanding of that higher, more fulfilling path, the Enneagram may encourage us to pursue it.

All of us are looking for answers to some of life's most difficult problems. We may well express it in different ways, but at some common human level we all are seeking a way to lead richer, more fulfilled, and graceful lives — and to help others do the same. While the Enneagram does not have all the answers, to be sure, it can help us identify how (and why) so many people often go wrong and bring unhappiness and various kinds of destructiveness on themselves and others.

The personality types of the Enneagram identify the chief features of our inner landscape — where the precipitous cliffs, arid deserts, and treacherous quicksands of the soul lie, as well as where the fertile oases, resourceful forests, and life-producing springs are within us. We are free to go to those places or not, free to fall into the many potential traps of psychic quicksand or not, free to scale the heights and move into new territory or not. Thus, understood and used properly, the Enneagram is not merely a map of our states of personality but a map that points the way toward what lies beyond us, *once we have transcended ourselves.*

Moreover, the Enneagram is an interpretation of human personality so encompassing that it takes us to the threshold of the spiritual. It is not out of place to talk about spirituality or the practice of virtue in regard to the Enneagram, since the virtues are the sources of many of the goods that we seek in our daily lives — and are the traits we find in the healthy Levels of Development of each type. The practice of virtue (which, in one form or another, is demanded by all forms of spirituality) is not only a religious issue. Learning how to be virtuous is what we (perhaps unwittingly) learn from the Enneagram so that we can lead a good life — one that is profoundly fulfilled and that allows us to make valuable contributions to the world. When we are healthy, we are being virtuous, and are moving out of ego states toward states of higher functioning and integration. To move in the Direction of Integration is to live out of our essence, as an expression of our best and truest self.

At its deepest, therefore, the Enneagram is not only profound psychology but a means to a deeper, more genuine spirituality. If you learn to transcend your ego, then you are already on a spiritual path, whether you call it that or not, because no spiritual path can be followed without self-transcendence. Thus, the Enneagram itself is not a form of spirituality but a means to spirituality of all kinds. It is psychology so profound and encompassing as to have spiritual overtones. Its insights resonate with the insights we find in many different religious traditions.

Turning evil into good, the dross of our lives into pure gold, is the most profound alchemy. Gurdjieff claimed that the Enneagram is in fact the long-sought "philosopher's stone" that catalyzes lead into gold. From our point of view, the process of turning lead into gold is what we are also concerned with here: the transformation of ourselves and our lives into something more fit for higher purposes—

although we cannot always be certain precisely what those purposes are.

In the end, however, the Enneagram is merely a tool and an intellectual system — simply a source of insight — and as such, it cannot work magic. Nevertheless, it can provide us with some of the wisdom we need to make good choices in our lives and the objectivity we need to transform ourselves. The rest, as usual, is up to us.

DON RICHARD RISO
New York City
Written for the eighth printing,
August 1989

Acknowledgments

This book did not take long to write, yet in another sense, it has been a long time in the making. It would have been impossible without the following people.

Some twelve years ago, when I started to study the Enneagram, Tad Dunne, S.J., suggested that I read the work of Karen Horney, and Bob Fecas encouraged me to continue to develop the descriptions of the healthy side of the personality types. Both suggestions have proved to be most helpful.

When I began lecturing about the Enneagram, the Reverend Richard Powers was extraordinarily generous about making lecture facilities available to me. Without the give-and-take of public presentations, I doubt that I would have been able to get the kind of confirmation of the Enneagram's validity which was useful and necessary at that time. Also helpful to me in a similar way, but in different circumstances, were Karl Laubenstein, Steve Rodgers, Priscilla Rodgers, Richard Hunt, S.J., and the members of Ruah, in Cambridge, Massachusetts.

Many of my friends have taken an interest in my work. I am grateful to them for their enthusiasm, which nurtured my fragile undertaking in those early years. The encouragement of Ruben St. Germain, Bob Cabaj, Irwin Montaldo, Robert Moore, Chuck Webb, Rose Mary

O'Boyle, and Jeff Posner has been especially important to me. I would also like to thank Hugh P. Finnegan, Ann L. MacDougall, Diana A. Steele, Erwin Mayr, and Dick Kalb for reading early drafts of the manuscript and commenting on them. Thanks also to Mark S. Desveaux for the line drawings and wonderfully realized caricatures of the personality types, and to Gene Bagnato for my photograph.

There are a number of others whose names, for entirely personal reasons, I would like to invoke here. They are Beverly Moreno Pumilia, Jeff and Gertrude Moreno, Dominick and Virginia Riso, Agnes Bazzle, Sister Thérèse of the Angels, Harry Claypool, Rob Bliss, Charles Aalto, Terri Kyller, Brent BecVar, Bruce MacClain, John Lush, Lester Wolff, Philip Stehr, Louisa and Sandy Arico, Bill and Lynette Rice, Robert Drez, Brother Brendan, S.C., as well as August Coyle, Joseph Tetlow, Edward Romagosa, Youree Watson, Daniel Creagan, Pat Byrne, and Peter Sexton — these last of the Society of Jesus.

I have a number of people to thank at Houghton Mifflin, doubtless many more than I realize. My first editor, Gerard Van der Leun, has since left Houghton. He taught me to say more by writing less. After his departure I was fortunate to be assigned to Ruth Hapgood, who has proved to be a beacon of wisdom, good cheer, and patience. I thank her especially for her forbearance in letting this book become itself. Geraldine Morse, my manuscript editor, improved the book greatly, saving me from untold error and embarrassment.

Above all, my thanks go to Austin Olney of Houghton Mifflin. Austin saw this book's potential when the manuscript was little more than a sketch. To say that he has been kind, supportive, and understanding is to say much too little. This book would not be in your hands now were it not for him.

Over the years I have received some of the best advice — and innumerable ideas and suggestions — from my agent and lawyer, Brian Lawrence Taylor, and from Patricia D. Walsh and James Peck, S.J. Their interest in my work has been more valuable to me than they know. The fact that these three people of rare intelligence also believed in the Enneagram helped sustain me in dark hours. Finally, my most profound thanks go to my family for all that they are. I wish it were possible to reveal everything that they have done for me, but I have not yet fathomed it myself. It will have to be enough to say that without their constant love, help, and understanding, this book would not exist.

Contents

PART I

Know then thyself, presume not God to scan;
The proper study of mankind is man.

—Alexander Pope, *An Essay on Man*

Chapter 1

Understanding Personality Types

WHAT IS THE POINT of understanding personality types? Since everyone is unique, the idea of cramming people into categories seems odious. And even if personality types were somehow theoretically valid, they would probably be either too academic to be helpful in our daily lives or too vague to be meaningful — grab bags anyone can read anything into.

These are valid objections, but they miss the mark. There are a number of good reasons to study personality types, the most important of which is that human beings are inherently interesting — and dangerous. Our fellow human beings compel our attention because they are easily the most changeable, infuriating, pleasurable, and mystifying objects in the environment. It would be impossible for most of us to spend a day without coming into direct or indirect contact with dozens of people — family, friends, people on the street, at the office, on television, in our fantasies, and in our fears. People are everywhere, having all sorts of impacts on us — for better or worse.

Most of the time we navigate the shoals of interpersonal life without coming to grief, but there have no doubt been times when we suddenly became aware that we did not really know the people we thought we knew. There may even have been times when we realized that we did not know ourselves. The behavior of others — and even our own behavior — is, at times, strange and unsettling. Odd things keep popping up, or seem to be out of place. Some of these surprises can be pleasant, but some are decidedly unpleasant, having calamitous effects on us far into the future. This is why, if we are too unthinking about the personality types in which human nature expresses itself, we run the risk of disaster. The person we thought we knew may turn out to be a monster or hopelessly self-centered. We may find that we have been callously used or that our legitimate needs have been selfishly ignored. Unless we have insight, we can be terribly abused. The opposite is equally true: unless we have insight, we may overlook a diamond in the rough or be too quick to get out of a relationship which is actually worth saving. Without insight, we may be hurt or foolish, and either way end in unhappiness.

Thus, becoming more perceptive is worthwhile, if only to avoid painful consequences. Understanding ourselves and others should make us happier.

The problem is, however, that while everyone wants insight into others, few people are as willing to look so intently at themselves. We want to know what makes other people tick, yet we are afraid to discover anything upsetting about ourselves. Today's competitive culture has shifted the emphasis of the ancient injunction of the oracle at Delphi from "know thyself" to "psych out the other guy." We would like to be able to figure out people as if we had X-ray vision, while not wanting others to see our weaknesses and shortcomings. We do not want anyone, including us, to see us as we really are. Unfortunately, something necessary and valuable — looking at ourselves with the same objective eye with which we view others — has been lost.

We have everything upside down. To correct this, we should remember Kierkegaard's advice. He suggested that we become subjective toward others and objective toward ourselves. That is, when we judge the actions of others, we should put ourselves in their place, trying to understand how they see themselves and their world. And when we judge ourselves, we should see ourselves as others see us, overcoming the ease with which we find extenuating circumstances for ourselves. Of course, Kierkegaard's suggestion is very difficult to put into practice. We need to cut through self-love and self-deception when we look at ourselves, as well as cynicism and defensiveness when we examine others. We must have courage toward ourselves and empathy toward others.

How can we acquire the knowledge and sensitivity we need? How can we begin to make sense of the vast diversity of human personality? How can we develop insight so that we can lead fuller, happier lives?

The answer is paradoxical: we will discover that we cannot really know anyone else until we know ourselves, and we cannot really know ourselves until we know others. The solution to this seeming conundrum is that understanding ourselves and understanding others are really two sides of the same coin — understanding human nature.

Because such a vast amount of territory is covered by human nature, it would be useful to have an accurate map of that familiar, yet ever unexplored territory. It would be helpful to have a reliable means of charting who we are and where we are going so that we will not lose our way.

I believe the Enneagram (pronounced "ANY-a-gram") is the map of human nature which people have long sought. Although the Enneagram is ancient, it is remarkably contemporary because hu-

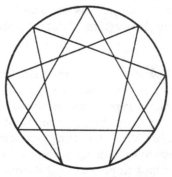

The Enneagram

man nature has not changed. The Enneagram, which has been transmitted to us from history's unknown masters of wisdom, represents a profound understanding of human nature, something needed as much now as it was in the past. It has been kept alive because it works. The Enneagram would not have been preserved in the oral tradition of the East if people had not felt that it was truly worth preserving. The purpose of this book is to introduce the general reader to this remarkable system.

Psychology has been wrestling with the problem of discovering a workable personality typology (a way of classifying human nature) which is accurate and practical, theoretically comprehensive and elegant. Beginning at least with Hippocrates in the fifth century B.C., Greek philosophers recognized that personality types exist in some form or other. However, no one has been able to discover the *fundamental* categories which human nature assumes, the basic personality types themselves.

Different classifications have been proposed over the centuries, although none has been without problems, inaccuracies, or contradictions. Many typologies do not do justice to the great variety of human nature — they employ too few categories, they are too abstract, or they concern themselves only with different kinds of neurosis and not with normal behavior. Not only has discovering the individual personality types been an enormous conceptual problem, it has been even more difficult to discover a system which indicates how the types are related to each other, thereby revealing how people change and grow. Finding a personality typology which truly does justice to human nature was an unsolved problem — until the discovery of the Enneagram. That is the argument of this book.

Every psychological system has an organizing principle. If we look briefly at some other systems, we see, for example, that Freud's three different character types emphasize the belief that psychic energy is fixated during early child development around the mouth, the anus, or the phallus. These fixations yield oral, anal, and phallic types, which correspond to Enneagram types. Another Freudian approach to character types emphasizes the dominance of the ego, the id, or the superego in the personality. The latter is a more sophisticated application of Freud's concepts, one which theorists have found difficult to apply, although it also correlates with the Enneagram, as we shall see.

Jung's typology delineates eight types based on how a person's psychological *attitude*, extroversion or introversion, is modified by one of four basic mental *functions* which Jung posits — feeling, thinking, sensation, or intuition. Thus, Jung describes an extroverted feeling type and an introverted feeling type, an extroverted thinking type and an introverted thinking type, and so on.

Karen Horney developed character descriptions based on her clinical observations of interpersonal orientations — that a person could be considered as fundamentally "moving toward others," "moving away from others," or "moving against others." She did not work out all the subtypes within these three general categories, but had she done so, her system probably would have yielded nine personality types, just as the Enneagram does. (There will be more about Freud, Jung, and Horney in the Theory chapter, particularly about the correspondence of their typologies to the Enneagram personality types.)

The organizing principle of the Enneagram is simple: nine personality types result from three personality types in each of three groups, or Triads. The Enneagram's three Triads specify whether your fundamental psychological orientation, which includes positive and negative traits, has to do with your emotions (if so, you are in the *Feeling* Triad) or with your ability to act (if so, you are in the *Doing* Triad) or with how you relate to the world (if so, you are in the *Relating* Triad).

We can characterize the resulting nine personality types very simply for now; they will become more sophisticated later on. In the Feeling Triad, the types are the *Helper* (the Two — the encouraging, possessive, manipulative type), the *Status Seeker* (the Three — the ambitious, pragmatic, narcissistic type), and the *Artist* (the Four — the sensitive, introverted, depressive type). In the Doing Triad, we see the *Thinker* (the Five — the perceptive, analytic, reductionistic type), the *Loyalist* (the Six — the committed, dutiful, passive-aggressive type), and the *Generalist* (the Seven — the sophisticated, hyperactive, excessive type). And in the Relating Triad, we find the *Leader* (the Eight — the self-confident, aggressive, confrontational type), the *Peacemaker* (the Nine — the receptive, easygoing, complacent type), and the *Reformer* (the One — the rational, orderly, perfectionistic type).

You may be able to find your own personality type from these brief designations. If not, do not worry. You will learn how to identify your personality type, or that of someone else, in the Guidelines chapter. Since there is a full chapter about each of the nine basic personality types, there is much more to become acquainted with. (To get a quick idea of any of the personality types, turn to the Caricature and Profile at the beginning of each description. The Profile lists many of the major traits of each type.) There will also be more about the three Triads of the Enneagram and how they produce the nine basic personality types, and many personality subtypes, in the Guidelines, and even more about them in the Advanced Guidelines.

As you might expect, how the Enneagram works is complicated and subtle. Considering your personality type as the result of one of the fundamental orientations (feeling, doing, or relating) is but one possible level of analysis with the Enneagram. By the end of this book you will see that we can approach the nine personality types from Freudian, Jungian, Hornevian, or other viewpoints because the Enneagram operates on different levels of abstraction simultaneously. It bridges the gap between approaches to personality which emphasize depth psychology and those which emphasize behavior. The insights we can obtain from the Enneagram range from the most abstract generalizations about human nature to highly specific descriptions of each personality type. And yet, as complex as the Enneagram is, paradoxically, it is easy to understand.

Furthermore, while the nine personality types of the Enneagram form discrete categories, you should not think of them as iron-clad entities. You will find that the Enneagram is open-ended and extraordinarily fluid, like human beings themselves. Movement and change — development toward either integration or disintegration — are essential aspects of this remarkable system. And because the Enneagram's descriptions of the personality types range from the highest levels of health and integration to the lowest stages of neurosis, they not only describe behavior, but predict it as well —something which can be extremely useful.

Because an introductory book should be relatively simple, it is not possible to present all the complexities of the Enneagram here.

Many of the most advanced, theoretical aspects of the Enneagram have either been omitted or touched on only briefly.

I have also omitted specific suggestions about how you can use each of the personality descriptions themselves. Even so, interested readers will be able to apply the descriptions to many different situations in their lives. For example, psychologists and psychiatrists will be able to diagnose the problems of their clients more accurately, and patients will be able to save time and money in therapy by gaining insight into themselves more quickly. The Enneagram will also give patients and therapists a common language with which to discuss their problems and their progress, no matter which school of psychotherapy they adhere to.

Lawyers will be better able to understand clients, as well as assess their credibility and their capacity to cooperate in legal matters. The Enneagram will help them particularly in situations such as divorce and child custody cases where personality factors are important. Physicians will have more insight with which to counsel their patients, particularly those whose physical ailments are compounded by psychological problems. Clergymen can be more psychologically attuned to others in pastoral work. While this book does not deal with spiritual direction as such, there are common areas between the psychological and the spiritual, since both build upon the whole person. Teachers can become more perceptive of their students. Different personality types have different natural aptitudes, different approaches to learning, and different ways of interacting with other students.

Personnel directors and businessmen can become better managers by being more aware of their employees' personality types. Job satisfaction and productivity increase when employees feel that management understands their personal needs and takes them into consideration. Hiring officers and those in charge of building effective teams for all purposes — from the boardroom to the assembly line — will find it valuable to have greater insight into the personality types of the individuals they consider. Understanding personality types can also be useful to journalists, politicians, and those in advertising. In short, understanding personality types is useful to anyone who has a personality (and who does not?) or who is interested in the personalities of others (and who is not?).

Despite its many practical applications, this is really a book which has been written for you, the individual, to use in your personal life.

However, I should say that this is not a typical self-help book: it does not promise miracles. It is not possible to write a psychological "cookbook" for becoming a healthy, fulfilled individual. Becoming a whole human being is, by definition, an ideal toward which we strive, a process which goes on as long as we live. Books can provide valuable information and advice, they can give us new insights, they can encourage. But knowledge alone is not enough to change us. If it were, the most knowledgeable people would be the best people, and we know from our own experience that this is not so. Knowledge would be virtue, and it is not. Knowing more about ourselves is but a means toward the goal of being happy and leading a good life, but the possession of knowledge alone cannot bestow virtue, happiness, or fulfillment on us. Books cannot provide answers to all the problems which confront us or impart the courage necessary if we are to persevere in our search. For these things, we must look both within and beyond ourselves.

Furthermore, this book is not, and cannot be, the last word on either the Enneagram or personality types. There will always be more to be said, new connections to be made, and new understandings to be reached. Perhaps the mysteries of the psyche can never be fully described because they may never be fully understood. How can human beings stand outside of themselves to study human nature in a totally objective way? How can we ever be completely subjective toward others and objective toward ourselves, as Kierkegaard suggests? Psychologists who try to describe human nature are themselves human beings subject to all the distortions and self-deceptions of which humans are capable. No one has a "God's-eye view" of the whole of human nature, so no one can say with absolute confidence what it all means. This is why there will always be an element of faith to psychology, not necessarily religious faith, to be sure, but a set of beliefs about human beings which go beyond what can be demonstrated scientifically.

This is why attaining some kind of final, objective truth about ourselves is probably impossible. What may be more important than arriving at ultimate answers is being searchers on the quest. Through the process of honestly seeking the truth about ourselves, we gradually transform ourselves from who we are into who we can be — into persons who are fuller, more life-affirming, and self-transcending.

Chapter 2

Origins

ONE OF THE MAIN PROBLEMS with introducing the Enneagram is that its exact origins are lost to history. No one really knows precisely who discovered it or where it came from. Some writers maintain that the Enneagram first surfaced among certain orders of the Sufis, a mystical sect of Islam which began in the tenth and eleventh centuries; others speculate that it may have originated as long ago as 2500 B.C. in Babylon or elsewhere in the Middle East. But these are mere speculations.

It seems that men have always been in search of the secret of perpetual self-renewal. We find it in one of the oldest legends preserved by man: in the story of Gilgamesh the Sumerian hero and his pilgrimage in search of the secret of immortality. At about the time that the Gilgamesh epic was compiled from earlier song, some 4,500 years ago, there arose in Mesopotamia a brotherhood of wise men who discovered the cosmic secret of perpetual self-renewal and passed it down from generation to generation. For a long time it was preserved in Babylon: 2,500 years ago it was revealed to Zoroaster, Pythagoras and other great sages who congregated in Babylon at the time of Cambyses (the Persian king who conquered Egypt in 524 B.C.). Then the custodians of the

tradition migrated northward and about a thousand years ago
reached Bokhara [in what is now Uzbekistan in the USSR] across
the river Oxus.

In the fifteenth century, [Islamic] mathematicians trained in
their schools discovered the significance of the number zero and
created the decimal system which all the world now uses. It was
observed at the time that a new kind of number appeared when
one was divided by three or seven. This we now call a recurring
decimal. . . .

These properties were combined in a symbol that proved to
have amazing significance. It could be used to represent every
process that maintains itself by self-renewal, including of course,
life itself. The symbol consists of nine lines and is therefore called
the Enneagram. (J. G. Bennett, *Enneagram Studies*, 1–3.)*

Ennea is the Greek word for nine, and so *Enneagram* is a Greek
word roughly meaning "a nine diagram." A plausible conjecture
about its origins is that the Enneagram is based on ancient mathematical discoveries — Pythagorean and Neoplatonic, or earlier —
and was passed on to the West with other Greek and Arabic learning during the fourteenth or fifteenth centuries by the Moslems. It
is said to have been used at this time by the Islamic mystics, the
Sufis, particularly by the Naqshbandi Brotherhood. If the Enneagram
did not appear in its present form when the Sufis came across it,
they may have developed it according to discoveries in Arabic
mathematics and used it to advance self-knowledge for individuals
within their secret brotherhoods and as a way of establishing harmony in society at large.

I concluded . . . that this symbol and the ideas for which it stands,
originated with the Sarmān [or "Sarmoun" Brotherhood, a wisdom school reputedly in Babylon] society about 2,500 years ago
and was revised when the power of the Arabic numeral system
was developed in Samarkand in the fifteenth century. . . .

There are endless possibilities of interpretation of this remarkable symbol. The simplest is given by numbering the points on
the circumference from 1–9 which gives the triangle numbers 3,
6, and 9, and the hexagon 1–4–2–8–5–7 which is the well-known
recurrent sequence that gives the remainder when any integer is
divided by seven. This property arises only in a decimal number

* Citations for this and all other quotations are given in the Bibliography.

system, which suggests that it was discovered only after the mathematicians of Central Asia had founded the modern theory of numbers by giving zero a separate symbol. Whereas the belief that the number seven is sacred probably goes back to Sumerian times, the form of the enneagram is likely to have been developed in Samarkand in the fourteenth century [*sic*]. This would account for its absence from Indian or European literature. However, Gurdjieff asserted that it was far more ancient and attributed it to the Sarmān Brotherhood. Both versions may be true. (J. G. Bennett, *Gurdjieff: Making a New World,* 293–294.)

No matter how or where it was used by the secret brotherhoods of the Sufis, the Enneagram was totally unknown in the West until quite recently. The credit for transmitting the Enneagram goes to George Ivanovitch Gurdjieff (ca 1877–1949), an adventurer, spiritual teacher, and seeker of what might be called practical secret knowledge about human nature. Despite the many books written about his life and the many investigations into the sources of his teachings, Gurdjieff still remains an enigma: some people think that he was little more than a charlatan, while others feel that his importance as a spiritual guide and practical psychologist has been vastly underrated. It is difficult to get to the truth of these opposing opinions, since Gurdjieff was secretive about his activities, purposely cultivating a charismatic and mysterious aura about himself. What is undoubtedly true, however, is that he had a profound impact on everyone who met him. His disciples have been debating about him and the meaning of his vast, complex system of thought since he died.

Although Gurdjieff was unclear about how and where he discovered the Enneagram, it was nevertheless through his transmission that the Enneagram became known in Europe in the 1920s, first at his school outside Paris near Fontainebleau, The Institute for the Harmonious Development of Man. The Enneagram was subsequently transmitted, along with the rest of Gurdjieff's teachings, through small private study groups in London, New York, and around the world.

In his authoritative book *The Harmonious Circle,* about Gurdjieff and his immediate group of disciples, James Webb attempts to sort out the facts of the Enneagram's history.

The most important use which Gurdjieff made of number symbolism is the figure of the enneagram, which he said contained and symbolized his whole System. His enneagram consists of a circle with the circumference divided into nine points which are joined to give a triangle and an irregular six-sided figure. Gurdjieff said that the triangle represented the presence of higher forces and that the six-sided figure stood for man. He also claimed that the enneagram was exclusive to his teaching. "This symbol cannot be met with anywhere in the study of 'occultism,' either in books or in oral transmission," [P.D.] Ouspensky reports him as saying. "It was given such significance by those who knew [i.e., by his Sufi teachers], that they considered it necessary to keep the knowledge of it secret." . . .

Because of the emphasis which Gurdjieff placed on this diagram, his followers have sought high and low for the symbol in occult literature. [J.G.] Bennett claims that it cannot be found anywhere; and if disciples of Gurdjieff have in fact discovered the figure, they have kept it very quiet.* (Webb, 505.)

Gurdjieff perhaps was purposely unclear about the origins of the Enneagram because one of his teaching methods was to make everything difficult for his students so they would discover as much as possible on their own. Whatever the truth of the matter, as Webb continues to examine the Enneagram's historical sources, he makes an interesting discovery.

The enneagram forms the center of the magnificent frontispiece to the *Arithmologia* published in Rome by the Jesuit priest, Athanasius Kircher, in 1665. Kircher (1601–80) is a figure of great significance for the origins of Gurdjieff's ideas. He was typical of

---

* This is not the place for a lengthy bibliography on Gurdjieff or his work; the interested reader will have no problem finding information about him. For a full and critical account of Gurdjieff, see Webb, *The Harmonious Circle*. Also see Kathleen Riordan Speeth, *The Gurdjieff Work*, 9, for the Sufi origins of the Enneagram among the Naqshbandi Brotherhood; Speeth and Friedlander, *Gurdjieff, Seeker of the Truth*, for an informative account of Gurdjieff's travels in the Near East in search of wisdom; P. D. Ouspensky, *In Search of the Miraculous*, 286–290; and Maurice Nicoll, *Psychological Commentaries on the Teaching of Gurdjieff and Ouspensky*, vol. II, 379 ff., for more on the Enneagram, its structure, and particularly the esoteric meaning of the numerical sequence 1–4–2–8–5–7–1, and related matters. For an attempt at applying the Enneagram to topics other than personality, see Bennett, *Enneagram Studies*. Those interested in a strictly Gurdjieffian viewpoint will find this book of interest.

the Renaissance man of learning and a prototype of the scholarly Jesuit of later days. . . .
In the *Arithmologia*, there is a figure called an "enneagram" composed of three equilateral triangles. (Webb, *The Harmonious Circle*, 505–7.)

Although Webb calls Kircher's figure an "enneagram," it is important to note that it is comprised of three equilateral triangles and is not Gurdjieff's single equilateral triangle with an inner hexagon. This makes a crucial difference, but having noted the difference, Webb glosses over its significance.

Webb continues with a discussion of the Cabala and the occultist Ramon Lull, then moves on to a discussion of esoteric Christianity, esoteric Buddhism, the occult revival of the nineteenth century in Europe and Russia, including Rosicrucianism, and to other movements, all of which Webb speculates, and in some instances is able to show, had various degrees of influence on Gurdjieff. But at the end of this lengthy discussion, which is certainly beyond the scope of this book even to condense, Webb seems to have lost sight of his attempt to explain the origins of the Enneagram in Gurdjieff's thought and has gone on to other matters. In the end, then, the answer to the Enneagram's historical origins remains a mystery.

And, in any event, investigating Gurdjieff's sources for the Enneagram, while historically interesting, is something of a digression since Gurdjieff's delineation of the three "different kinds of men" is quite different from my descriptions of the nine personality types. I have seen little to suggest that Gurdjieff ever developed descriptions of the nine personality types. (Seminal descriptions of these have come from Oscar Ichazo, Claudio Naranjo, and the Jesuits, as we will see shortly.) Thus, while we must credit Gurdjieff with first making the Enneagram known in the West, saying anything more about his particular interpretation of it here would take us very far afield.*

The delineation of the nine personality types presented in this book derives in part from work done on the Enneagram by Oscar Ichazo, the founder of the Arica Institute. While Ichazo agrees with Gurdjieff

---

* For more about Gurdjieff's interpretation of personality types, see Webb, *The Harmonious Circle*, 139 ff., and Speeth, *The Gurdjieff Work*, 31 ff.

that the Enneagram is ancient, he maintains that he learned it from Sufi teachers in the Pamir in Afghanistan, who taught him their secrets before he became acquainted with Gurdjieff's writings.*

Ichazo first began teaching the Enneagram at the Institute for Applied Psychology in La Paz, Bolivia, as part of his larger system of human development and later, in the 1960s, taught in Arica, Chile. Ichazo came to the United States in 1971, founded the Arica Institute, and continued teaching. According to its brochure, the Arica Institute "teaches a science of human development which systematically develops the full potential of a human being. It synthesizes Eastern mysticism and Western psychological traditions to present a body of theory and method precisely designed to deal with the realities and stresses of our technological society." Among those who first learned Ichazo's system were Americans from the Esalen Institute in Big Sur, California, including John Lilly, M.D., and psychiatrist Claudio Naranjo, M.D.†

The interpretation of the Enneagram I present here diverges from Ichazo's approach on a number of important points, particularly in my attempt to make the "ego fixations" (as Ichazo calls the personality types) more comprehensive and useful, as well as to bring the personality types into clearer coherence with modern psychology.

In fact, Ichazo's approach to the Enneagram and mine are really quite different. Ichazo's interpretation of the Enneagram includes material on the ego fixations, the "traps" of each ego fixation, the "holy ideas," the passions and virtues, the centers of the body (the Path, Oth, and Kath — roughly equivalent to the head, heart, and belly, respectively), the physical organs and systems of the body as they relate to attaining enlightenment, the "mentations" (symbolic ways of thinking about the body), astrological signs, mantras, and

---

* For more about Ichazo's approach to the Enneagram, see Sam Keen, "We have no desire to strengthen the ego or make it happy," in *Interviews with Oscar Ichazo*, 8 ff.; Dorothy De Christopher, "I am the root of a new tradition," in *Interviews with Oscar Ichazo*, 144 ff.; John C. Lilly and Joseph E. Hart, "The Arica Training," in *Transpersonal Psychologies*, 333 ff. This article is highly recommended to anyone who is interested in Ichazo's interpretation of the Enneagram.

† See John Lilly, *The Center of the Cyclone*, 126 ff., for a description of his encounter with Ichazo.

much more, which I do not go into. Those who wish to do so can find Arica groups in most large North American cities.

It is an interesting historical coincidence that Athanasius Kircher, to whom James Webb credits great influence on Gurdjieff, was a Jesuit — and that the development of the Enneagram and its transmission to thousands of people has largely been the work of Jesuits.

In the early 1970s, several American Jesuit priests — most notably the Reverend Robert Ochs — learned the material from Claudio Naranjo at the Esalen Institute. Shortly thereafter, the Jesuits began to adapt the Enneagram to their counseling needs for the seminarians and laymen with whom they came into contact. Before the Jesuits became involved with the Enneagram, as far as I can tell, the descriptions of the nine personality types were transmitted orally, from teacher to student. It was only in 1972–1973 that the first brief notes on the personality types were written down and passed around in informal seminars at Jesuit theological centers, particularly those at the University of California at Berkeley and Loyola University, Chicago.

When I encountered the Enneagram in 1974 in Toronto, Canada, the core of the "Jesuit material" consisted of nine one-page impressionistic sketches of the personality types. These pages contained the seeds of this book.

At first I was skeptical about what I saw of the Enneagram. Like most newcomers, I especially disliked being pigeonholed by others who — rather too quickly for my taste — assigned one of the "Sufi numbers" to me. At the time I was a Jesuit seminarian studying theology at the University of Toronto, and the other Jesuits with whom I lived referred to the Enneagram personality types as the Sufi numbers rather than to personality types One, Two, Three, and so forth. They used the Enneagram to get a quick fix on each other, much as they might have used astrological signs had they been inclined to that ancient typology.

My first impression was that the Enneagram, like much that was coming out of California in the seventies, was a fad, and I resisted becoming involved with it. But as I listened to people talk about the Sufi numbers, I began to be intrigued; soon I was able to see beyond the glib use of the system to the genuine insights it contained.

My "conversion" to the Enneagram came suddenly. In the winter of 1974, I woke up one morning before dawn and, for no particular reason, reached for the looseleaf binder in which I had collected information on the Enneagram from other Jesuits. Back under the blankets, I began to read in earnest, concentrating for the first time on the nine impressionistic sketches of the personality types. I was soon able to spot my own type among them, and before long I began to gain some insights into the personalities of the other seminarians, my family, and friends. When I finally got out of bed a couple of hours later, I realized that there was more to this system than I had thought, and I wanted to know more about it.

Even though many of the details of the Enneagram as a psychological system had not been worked out, I was still able to intuit the essential correctness of the personality types. The Enneagram seemed to categorize people in a way which made sense. For the first time in my life, I could see that there actually are "personality types" — that while people are unique, they also belong to a larger class of which they are particular examples, like different kinds of primates in the animal kingdom. I felt that I no longer was at the mercy of the unknown: it was possible for me to see more deeply into people by understanding which personality type an individual belongs to. This was a revelation.

I was not alone in my enthusiasm for the Enneagram. As more people became acquainted with it, interest in the Enneagram grew. Some Jesuits taught it to their friends and acquaintances informally, while others began to include presentations of the Enneagram on the roster of offerings at retreat houses. Awareness of the Enneagram quickly began to spread beyond Jesuits to other religious and nonreligious circles throughout the United States, Canada, and Europe, particularly among New Age, human potential groups. Nevertheless, what was still lacking was a clear conception of how the Enneagram worked, as well as an accurate description of the personality types themselves.

Since the Enneagram seemed to be valid, I thought that it must be consistent with the findings of modern psychology, because both were trying to describe the same thing — human beings. After using the Enneagram in my personal life for about two years, I was sufficiently convinced of its validity and usefulness to attempt to interpret it according to modern psychology.

I soon found that correlating the Jesuit Sufi numbers to psychology would be difficult for a number of reasons. As you have seen, the development and transmission of the Enneagram has been a long and mysterious affair. There was no one source or tradition to consult. Indeed, it became clear to me that the three main traditions of transmission of the Enneagram — Gurdjieff, Ichazo, and the Jesuits — were quite different. Furthermore, when I began to work on the Enneagram in 1975, very little had been written about it, a fact which is almost as true today as it was then.

A diagram of the lines of transmission which we have seen so far may help to clarify the history of the Enneagram.

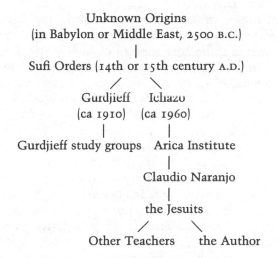

Unknown Origins
(in Babylon or Middle East, 2500 B.C.)
|
Sufi Orders (14th or 15th century A.D.)
/ \
Gurdjieff   Ichazo
(ca 1910)   (ca 1960)
| |
Gurdjieff study groups   Arica Institute
|
Claudio Naranjo
|
the Jesuits
/ \
Other Teachers   the Author

The Transmission of the Enneagram

Finding material on the Enneagram was not the only difficulty. As different teachers presented the material, they usually added something of their own as they passed it on to their students. Students in turn frequently became teachers of the Enneagram, and they also added their insights. For better or worse, the material was constantly changing, and many different interpretations began to emerge, even within the Jesuit stream of transmission.

While some of these additions represented an advance in understanding the personality types, others did not. For example, some teachers specify certain colors and animals to symbolize each of the personality types, an approach which may be poetically allusive were it not for the fact that other teachers change the colors and animals arbitrarily. More important, different interpretations flatly contradict each other about basics, such as the Directions of Integration and Disintegration, and, most important of all, some teachers misattribute traits from one personality type to another. The result is that much of what is being taught about the Enneagram is garbled: it still rings true, but not quite enough to be very useful to people in their daily lives.

As if all these problems were not enough, the traditional Enneagram materials also tended to be negative, focusing almost exclusively on the unhealthy aspects of each personality type. Of course, understanding our unhealthy tendencies is extremely helpful because what is negative about us causes more problems for us and others than what is positive. But I soon realized that if the Enneagram were to become valuable to people, it should not be so negative and depressing. The personality types would have to describe the whole person, not just neurotics.

I therefore decided to try to develop the healthy and average traits for each personality type. I did not realize what a monumental task I had set for myself. Indeed, the bulk of my work over the years has involved discovering and sorting out the hundreds, perhaps thousands, of traits which characterize the personality types, and then discovering how those traits fit within each type to produce a unified whole. Relying on the psychological principle that neuroses grow out of distortions and conflicts in *normal* modes of behavior, I eventually discovered how the healthy, average, and unhealthy traits form *a continuum of traits* for each type. (There will be more about the Continuum in the next chapter, which gives guidelines to the basic theory of the Enneagram.)

In short, I have retained the essence of the Enneagram — its delineation of the nine personality types — while remaining skeptical of the many garbled interpretations and misattributions which have accumulated around it. I have also eliminated the esoteric elements which were originally part of the traditional teaching, along with whatever interpretations seemed to be neither useful nor accurate.

What did not make sense or what was not helpful has not been retained. Even so, the more I cleared away the accretions surrounding the Enneagram, the more obvious it was that this typology deserved to be more widely known and used.

Finally, there is, at present, no scientific proof for the nine personality types. I have not done any formal research on them other than to use my own observation, intuition, and reading from the last twelve years. It has been said that psychology is as much an art as it is a science, and my interests lie more on the humanistic side of the truth of psychology than in its scientific proof.

Moreover, each body of knowledge has its own kind of proof. The proof of the truth of a proposition about art is certainly different from that of a proposition about history, just as history's proof is different from that of physics and the other hard sciences. It seems to me that the proof of the Enneagram's accuracy lies not so much in empirical validation, although I am sure it can withstand scientific scrutiny, as in its ability to describe people in a way which deepens their understanding of themselves and others. In the last analysis, either the descriptions of the personality types in this book have the ring of truth about them or they do not; either the Enneagram makes sense in your own experience, or it does not. Those who take the time will find themselves in these pages. You will experience a shock of recognition when you discover your own personality type — the most important proof of the Enneagram's accuracy there is.

Some rather good advice comes from Gurdjieff about all esoteric systems. It also applies to a good deal of psychology — and, of course, to the Enneagram.

The fact of the matter is that in occult literature much that has been said is superfluous and untrue. You had better forget all this. All your researches in this area were a good exercise for your mind; therein lies their great value, but only there. They have not given you knowledge. . . . Judge everything from the point of view of your common sense. Become the possessor of your own sound ideas and don't accept anything on faith; and when you, your self, by way of sound reasoning and argument, come to an unshakable persuasion, to a full understanding of something, you will have achieved a certain degree of initiation. (Quoted in Webb, *The Harmonious Circle*, 500.)

It is worthwhile applying Gurdjieff's advice to this book: "Become the possessor of your own sound ideas and don't accept anything on faith." If the Enneagram is to have value in your life, it will be because *you* have worked through it and made it a part of yourself. If you find yourself in these pages — if these descriptions ring true in your own experience — then the effort which has gone into them will have been worthwhile.

Chapter 3

Guidelines

IT IS NECESSARY to know merely a handful of concepts to understand how the Enneagram works. Because many distinctions are required to describe personality types, however, the theory of the Enneagram is ultimately subtle and complex. This chapter is not concerned with all the nuances of the Enneagram; instead, it will introduce you to the practical points you must know to read the descriptions.

The explanations in this chapter have purposely been kept as simple as possible. They will introduce you to the more complex ideas which will be discussed at the end of the book in Chapters 13 and 14, Advanced Guidelines and The Theory of the Enneagram.

THE STRUCTURE OF THE ENNEAGRAM

Although the Enneagram may look confusing at first glance, its structure is actually simple. There are nine equidistant points on the circumference of the circle. Each point is designated by a number from one to nine, with nine at the top, by convention and for symmetry. Each point represents one of the nine basic personality types. They are interrelated with each other in certain specific ways, as indicated by the inner lines of the Enneagram. It will help you to understand how the Enneagram is constructed if you sketch it yourself.

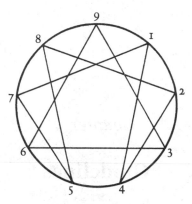

The Enneagram

Note that points Three, Six, and Nine form an equilateral triangle. The remaining six points are connected in the following order: One connects with Four, Four with Two, Two with Eight, Eight with Five, Five with Seven, and Seven with One. These six points form an irregular hexagram. I will discuss the meaning of these sequences of numbers shortly.

THE TRIADS

On the simplest level of analysis, the Enneagram is an arrangement of nine personality types *in three Triads.* There are three personality types in the *Feeling Triad,* three in the *Doing Triad,* and three in the *Relating Triad,* as shown below. Each Triad consists of three personality types which are best characterized by the assets and liabilities of that Triad. For example, personality type Two has particular strengths and liabilities involving its feelings, which is why it is one of the three types in the Feeling Triad. The Seven's

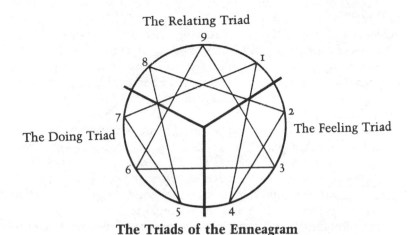

The Triads of the Enneagram

assets and liabilities involve doing, which is why it is in the Doing Triad, and so forth for all nine personality types.

The three personality types of each Triad are not arbitrary. Each type results from a "dialectic" consisting of a thesis, antithesis, and synthesis of the psychological faculty characterizing that Triad. In each Triad, one of the types overdevelops the characteristic faculty of the Triad, another type underdevelops the faculty, and the third is most out of touch with the faculty. These relationships are depicted in the illustration below.

9 Most out of touch with relating

8 Overdeveloped relating	1 Underdeveloped relating
7 Overdeveloped doing	2 Overdeveloped feeling
6 Most out of touch with doing	3 Most out of touch with feeling
5 Underdeveloped doing	4 Underdeveloped feeling

The Dialectical Structure of the Triads

By going around the Enneagram Triad by Triad, you will see what this means. For example, in the Feeling Triad, the Two has overdeveloped its feelings, expressing only its positive emotions while repressing its negative ones. The Three is most out of touch with its feelings, projecting an image which substitutes for genuine feelings. The Four has underdeveloped the personal expression of its feelings, revealing itself indirectly through some form of art or aesthetic living.

In the Doing Triad, the Five's ability to do is underdeveloped: it substitutes thinking for doing, endlessly going around in ever more complex, yet isolated, thoughts. The Six is most out of touch with its ability to act on its own without the approval of an authority figure of some sort. And the Seven has overdeveloped its ability to act, becoming hyperactive and manic until it flies out of control.

In the Relating Triad, the Eight has overdeveloped its ability to relate to the environment, seeing itself as bigger than everyone else. The Nine is most out of touch with its ability to relate to the environment as an individual since it identifies with another, living through someone else rather than becoming independent. And the One has underdeveloped its ability to relate to the environment in the sense that it feels less than an ideal which it constantly strives to attain.

I refer to the three types on the equilateral triangle — the Three, Six, and Nine — as the "primary" personality types because they have the most trouble and are the most blocked in some way with feeling, doing, or relating. The remaining six personality types — the One, Four, Two, Eight, Five, and Seven on the hexagram — are the "secondary" types because they are more mixed and not as out of touch with feeling, doing, or relating. In the Advanced Guidelines we will see more of what this means and why making this distinction is important.

No matter which Triad the basic personality type is in, everyone has the ability to feel, do, and relate to the environment. We become one of the nine personality types because our psychological development, beginning in childhood, has emphasized one faculty over the remaining two. But this does not mean that the remaining two faculties are not also a part of us. They are, and we are who we are because all three faculties operate in an ever changing balance to produce our personality.

Focusing on your basic personality type within its Triad is but the first place to begin the process of self-understanding. Many other factors are also part of the picture, however, because the Enneagram is, at its most abstract, a universal symbol — a symbol of each of us.

THE BASIC PERSONALITY TYPE

The simplest way to think of the Enneagram is as a configuration of nine distinct personality types, with each number on the Enneagram denoting one type. Everyone has emerged from his or her childhood as a unique member of *one* of the personality types, and his or her psychological potentials have either developed or deteriorated from that starting point.

The personality types, and their relationships with each other, can be represented schematically. One of the nine points on the circumference of the Enneagram denotes a particular personality type which characterizes you more accurately than any other type. This is your *basic personality type*, which you will be able to identify shortly.

It is commonly accepted by psychologists that personality is largely the result of the relationship a child has with its parents or other significant persons. By the time the child is four or five years old, its consciousness has developed enough for it to have a separate sense of self. Although its identity is still very fluid, a child at this age is beginning to establish itself and find ways of fitting into the world on its own. Doubtless, there are genetic factors which predispose a child to have (practically from birth) a certain temperament, as the physical basis of personality is called. However, science has not been able to say precisely what genetics are involved, and in any event, each basic personality type of the Enneagram represents the overall way in which the child has consciously and unconsciously adapted itself to its family and the world. In short, which basic personality type a person has represents the total outcome of all childhood factors that have gone into the formation of the child's personality, including genetics. Since there is more about the childhood origins of each personality type in the descriptions and in the Theory, I will not go into any detail about them here.

However, several more points should be made about the basic personality type itself. First, people do not change from one basic personality type to another. Each person is a unique individual within that larger group and, in the last analysis, remains that type for the rest of his or her life. In reality, people do change in many ways throughout their lives, but their basic personality type does not change.

Second, the descriptions of the personality types are universal and apply equally to males and females, since no type is inherently masculine or feminine. Questions about sexual roles and purely biologically based sexual differences are important, but they are beyond the scope of this book. In any event, much of what we associate with masculinity or femininity results from cultural expectations and learned behaviors which are not inherent in human nature.

Third, not everything in the description of your basic type will apply to you all the time. This is because people fluctuate among the healthy, average, and unhealthy traits that make up their personality type. For example, if you are fundamentally healthy, the unhealthy traits will not be applicable, and vice versa. However, as you get to know yourself more objectively, you will recognize that all the traits of your personality type are genuine tendencies inherent in yourself. If you were to become healthy or unhealthy, you would do so in the way the Enneagram predicts.

Fourth, as we have seen, the Enneagram uses *numbers* to designate each of the personality types. There are several things to understand about the use of numbers. The principal reason for their use is that they are indeterminate. Because they are value neutral, they imply the whole range of traits for each type without indicating anything either positive or negative about it. Using numbers is an unbiased, shorthand way of indicating a lot about a person. Unlike the labels used in psychiatry, numbers are helpful without being pejorative.

In psychiatric terminology, for example, personality types are always designated by their pathological characteristics: the obsessive type, the depressive type, the psychopathic type, the antisocial type, and so forth. While the Enneagram encompasses the pathological aspects of each personality type, it also indicates the healthy and average traits — and it is clearly not appropriate to use pathological labels for average or healthy people. Furthermore, it is more encouraging to think of yourself as a Five, for instance, rather than as a paranoid type, or as a Seven rather than as a manic-depressive type, and so on, especially if you are normal and not neurotic. In short, because the Enneagram comprehends more than the standard psychiatric designations, it is appropriate that its categories be as neutral and unbiased as possible. The use of numbers fulfills this function.

The last point to make about numbers is that the numerical ranking of the personality types is not significant. A larger number is no better than a smaller number; it is not better to be a Nine than a Two because nine is a bigger number.

Fifth, no personality type is inherently better or worse than any other. Each type has its particular strengths and weaknesses, and it is extremely useful to know what they are. While all the personality types have assets and liabilities, some types are usually more desirable than others in any given culture or group. You may not be pleased with your personality type; you may feel that your type is handicapped in some way which dissatisfies you. However, as you learn more about all the personality types, you will discover that each is limited in particular ways, and each has its unique capacities. If some personality types are more highly esteemed in modern Western society than others, it is because of the qualities the society rewards, not because of any superior value of those types.

For example, the aggressive, self-assured, extroverted types are highly valued in our competitive, materialistic, success-oriented society, while the introverted, person-oriented, easygoing types tend to be regarded as second-class citizens. If you feel that your personality type is in the latter group, remember that the more socially desirable types also have limitations, while the types that receive fewer social rewards have assets which make them valuable, too. The ideal is to become *your best self*, not to envy the strengths and potentials of others.

IDENTIFYING YOUR BASIC PERSONALITY TYPE

Applying these concepts to yourself will make them more concrete. Which of the following nine roles fits you best most of the time? Or, to put it differently, if you were to describe yourself in one word, which of the following words would come closest?

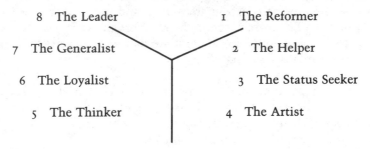

9 The Peacemaker

8   The Leader   1   The Reformer

7   The Generalist   2   The Helper

6   The Loyalist   3   The Status Seeker

5   The Thinker   4   The Artist

We will now expand these one-word descriptions. Read the following four-word descriptions to see if you still feel comfortable with the type with which you have tentatively identified yourself. Keep in mind that these traits are merely highlights and do not represent the full spectrum of each personality type.

The *Two* is caring, generous, possessive, and manipulative.
The *Three* is self-assured, competitive, narcissistic, and hostile.
The *Four* is creative, intuitive, introverted, and depressive.
The *Five* is perceptive, analytic, eccentric, and paranoid.
The *Six* is likable, dutiful, dependent, and masochistic.
The *Seven* is accomplished, impulsive, excessive, and manic.
The *Eight* is self-confident, forceful, combative, and destructive.
The *Nine* is peaceful, reassuring, passive, and neglectful.
The *One* is principled, orderly, perfectionistic, and punitive.

We will now look at the main assets and liabilities of each type to discover why each is in the Feeling, Doing, or Relating Triad. Although the following short descriptions are still simple, see if the personality type you have tentatively chosen still fits you best. If it does not, consider the next most likely possibility.

IN THE FEELING TRIAD: PERSONALITY TYPES TWO, THREE, AND FOUR

These three personality types have common assets and liabilities which involve their *feelings*. When these types are healthy, their feelings are the focus of what is admirable about their personalities, enabling them to become highly valued for their interpersonal qualities. When they are unhealthy, however, their emotions are out of balance in one way or another.

Healthy Twos' strengths result from the ability to sustain positive feelings for others. Healthy Twos are compassionate, generous, loving, and thoughtful; they go out of their way to be of service to people. However, average Twos are possessive and controlling. They want to be loved but intrude on others too much. And unhealthy Twos deceive themselves about the presence of their negative feelings, particularly aggression. They want others to see them as loving and good all the time even when they manipulate people and act selfishly.

Healthy Threes' strengths involve the ability to adapt to others. Healthy Threes quickly learn what will make them attractive and desirable. They are able to motivate others to want to be like them because they are genuinely admirable in some socially valued way. Average Threes, however, are the most out of touch with their emotions and with their individuality. They are chameleons, projecting an image which others will applaud. Unhealthy Threes get hostile and extremely malicious if they do not get the admiring attention they desire.

Healthy Fours' strengths involve intuitive self-awareness. Healthy Fours are very personal, revealing and communicating their feelings in ways that enable others to get in touch with their own emotions. However, average Fours become too aware of their feelings, especially their negative ones, withdrawing from others and living too much in their imaginations. Unhealthy Fours are extremely depressed and alienated from others, tormented by self-doubt and self-hatred. They become suicidal when they can no longer cope with reality.

The Two, Three, and Four have common problems with *identity* and with *hostility*, which they take out either on themselves or on others, depending on the personality type.

IN THE DOING TRIAD: PERSONALITY TYPES FIVE, SIX, AND SEVEN

These types have common assets and liabilities which involve *doing*. When these types are healthy, their ability to accomplish things is unequaled by the other personality types: they are frequently responsible for outstanding practical or scientific achievements.

When they are unhealthy, however, their ability to act is out of balance in one way or another.

Healthy Fives' assets make them the most profoundly perceptive of the personality types. Healthy Fives are extremely knowledgeable about some aspect of their environment and are capable of brilliant, original, inventive solutions to problems. However, average Fives want complete certitude before they act, so they tortuously think through everything before they do anything, getting stuck in thinking rather than doing. As a result of thinking too much, unhealthy Fives create more problems for themselves than they solve because they have become so completely isolated from reality. They are unable to know what is real or unreal, true or untrue.

Healthy Sixes' strengths involve the ability to form strong emotional bonds with others. When healthy Sixes act, it is to everyone's mutual benefit. They are committed to others, loyal and faithful friends, and they look for the same qualities from others. Average Sixes, however, look outside themselves too much for "permission" to act from an authority figure or belief system which will tell them what to do. Unsure of themselves unless the authority is on their side, they nevertheless feel they must assert themselves against the authority to prove their independence. Unhealthy Sixes succumb to anxiety and feelings of inferiority and insecurity, self-destructively bringing about the very consequences they most fear.

Healthy Sevens' assets involve the ability to do many things exceptionally well. Healthy Sevens are exuberantly enthusiastic about the environment, becoming extremely accomplished in a wide variety of activities. However, average Sevens overdo everything in an unending search for new sensations, although, ironically, the more they do, the less they are satisfied. They greedily want more of everything so they will not feel deprived. Unhealthy Sevens become self-centered, demanding that others cater to their whims. They become dissipated escapists and fly compulsively out of control.

The Five, Six, and Seven have common problems with *insecurity* and *anxiety* which they handle in different ways, depending on the personality type.

IN THE RELATING TRIAD: PERSONALITY TYPES EIGHT, NINE, AND ONE

These three personality types have common assets and liabilities which involve *relating*. When they are healthy, these types relate to their environment and to others exceptionally well, frequently as leaders of one kind or another. However, when they are unhealthy, they are out of balance with how they relate to the world and other people.

Healthy Eights' strengths are based on their seeing themselves as more powerful than anyone else. They can use their immense self-confidence, courage, and leadership abilities to inspire others to great accomplishments. Average Eights, however, tend to dominate everything in the environment too aggressively, since they look after only their own self-interest and do not respect the rights and needs of others. Unhealthy Eights relate to their environment as bullies and tyrants, ruthlessly destroying anyone and anything that stands in their way.

Healthy Nines' assets are based on the ability to identify intimately with a person or belief. The receptiveness, optimism, and peacefulness of healthy Nines are reassuring to others, enabling others to flourish because Nines create a harmonious atmosphere for everyone. However, average Nines undermine their own development (and their ability to deal with reality) by idealizing the other — whether a person or an abstraction — too much. And unhealthy Nines become dangerously fatalistic and neglectful as they cling to what has become little more than illusions about reality from which they have dissociated themselves.

Healthy Ones' strengths involve the ability to relate objectively to the environment. Healthy Ones are reasonable, fair-minded, and conscientious, guided by principles which give them strong consciences and a clear understanding of right and wrong. However, average Ones are out of balance with their emotions, which they try to control too much. They strive for nothing less than absolute perfection, finding it difficult to accept anything as it is because it can always be better. Unhealthy Ones are intolerant and self-righteous, becoming obsessed about the evil they find in others while ignoring their own contradictory actions. They can be cruel and merciless toward others.

The Eight, Nine, and One have common problems with *repression* and *aggression*, which they handle in different ways, depending on the personality type.

If you still cannot decide what your personality type is, at least try to narrow the possibilities to two or three of the most likely candidates. Your basic type should finally become clear when you read the full descriptions.

A common problem is that people tend to pick the personality type they would like to be rather than the one they actually are. You can avoid this by trying to be objective about yourself, although this is one of the most difficult things to achieve. However, the more you understand the descriptions — and yourself — the more you will see that one personality type really does describe you better than any of the others. Give yourself time to find out which one it is.

You may find yourself responding to one or two traits from each type, seeing yourself in all of them, but in no one type in particular. While you may be able to find a little of yourself in all the types, when you read the description of your own personality type, *you will know it*. You may feel chills run down your spine, or an uneasy feeling in the pit of your stomach. This will be your subconscious telling you that something is hitting home.

While the descriptions are not difficult to understand intellectually, they may be difficult to deal with emotionally. Some people have found that they become anxious or depressed as they read the description of their own type. Seeing yourself revealed in these pages can be elating. It can also be disturbing.

If you become anxious as you read the description of your type, it might be useful to put the book aside until you have thought about what you found upsetting. One of the most helpful things about reviewing the descriptions is that it will help you recognize the changes you need to make in your life. Changing yourself takes time and the willingness to confront unpleasant truths about yourself, but it is the only way to rid yourself of troublesome habits and self-defeating patterns of behavior. And, as you will see for yourself, the very process of reflecting on the description of your personality type can be cathartic: the more you go over this material and apply it to yourself, the more freeing the process becomes.

THE WING

Now that you have tentatively identified your basic personality type, we can begin to make some refinements. It is important to understand that no one is a "pure" personality type. Everyone is a unique mixture of his or her basic type and *one* of the two types adjacent to it on the circumference of the Enneagram. One of the two types adjacent to your basic type is called your *wing*.

Your basic type dominates your overall personality, while the wing complements it and adds important, sometimes contradictory, elements to your total personality. The wing is the "second side" of your overall personality, and you must take it into consideration to understand yourself or someone else. For example, if you are a personality type Nine, you will have *either* a One-wing or an Eight-wing, and your total personality can best be understood by considering the traits of the Nine in some unique blend with the traits of either the One or the Eight.

Obviously, it is necessary to determine your basic personality type *before* you can determine which wing you have. And in order to determine your wing, you have to know which traits comprise the two types adjacent to your basic type. The best way to diagnose your wing is by reading the full descriptions of the two possible types, and by seeing which one applies to you best. To help get this process going, I have included a brief discussion of some of the major traits of the two wings at the end of each descriptive chapter.

You will see much more about the wing in the Advanced Guidelines, since it is one of the major elements which explains why two people who have the same personality type can still be very different.

DIRECTIONS OF INTEGRATION AND DISINTEGRATION

The next important concept you have to understand is what the lines on the Enneagram mean. The nine personality types are not static categories; they are open ended, allowing for psychological growth and deterioration.

The numbers on the Enneagram are connected in a specific sequence. The way the numbered points are connected is significant psychologically because the lines between each of the types denote the Direction of Integration (health, self-actualization) and the Direction of Disintegration (unhealth, neurosis) for each personality type. In other words, as you become more healthy or unhealthy, you can move in different "directions," as indicated by the lines of the Enneagram, *from your basic type.*

The Direction of Disintegration for each type is indicated on the Enneagram by the sequence of numbers, 1–4–2–8–5–7–1. This means that if a neurotic One deteriorates further, it will be to Four; a neurotic Four will deteriorate to Two, a neurotic Two will deteriorate to Eight, a neurotic Eight to Five, a neurotic Five to Seven, and a neurotic Seven to One. Likewise, on the equilateral triangle, the sequence is 9–6–3–9: a neurotic Nine will deteriorate to Six, a neurotic Six will deteriorate to Three, and a neurotic Three will deteriorate to Nine. You can see how this works by following the direction of the arrows on the Enneagram below.

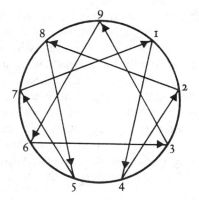

The Direction of Disintegration
1–4–2–8–5–7–1
9–6–3–9

The Direction of Integration is indicated for each type by the *reverse* of the above sequences. Each type moves toward increasing integration in a direction which is the opposite of its unhealthy direction. Thus, the sequence for the Direction of Integration is

1–7–5–8–2–4–1: an integrating One goes to Seven, an integrating Seven goes to Five, an integrating Five goes to Eight, an integrating Eight goes to Two, an integrating Two goes to Four, and an integrating Four goes to One. On the equilateral triangle, the sequence is 9–3–6–9: an integrating Nine will go to Three, an integrating Three will go to Six, and an integrating Six will go to Nine. You can see how this works by following the direction of the arrows on the Enneagram below.

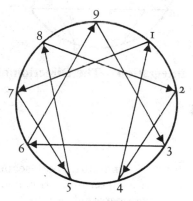

The Direction of Integration
1–7–5–8–2–4–1
9–3–6–9

Separate Enneagrams for the Direction of Integration and the Direction of Disintegration are unnecessary. Both directions can be shown on one Enneagram by eliminating the arrows and connecting the proper points with plain lines.

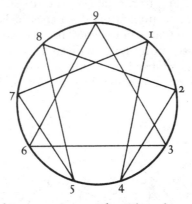

The Direction of Integration   **The Direction of Disintegration**
1–7–5–8–2–4–1   1–4–2–8–5–7–1
9–3–6–9   9–6–3–9

It will be helpful for you to memorize both sequences of numbers so that you know the Direction of Integration and the Direction of Disintegration for any given personality type.*

It is important to understand that the Directions of Integration and Disintegration are metaphors for psychological processes occurring in everyone. There is no literal movement around the Enneagram; rather, this is a symbolic way of indicating how a specific personality type will either integrate or disintegrate beyond the state it is in.

A brief example will illustrate what these movements mean. At personality type Six, one line is drawn to Nine, and another to Three. This means that if the Six were to become healthy and begin

---

* An easy way to memorize both sequences of numbers is to remember the *unhealthy* sequence and then reverse it for the healthy one. A trick to help you remember the unhealthy sequence (1–4–2–8–5–7) is to group these six numbers in pairs: each pair is approximately twice the preceding pair. Thus, the first two (1–4, or "14") when doubled is "28," and when that is doubled, it becomes "57." (It is really 56, of course, but this does not harm the mnemonic. So: 14 — 28 — 57, or 1–4–2–8–5–7.)

to actualize his potentials, he would move to Nine, the Direction of Integration specified by the Enneagram, activating what personality type Nine symbolizes for the Six. When the Enneagram predicts that a healthy Six will move to Nine, we find that this is precisely the kind of psychological development we see in individuals who are Sixes. Many of the Six's problems have to do with insecurity and anxiety, and when the Six moves to Nine, he or she becomes relaxed, accepting, and peaceful. The Six at Nine is more self-possessed and less anxious than ever before.

Conversely, the line to Three indicates the Six's Direction of Disintegration. If a Six were to become not merely neurotic, but even more unhealthy, he or she would do so by "going to Three." The Six's anxiety has made him extremely suspicious of others, and his feelings of inferiority and insecurity are rampant. A move to Three marks a neurotic Six's need to bolster his self-esteem by an extreme narcissistic overcompensation. The Six at Three will maliciously strike out at people to prove how tough he can be, and to triumph over anyone he thinks has threatened him. In short, the Six at Three becomes dangerously aggressive and psychopathic.

No matter what your basic personality type, be aware that the types in *both* your Directions of Integration and Disintegration have an influence on you. To obtain a more complete picture of yourself (or someone else), you must take not only your basic type and wing into consideration, but also the two types in your Directions of Integration and Disintegration. The traits of those *four types* blend into your total personality; a unique mixture of these four types gives you the fullest picture of yourself. For example, no one is simply a personality type Two. Anyone who is a Two has either a One-wing or a Three-wing, and the Two's Direction of Disintegration (Eight) and its Direction of Integration (Four) also play important parts in its overall personality.

Also keep in mind that it is possible for an unhealthy person to manifest some of the elements of a move to its Direction of Disintegration before reaching the final stage of deterioration in neurosis. For example, an average Six can have moments of arrogance and contempt for people as overcompensation for growing inferiority feelings. Although arrogance and contempt are traits of the Three, they show up as early warning signals in the Six's behavior before the Six actually becomes neurotic.

If you want more information than I have given in the brief descriptions of the Directions of Integration and Disintegration for any of the personality types, you can read the appropriate section in each type's Direction of Integration or Disintegration and make the application yourself. For example, to know more about what it means for a Two to integrate to Four, read the description of the healthy Four with the healthy Two in mind. Or if you want to know more about what is involved in a Nine disintegrating to Six, read the description of the unhealthy Six, applying the traits to the unhealthy Nine, and so forth for all the types. The basic idea is that when a type integrates, it appropriates the *healthy* traits of the type in its Direction of Integration, and when it deteriorates, it appropriates the *unhealthy* traits of the type in its Direction of Disintegration.

The Enneagram is able to predict integrated or disintegrated traits because these states are foreshadowed in the dynamics of the person's basic personality type. The Direction of Integration for each personality type is a natural outgrowth of the healthiest qualities of that type, so it is connected to another type by a line on the Enneagram to indicate that interrelationship. In a sense, then, you can think of each personality type as flowing into the next because the type in the Direction of Integration marks a higher development of the prior type, just as the type in the Direction of Disintegration marks its further deterioration.

Ultimately, the goal is to move completely around the Enneagram, integrating what each type symbolizes and acquiring the active use of the healthy potentials of *all the types*. The ideal is to become a balanced, fully-functioning human being, and each of the types of the Enneagram symbolizes different important aspects of what we need to achieve this end. Therefore, which personality type you begin life as is ultimately unimportant. What matters is what you do with your personality type and how well (or badly) you use it as the beginning point for your development into a fuller, more integrated person.

THE CONTINUUM OF TRAITS

There is an overall structure to each personality type. As you will see, the analysis of each type begins with a description of its healthy traits, then moves to its average traits, and then to its unhealthy traits. That structure is the Continuum of Traits which forms the personality type.

To understand an individual accurately, you must not only perceive his or her basic type and wing, but you must also perceive where the person lies along the Continuum of Traits of the basic personality type. In other words, you have to diagnose whether the person is healthy, average, or unhealthy. This is important because, for example, two people of the same basic personality type and wing will still differ significantly if one of them is healthy and the other unhealthy. (Where a person lies along the Continuum of Traits of his or her *wing* is also important, but since this can be difficult to perceive, I am not emphasizing it here.)

The concept of a personality "continuum" is not an academic one; it is something we intuitively use every day. One of the things we have no doubt noticed about ourselves (and others) is that we change constantly — sometimes for the better, sometimes for the worse. Understanding the concept of the Continuum makes it clear that when we do so, we are shifting within the spectrum of traits which make up our personality type. You will see more about how and why we move along the Continuum in the Advanced Guidelines chapter.

The Continuum for each of the basic personality types may be thought of as pictured below in the illustration of the Continuum of Traits.

The Continuum is comprised of the *Levels of Development*. It may help you to think of the Continuum as a photographer's gray scale, which has gradations from pure white to pure black with many shades of gray in between. On the Continuum, the healthiest traits appear first, at the top, so to speak. As we work down through the Continuum, we progressively pass through each Level of Development marking a distinct shift in the personality's deterioration to the pure black of neurosis at the bottom.

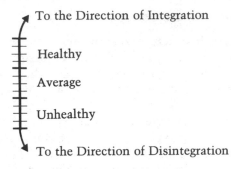

To the Direction of Integration

Healthy

Average

Unhealthy

To the Direction of Disintegration

The Continuum of Traits

Briefly, there are nine Levels of Development within each personality type — three in the healthy section, three in the average section, and three in the unhealthy section. The traits which appear at each of the Levels of Development are not arbitrary; they are arrayed in clusters at each Level. As you read the description of each personality type, you will, in effect, be seeing some of the most important traits from each of those clusters at each Level along the Continuum from health to neurosis.

The Continuum helps to make sense of each personality type as a whole by providing a framework upon which to place each healthy, average, and unhealthy trait. The Continuum is also worth understanding because it is only from its healthy end that we are able to move in the Direction of Integration, just as it is only from its unhealthy end that we deteriorate into the Direction of Disintegration. In other words, we must become healthy before we can integrate further, just as we have to be neurotic before we can deteriorate into borderline states, psychosis, or schizophrenia. We cannot simply leap from neurosis to integration — or from health to instant neurosis. Integration, like disintegration, is a *process* which takes time to accomplish. We can learn to be healthy just as, in different ways and for different reasons, we learn to be unhealthy.

GETTING STARTED

We can now turn to the descriptions of the nine personality types, which may be read in any order.

It might be helpful to understand the organization of the descriptions. Each chapter opens with a Caricature and Profile of the type to give you an impression of its most important traits. The Profiles are particularly useful, since they give you fifty or more key adjectives which you can use as a checklist to see if the personality type under consideration applies to you or someone else.

Next comes an Overview, a short essay presenting the principal psychological dynamics of the type being described. In the Overview, you will see how the personality type compares and contrasts with other types in its Triad, what its childhood origins are, how it correlates to the Jungian and other typologies, and most important, the major themes that will be developed more systematically in the longer analysis which follows. The Overview can be read as an independent short essay on each type or as a review after you have finished the analysis.

The more systematic description — the analysis of the personality type — follows the Overview. It begins with the *healthy* traits, then moves into the *average* traits, and then into the *unhealthy* traits. In other words, the description *gets progressively more negative* as it traces the deterioration of the type along the Levels of Development.

The analysis ends with a discussion of what will happen to the type if it continues in its unhealthy direction on the Enneagram — its Direction of Disintegration — as well as a description of what it will become if it moves toward increasing health — its Direction of Integration. Following these two sections is a brief description of the two major subtypes for each personality type — its wings — with examples of famous people, real or fictional, and some final thoughts about the type as a whole.

The examples of well-known people are educated guesses based on intuition, observation, and reading. They are offered as illustrations of the diversity of the personality types, with no implication about their state of health or neurosis. Remember that each of these people may have been healthy, average, or unhealthy at various times in their lives, and that each may have moved to his or her Direction of Integration or Disintegration. Above all, remember that there is an enormous amount of individual diversity, including intelligence, talent, and experience, among those illustrating any given type. But even taking these various factors into consideration, the famous people are included because, by understanding how they exemplify the different personality types, you will be able to see both what is common to them all and what a vast range of psychological territory is covered by each type. No two people are precisely alike, yet there are deep similarities between all people of the same personality type.

The last point about the descriptive chapters is that the quotations in parentheses are included to give the personal flavor of each of the types. Unless otherwise noted, these statements are not specific quotations.

You may be able to figure out your own type and those of a few close friends very quickly, or you may find it difficult to "categorize" people and not know where to begin. Either state is normal. It is not always apparent which type someone is, and it takes time to sharpen your skills. Remember that you are like a beginning medical student who is learning to diagnose a wide variety of conditions, some healthy and some unhealthy. It takes practice to learn to identify the major symptoms and apply them to the proper syndromes.

You might also keep in mind that while some people have an aptitude for psychological insight, others simply do not. If you find that your psychological aptitude is undeveloped, do not be discouraged. Read the descriptions carefully, going back to them when you need to check something or as new insights occur to you. You will probably be surprised at how quickly you get better at it.

There is really no secret to learning how to "type" people. You must learn which traits go with each type and observe how people manifest those traits. This is tricky because there are many subtypes and quirks to the personality types, as you will see. Also, different types can sometimes seem similar. For example, several of the types can be bossy. Even though they order people around, they do so in different ways and for different reasons. Eights boss people around as if saying, "Do as I say because I have power over you and I will punish you if you disobey me!" Ones boss others around as if they were saying, "Don't argue with me: just do as I say because I am right." Eights appeal to their power and ability to do harm in retaliation for not getting their way, whereas Ones invoke their infallibility to justify telling other people what to do. Under various circumstances, other types can also be bossy. Twos can be domineering, bossing people around as if they were saying, "You really don't want to hurt me, do you? You may as well do what I'm asking." Sixes can exhibit a blustering aggressiveness toward people, and Sevens can boss others around by demanding that others give them what they want, and so forth.

This is why you should not focus on a single trait in isolation and try to make a diagnosis based on that. It is necessary to see each type as a whole — its overall style and approach to life and its basic motivations. A lot of elements must be put together before you can type someone accurately.

For better or worse, there is no easy, automatic way to diagnose either yourself or others. It takes time, sensitivity, the ability to observe, and an open mind — unfortunately, more than most people are willing, or able, to bring to their relationships, although these are among the very qualities you will be able to develop with the help of the Enneagram.

The ultimate purpose of the Enneagram is to help each of us become a fully-functioning person. It helps us to see ourselves more clearly so we can become better balanced and integrated individuals. However, the Enneagram does not promise perfection, nor does it counsel us to become world-denying ascetics. In the real world, healthy people do not live in a constant state of Zen-like enlightenment, nor do they ever achieve total personhood — whatever that might mean. No matter how healthy or happy we become, we will always be incomplete and limited. Instead of fleeing from life into Nirvana or trying to become superior to life in a quest for an impossible perfection, we must learn to rise to the tremendous challenge of becoming, and being, fully human.

Attaining the goal of a full, happy life, ripe with experiences well used, means that each of us will become a paradox — free, yet constrained by necessity; shrewd, yet innocent; open to others, yet self-reliant; strong, yet able to yield; centered on the highest values, yet able to accept imperfection; realistic about the suffering existence imposes on us, yet full of gratitude for life as it is.

The testimony of the greatest humans who have ever lived is that the way to make the most of ourselves is by transcending ourselves. We must learn to move beyond self-centeredness to make room within ourselves for others. When you transcend yourself, the fact will be confirmed by the quality of your life. You will attain — even if only momentarily — a transparency and a radiance of being which result from living both within and beyond yourself. This is the promise and the excitement of self-understanding.

PART II
The Nine Personality Types

Chapter 4

Type Two: The Helper

The Two in Profile

Healthy: Becomes unselfish, disinterested, and altruistic, giving unconditional love to others. Empathetic, compassionate, caring, warm, and concerned. Encouraging, generous, and giving: a helpful, loving person.

Average: Emotionally demonstrative, gushy, friendly, full of good intentions about everything. Gets overly intimate, enveloping, and possessive: the self-sacrificial, mothering person who cannot do enough for others. Self-important: feels he or she is indispensable, but overrates his efforts in others' behalf. Overbearing, patronizing.

Unhealthy: Can be manipulative and self-serving, instilling guilt, putting others in his debt. Self-deceptive about his own motives and behavior. Domineering and coercive: feels entitled to get anything he wants from others. The "victim and martyr": feels abused, bitterly resentful and angry, resulting in hypochondria and psychosomatic problems.

Key Motivations: Wants to be loved, to express his or her feelings for others, to be needed and appreciated, to coerce others into responding to him, to vindicate his claims about himself.

Examples: Mother Teresa, Mahatma Gandhi, Eleanor Roosevelt, Leo Buscaglia, Bill Cosby, Luciano Pavarotti, Sammy Davis, Jr., Mr. Rogers, and the Jewish Mother stereotype.

An Overview of the Two

Because it has so many facets, love is difficult to define. It means different things to different people in different kinds of relationships. The word can be used to cover a multitude of virtues as well as vices. Of all the personality types, Twos think of love in terms of having positive feelings for others, of taking care of others, and of self-sacrifice. These aspects of love are undoubtedly important parts of the picture. But what Twos do not always remember is that, at its highest, love is more closely aligned with realism than with feelings. Genuine love wants what is best for the other, even if it means risking the relationship. Love wants the beloved to become strong and independent, even if it means that the Two must withdraw from the other's life. Real love is never used to take away from others what they would not freely give. Love outlives a lack of response, selfishness, and mistakes, no matter who is at fault. And it cannot be taken back. If it can be, it is not love.

Twos believe deeply in the power of love as the prime source of everything good in life, and in many ways they are right. But what some Twos call "love" and what is worthy of the name are very different things. In this personality type, we will see the widest possible uses of love, from disinterested, genuine love, to the flattering effusions of "pleasers," to the manipulations of a Jewish mother (although one does not have to be Jewish or a mother to use love to manipulate others). There is the greatest variety among those who march under the banner of love, from the most selfless angels to the most hate-filled devils. Understanding the personality type Two will help us understand how they got that way.

IN THE FEELING TRIAD

Although Twos have strong feelings for others, they have potential problems with their feelings. They tend to overexpress how positively they feel about others, while ignoring their negative feelings altogether. They see themselves as loving, caring people, yet all too often they love others only to have others love them in return. Their "love" is not free: expectations of repayment are attached.

Healthy Twos, however, are the most considerate and genuinely loving of all the personality types. Because they have strong feelings and sincerely care about others, they go out of their way to help people, doing real good and serving real needs. But if they become unhealthy, Twos deceive themselves about the presence and extent of their aggressive feelings, not recognizing how manipulative and domineering they can be. As we shall see, unhealthy Twos are among the most insidious of the personality types because they are extremely selfish in the name of utter selflessness. They do terrible harm to others while believing that they are completely good.

The essence of the problem is that even average Twos cannot see themselves as they really are, as persons of *mixed* motives, conflicting feelings, and personal needs which they want to fulfill. Instead, they see themselves only in the most glowing terms, ignoring their negative qualities as they gradually become self-deceptive. What is difficult to understand about Twos is how they can deceive themselves so thoroughly; what is difficult to deal with in them is the manipulative way in which they go about getting what they want. The worse they get, the more difficult it is to square your perception of them with their totally virtuous perception of themselves. They constantly exonerate themselves and demand that you do the same — indeed, they demand that you accept their interpretation of their actions against your own judgment, and sometimes even contrary to the plain facts.

Twos correspond to the extroverted feeling type in Jung's typology. Unfortunately, it is not one of his most insightful descriptions; nevertheless, the following traits are worth noting.

Depending on the degree of dissociation between the ego and the momentary state of feeling, signs of self-disunity will become clearly apparent, because the originally compensatory attitude of

the unconscious has turned into open opposition. This shows
itself first of all in extravagant displays of feeling, gushing talk,
loud expostulations, etc., which ring hollow: "The lady doth pro-
test too much." It is at once apparent that some kind of resistance
is being over-compensated, and one begins to wonder whether
these demonstrations might not turn out quite different. And a
little later they do. Only a very slight alteration in the situation
is needed to call forth at once just the opposite pronouncement on
the selfsame object. (C. G. Jung, *Psychological Types*, 357–358.)

What Jung describes is the ambivalence of the Two's feelings —
the ability to shift from apparently totally positive feelings for others to highly negative ones. As we trace the deterioration of the
Two along its Continuum of Traits, we can see that healthy Twos
really do love others genuinely. But average Twos have mixed feelings: their love is nowhere near as pure or selfless as they think it
is. And in unhealthy Twos, the opposite of love is operative: hatred
finds nourishment in burning resentments against others. Jung is
not correct in saying that "only a very slight alteration in the situation is needed to call forth at once just the opposite pronouncement on the selfsame object," since hatred is at the other end of the
spectrum from genuine love. But what is true is that step by step, as
Twos deteriorate along the Continuum toward neurosis, this is precisely what happens.

PROBLEMS WITH HOSTILITY AND IDENTITY

Twos, Threes, and Fours have a common problem with hostility,
although they manifest it in different ways. Twos deny that they
have any hostile feelings whatsoever, concealing their aggressions
not only from others, but also from themselves. Like everyone else,
Twos have aggressions, but they protect themselves from realizing
their existence and extent because their self-image prohibits them
from being openly hostile. They act aggressively only if they can
convince themselves that their aggressions are for someone else's
good, never for their own self-interest. Average to unhealthy Twos
fear that if they were ever openly selfish or aggressive, not only
would their negative behavior contradict their virtuous self-image,
it would keep others away from them. They therefore deny to themselves (and to others) that they have any selfish or aggressive mo-

tives whatsoever, while interpreting their actual behavior in a way which is entirely favorable to themselves. They eventually become so practiced at this that they completely deceive themselves about the contradiction between their true motives and their real behavior. Unhealthy Twos become capable of acting both very selfishly and very aggressively, while, in their minds, they are neither selfish nor aggressive.

The source of their motivation is the need to be loved. However, Twos are always in danger of allowing their desire to be loved to deteriorate into the desire to control others. By gradually making others dependent on them, average Twos inevitably arouse resentments against themselves while demanding that others confirm only how virtuous they are. When interpersonal conflicts arise, as they inevitably do because of their attempts to control others, average to unhealthy Twos always feel "more sinned against than sinning." They see themselves as martyrs who have sacrificed themselves selflessly without being appreciated for it in the least. Their aggressive feelings and resentments eventually manifest themselves in psychosomatic complaints and physical illnesses which force others to take care of them because they have become broken down invalids — all in the name of love.

Gaining the love of others is important to Twos because they fear that they are not loved for themselves alone. They feel that they will be loved only if they can earn love by always being good and by constantly sacrificing themselves for others. In a word, they fear that others would not love them *unless they made others love them.* (Twos could be briefly characterized as persons who, fearing that they are unloved, spend their lives trying to make people love them.) Naturally, that creates a deep source of hidden aggression, and if people do not respond to them as they want, average to unhealthy Twos become increasingly resentful. But since they cannot consciously own up to their aggressive feelings, they express them indirectly, in manipulative behavior they disavow. It is mind-boggling to see how badly unhealthy Twos treat others while justifying everything they do. But no matter how destructive their actions are, unhealthy Twos persuade themselves that they have nothing but love and the purest of good intentions at heart.

One of the major ironies of all Twos is that, unless they are very healthy, the focus of their attention is essentially on themselves, although they neither give this impression to others nor think of themselves as egocentric. Assertions to the contrary, even for average Twos the welfare of others is not primary. Rather, their positive feelings about themselves — as reinforced by the positive reactions of others — are what is important to them and what they are always angling for.

This is why Twos have a second problem in common with Threes and Fours, a problem with their identities. Other people do not see Twos as they really are, and, more important, Twos do not see themselves as they really are. There is an ever increasing disparity between the saintly self-image and the actual sinner, between the claims on the love of others which they make, and what they actually deserve.

CHILDHOOD ORIGINS

As children, Twos had ambivalent relationships to their fathers, or father figures, which were crucial in the development of their personalities. The ambivalence they have to their fathers sets the stage for an ambivalent orientation toward everyone who can give the love they want. (In Freudian terms, Twos have superego problems which also result from their ambivalent orientation to their fathers.)

Ambivalence to their fathers helps explain the fact that their self-esteem is conditional. Twos do not love themselves unconditionally, as Threes do, nor do they lack self-esteem, as Fours do. Rather, their self-esteem is based on the condition that they be absolutely good. They must see themselves as good so that they can maintain self-esteem and build an identity to which others will respond with the love they desire.

While there is certainly nothing objectionable about feeling good about themselves when they are genuinely good, their problems begin when they need to feel that they are good all the time. Even when they are far from good, Twos *must* see themselves as good for others — by virtue of their virtue, as it were. The irony is that their need to think of themselves as all-good is never more urgent than when they are self-centered, manipulative, and appallingly coercive.

Average to unhealthy Twos, therefore, do everything they can to be good in their own minds — and to get others to reinforce their assessment of themselves. This is why self-deception is so important to unhealthy Twos and why they can become so destructive of the emotional lives of others while remaining absolutely convinced of their own virtue.

However, when they are healthy, Twos are able to move beyond the needs of their egos to become caring, unselfish, and disinterested, in the most positive meanings of those words. But at the lower end of the personality Continuum, the "love" of unhealthy Twos is nothing more than a veneer for the desire to dominate others. They do not genuinely care for other people or concern themselves with their welfare; they are interested only in the gratification of their neurotic needs. Unhealthy Twos do evil in the name of good and can no longer tell the difference.

Analyzing the Healthy Two

THE DISINTERESTED ALTRUIST

At their best, healthy Twos are amazingly unselfish and altruistic, able to offer others a truly unconditional, continuing love with no strings attached. Their unconditional love allows Twos to love without concern for themselves and without necessarily being loved in return. "Getting a return" on their love is not what matters to them.

Truly unconditional love is both free and freeing: healthy Twos are free to love or not, and others are free to respond or not. Others are allowed to grow on their own terms, even if it means that they will grow away. Healthy Twos always remember that it is an immense privilege for others to allow them to be part of their lives, a gift others bestow on them, not something they can rightfully claim for themselves.

Very healthy Twos are as altruistic as human beings can be. They are unselfconscious about their goodness, not letting "their right hand know what their left hand is doing." They have immense reservoirs of good will and are absolutely delighted at the good fortune of others. Their attitude is that good is to be done, no matter who does it or who gets the credit for it. Very healthy Twos are not angry if someone else takes credit for something they have done. Good was done, other people have benefited, and that is all that matters.

At their best, therefore, healthy Twos are completely disinterested in the truest sense of the word: they do not act from self-interest. Their intentions and actions are purely directed toward the good of the other, with no ulterior motives. Their disinterest allows Twos to see the real needs of others clearly, without ego clouding the picture. As a result, an extraordinary directness is possible in all their relationships because ego and self-interest do not get in the way.

The paradox of very healthy Twos is that the more they give of themselves, the more there is to give. The more revered they are, the more humble they become. The more power people give them in their lives, the less they want. The less they think about themselves, the more others love them. Furthermore, virtue is not simply its own reward: the enduring reward of virtue is happiness. Very healthy Twos are happy to be good and are filled with an outflowing joy. They are among the most radiant human beings one can hope to find in life — radiating the inexpressible happiness which comes from truly being good and doing good for others.

Few people rise to this level of sustained altruistic love, and those who do, do not advertise it. Those few who do come as close to being saints as anyone becomes, although they are too humble to think of themselves this way. They would be embarrassed by any suggestion that they are saints because, good as they are, they know perfectly well how fragile their virtue is. Even so, when they are at their best, very healthy Twos present us with an example of the heights which human nature can attain. They have been victorious in the never-ending battle to transcend the ego to make room inside the self for the other. They have truly learned to love.

THE CARING PERSON

Even if they do not live at this high peak of disinterested altruism all the time, healthy Twos remain personally concerned for the welfare of others. Emotionally attuned to other people, they are the most empathetic of the personality types.

Empathy is the quality of being able to feel with another person, to experience his or her feelings as if they were your own. Empathy makes the feelings of others your feelings, their needs your needs. Being highly empathetic, healthy Twos are able to put themselves in the place of others, feeling compassion and concern. They have the strength to empathize with those who suffer. For example, when they hear about a disaster on television, their hearts go out to those who have been affected. The marital or job problems of their friends touch them deeply. Just knowing that someone else knows how you feel, that someone weeps with you, cares about you, takes your needs seriously, and will do all he or she can to help you, is itself a source of great comfort in times of trouble.

Because their emotions are engaged so strongly and so positively for others, healthy Twos are aware of themselves as empathetic, caring people. Their hearts rather than their heads are their main faculty, and because they are led by their hearts, they do not judge others or concern themselves with keeping a strict account of right and wrong.

Healthy Twos see themselves as good because, in fact, they are good. They see themselves as loving persons because, in fact, they are loving. They are well meaning, sincere, and warmhearted, and they recognize these strengths in themselves. Moreover, realizing that they sincerely care for others gives Twos an enormous amount of self-confidence, allowing them to venture "where angels fear to tread." Their confidence, however, is not primarily in themselves but in the value of the goodness they so deeply believe in.

It almost goes without saying, but healthy Twos are extremely generous. One of the most important forms of their generosity is their generosity of spirit, not primarily a material generosity (since a particular Two may be poor or of modest means), but more an attitude toward others. They are charitable and put a positive interpretation on everything, emphasizing the good they find in others. This is, in a sense, an irrational gift because it goes beyond reason: healthy Twos do not find fault with others even when there is fault to be found, not because they are not perceptive (far from it) but because they are much more attracted to what is positive and want to support those values. They are able to love the sinner, not the sin, a saving distinction.

THE NURTURING HELPER

Healthy Twos like to express how much they love others. Their strong, positive feelings for others naturally impel them into action. Service therefore is the keynote at this stage, and healthy Twos become giving people who take great satisfaction in helping others in many tangible ways. They serve those who are in need and cannot take care of themselves, feeding the hungry, clothing the naked, visiting the sick, volunteering for philanthropic work, using whatever means are at their disposal to help others.

Healthy Twos reach out to people, giving substantial help, even if it means going out of their way when it is inconvenient or difficult to do so. They are exceptionally thoughtful about the material, psychological, emotional, or spiritual needs of others. Twos are extraordinary in crisis situations because others know that they can count on them to help out. They are the kind of people you know you can call in the middle of the night for help. They are generous with their time, attention, money, and other resources —self-sacrificial in the best sense of the word. Indeed, people seek out healthy Twos because of their unique mixture of personal concern and practical helpfulness.

Healthy Twos have uniformly good effects on people because their love is so particular: they make others feel that someone really cares about what is best for them. They divine the good in others, and armed with this knowledge, are able to encourage and praise others sincerely, uplift spirits, and instill confidence. They build self-esteem because they give people the attention and appreciation they need to thrive.

Without trying to do so, healthy Twos exert an immense influence over others because few things in life are as powerful as instilling the feeling in others that someone good cares about them, believes in them, and is on their side. Expecting good from people and appreciating what they do nurtures self-confidence and creates a climate of expectation which enables others to do wonderful things.

Thus, healthy Twos are an archetype of the good parent, acting as parent figures, in the best possible sense, to everyone they meet. Good parents want what is best for their children. They actively look out for their welfare. Similarly, healthy Twos actively look out for the welfare of others — nurturing them, encouraging them, and empowering people to grow and discover their own strengths.

In a word, they are the embodiment of the ideal of charity in action. Healthy Twos may be saints — or not quite saints — but in either case, they try to be caring, loving, and helpful. This is their ideal, and in one degree or another, healthy Twos attain it.

Analyzing the Average Two

THE EFFUSIVE FRIEND

While healthy Twos are genuinely good, average Twos do less real good while talking more about their feelings and good intentions. Some reverse gear in their psyches has become engaged, and the attention they previously directed toward others begins to be focused on themselves. Their attention shifts away from doing real good onto having good feelings, principally about themselves. They do not recognize how overblown and histrionic their feelings are becoming or that they begin to have ulterior motives for what they say and do.

The helpful, nurturing person has become little more than effusively outgoing. Declarations of heartfelt feelings are the order of the day. Empathy has deteriorated into shamelessly wearing their hearts on their sleeves, as average Twos constantly tell everyone how they feel. They have a knack for meeting people easily, instantly regarding them as friends rather than acquaintances. Tactile people, they frequently give others a reassuring squeeze of the hand or an arm around the shoulder. They like to be physically close; kissing, touching, and hugging are natural extensions of their outgoing, histrionic style.

Of course, love remains their supreme value, and they want to love everyone. Love becomes their excuse, their rationale, their every motive, their only goal in life. If there is any type which is a Johnny-one-note about anything, it is the average Two talking about love. But it is also clear that when average Twos talk about love what they mean is that it is *their* love which is the solution to your needs.

Average Twos are confident that they have something valuable to share with others: *themselves* — their love and attention. They are completely convinced of the sincerity of their good will toward everyone, putting a favorable interpretation on everything they do. However, they are not so much good as they are faultlessly well-intentioned. An increase of ego is involved, although they take pains not to let this show, especially to themselves.

At this stage, average Twos are pleasers, gratifying others so that others will love them in return, although average Twos would not want (or be able) to admit this motive. They are convinced that they simply want to love others and to express how they feel. But when they overstate their appreciation of others, genuine appreciation deteriorates into flattery, the purpose of which is not appreciation of the other, but that the flatterer be appreciated for his praise.

Religion often plays an important part in their lives. Average Twos may well be sincerely religious and want to do good for others because of their religious convictions. However, religion is also very congenial to the way they view themselves. Religion reinforces their self-image of being well-intentioned and gives credibility to their assertions of sincerity. Religion also gives average Twos a vocabulary and a respected value system in which to talk about love, friendship, self-sacrifice, goodness, what they do for others, and how they feel about others — all of their favorite topics. Religion puts average Twos on the side of the angels so that few people, including, of course, average Twos themselves, dare to question their motives. Religion also appeals to their pride: they would secretly like to be thought of as savior figures and miracle workers. They have fantasies of their love conquering all, of killing the other person with kindness, and of winning over others through sheer goodness — all religious themes which make average Twos feel good about themselves.

The genuine appreciation of others that we find in healthy Twos has deteriorated into the beginning of an egocentricity which draws attention to itself in subtle ways. In all circumstances, they assert the depth of their feelings and how sincerely well-intentioned they are. And while their fine words seem to be directed toward others, average Twos are in fact their own most attentive audience. Hearing their fine sentiments makes them feel good, and since they are less genuinely helpful to others, average Twos have a lot of time to talk about how they feel. They like to share their feelings, encouraging others to reveal their inmost thoughts and intimate details about their personal lives. They talk incessantly about their friends (and about friendships) in embarrassingly explicit detail. ("Let's talk about us." "Why are you resisting me? Don't you love me anymore?")

Many people like the attention of average Twos, and average Twos know it. Their ability to lavish praise and flattery on people is a source of power, particularly over those who are hungry for approval. The approval they give, however, is not without cost.

THE POSSESSIVE "INTIMATE"

Given their interpersonal talents, it is not unusual for average Twos to gather a circle of people around themselves who become increasingly dependent on them. Average Twos would like to create an extended family, or a community, with themselves at the center so that others will regard them as important figures in their lives. They envelop people, making others feel that they are both part of a family and indebted to them for being invited to join it.

At this stage, they are the mothering type who can't do enough for you — the stereotypical Jewish mother — although average Twos of all religions and sexes are equally inclined to this behavior. They are forever feeding people, literally and emotionally, something which has a powerful effect on others. Few things are as disarming as a seemingly sincere interest in oneself, and average Twos are never more effective than with those who, for their own psychological reasons, are searching for a mother's love.

Average Twos see everyone as needy children hungry for love and attention, which they begin to press on others whether they seek it or not. They hover and interfere, giving unrequested advice, intruding into situations, and imposing themselves on people—making pests of themselves in the name of self-sacrificial love. The difficulty is that they are self-sacrificial to a fault, martyrs who invent needs to fulfill so that they can assume a greater position of importance to others. In short, they need to be needed.

They become busybodies, intrusively nosing into everyone's affairs. In adopting the role of the loving parent even to their peers, Twos make it their business to solve everyone's problems, from matchmaking to finding a job to giving advice about decorating an apartment. Because they want others to need them (their love, advice, approval, guidance), they do not hesitate to meddle, for the other's own good, of course. They also think nothing of asking pointed personal questions. Most people are usually too embarrassed (or too dependent on them) to rebuff their inquiries. The problem is that the flow of information is one-sided: average Twos always pry more out of others than they reveal about themselves. After all, they do not have problems: they are there to help you solve *your* problems.

Average Twos insinuate themselves into other people's lives very quickly; others invariably find it difficult to pull away. Unfortunately, average Twos begin to inflict themselves on others, who have to bear the burden of the Two's love — or really the Two's need to feel loved. Not surprisingly, their intrusiveness has negative effects on the very people they think they love. (The smothering mother's love suffocates.) But because their love is so relentlessly self-sacrificial, the beneficiaries of it are constrained from complaining about the quality of the Two's help.

As long as they are sacrificing themselves for others, average Twos feel that they have proprietary rights over them. They become possessive and extremely jealous of their friends — or protective of their "property," since it is difficult to tell the difference. They do not introduce their friends around or encourage them to get to know each other because they fear that their influence over them might diminish. They like it best when other people are in a crisis: they are not really happy if things are going well for others — or if people find out they can do without them. Average Twos do not know how to let go of people, a problem which only gets worse as they continue to deteriorate toward unhealth.

It is as if they are always holding court. It flatters Twos to be treated like a guru, someone to whom others come for advice about all sorts of personal matters. Naturally, others are expected to keep them informed about everything significant in their lives: they want to be the social switchboard through which every piece of important information must pass. They expect tangible responses from others as signs of success in their relationships. They expect to receive phone calls, invitations to dinner, cards for every conceivable occasion, thank-you notes, hearing that people miss and love them. To keep the flow of responses going, they stay in touch with old friends, spending a considerable amount of time maintaining their relationships — letting people know that they are thinking of them, worrying about them, praying for them, and so forth. Thus, while average Twos may still be thoughtful, it is in increasingly superficial ways: they remember birthdays and call frequently on the phone, but they begin to avoid getting tied down to the real needs of others so they can influence more people.

Ironically, their overinvolvement in the lives of others takes a toll on their genuine obligations, especially if they have families of their own. A problem with commitment surfaces. They become fickle, not so much because they drop one person to become deeply involved with another, but because they are constantly looking for love from yet another source. Since they want to be loved and appreciated by everyone, average Twos are constantly widening their circle of friends and acquaintances, doing yet more for others and inventing more needs to fulfill. When those who depend on them turn to them for help, they find that they are no longer there — they are off helping someone else.

Average Twos inevitably overextend themselves, helping too many people, sitting on too many committees, giving advice to too many friends, until they begin to feel burdened and physically worn out by their charity. Yet it is difficult for them not to be so involved, since that is how they maintain their sense of self. Furthermore, their histrionic qualities have not been outgrown, and as average Twos sacrifice themselves for others, they feel that they suffer because of their goodness. They dramatize every ache and pain, every inconvenience and problem which their kindliness has cost them. Illnesses, little breakdowns, and hypochondria become part of the picture.

The fact is that at this stage average Twos are not as loving as they think they are. They have strong egos, something they probably would not deny. (They have never claimed that they have no ego but that they are always well-meaning and loving.) They also have aggressive impulses on which they cannot act directly, as well as personal needs. Since they cannot risk being selfish and driving others away, they convince themselves that what they do is never for themselves but for everyone else. ("I was just doing it for you, trying to make your life easier.") Even the simplest, seemingly most spontaneous acts of kindness become loaded with unacknowledged ulterior motives.

Unfortunately, average Twos feel that they will be loved only if they are constantly doing things for people — in effect, bribing others to love them. Of course, Twos want a sincere response, but instead of allowing others to take the initiative, they prime the pump to get the kind of response they want. The irony is that when Twos receive the response they have maneuvered for, they never know whether they would have received it without their own prompting, so the response does not mean much. This raises a new anxiety: How much are they appreciated for themselves? It is a problem which Twos create — and then begin to chafe under.

THE SELF-IMPORTANT "SAINT"

Their point of view is understandable: average Twos feel that they have done many good things — they have taken a well-meaning interest in people, they have sacrificed themselves, they have taken care of people's needs — and they simply want to be appreciated for it. It seems to them that others completely take for granted the efforts they have made. They feel that no one values them, that others do not think about their needs or sacrifice themselves for them the way they have. Twos feel that others are ungrateful and thoughtless and must be reminded of how good they are.

The reason for this kind of behavior is that it is difficult for Twos to appreciate themselves — and keep their aggressive impulses under control — unless their value is reinforced by others. The person who was once so seemingly other-oriented has, at this stage, become egocentric under a veneer of modesty calculated to draw attention to itself. Twos at this stage are now altogether too self-important, patronizingly regarding themselves as indispensable to others, praising themselves, and becoming insufferably self-congratulatory — modestly talking about their many virtues.

Vainglory is the capital sin of average Twos. Very pleased with themselves, they never allow an opportunity to slip by without reminding others of how much people love them or how many friends they have and what good works they have done. ("Imagine someone like me becoming friendly with someone like you! People have told me that you are lucky to have me as a friend.") They drop the names of everyone they know, particularly if these are people of prominence. (Dropping names impresses others with how important Twos are as friends, sending the message that others had better value them since so many other people already do.)

Self-satisfied Twos may well not be aware of the extent of their pride. They like to impress others as selfless saints, calling attention to their virtue so that their good deeds will not go unnoticed — for the edification of others, of course. They like to shine in the eyes of others, be acclaimed for their virtues, and told what fine people they are, or even better, overhear themselves discussed in the most glowing terms. (Twos can, of course, proclaim their little human foibles, but God help anyone who accuses them of any serious faults.) The fact is that by now others have become mere appendages to their egos, little more than sources of gratification for their pride.

The servant has become the master. What self-important Twos do not see is that they expect others to be grateful to them constantly: an unending stream of gratitude, attention, and praise must flow in their direction. They expect that others will do favors for them as signs of their importance and that others will repay them — in cash or kind — for their previous self-sacrifices, real or only talked about. Having done a good deed sometime in the past, self-important Twos feel that the beneficiary is forever in their debt. The problem is that they grossly overvalue what they have done for others, while undervaluing what everyone else does for them. What others find particularly galling is that indispensable Twos take credit for everything positive in their lives, as if they alone were responsible for whatever success or happiness others have. Twos feel that others could not have done anything without their help ("You have me to thank for that.") and do not hesitate to say so.

Unfortunately, Twos do not see that their expectations of appreciation are much too high. They are bound to be disappointed and furious if others do anything short of handing over their very lives to them. But this creates a serious conflict: they are furious with others if others do not love them in return. Yet rehashing their claims to force others into loving them will likely only drive others away, making Twos feel the bitter sting of rejection even more acutely because they feel so self-important. Resentments smolder, becoming the prelude to manipulation, coercion, and revenge.

Analyzing the Unhealthy Two

THE SELF-DECEPTIVE MANIPULATOR

At this point Twos take a particularly nasty turn for the worse. Their aggressions have been strongly aroused, but because their aggressions conflict with their all-good self-image, Twos cannot express how they actually feel. The upshot is that unhealthy Twos have to express their aggressions indirectly, by manipulating others to give them the kind of loving response they desperately want. The irony is, however, that if they manipulate others, the responses they receive will never satisfy them.

Not feeling that they are loved not only hurts unhealthy Twos terribly, it calls into question their whole value system — the value of "love." If love does not have the power to get them what they want, then what does? Having loved and lost, they are furious about it. The answer is, of course, that what passes for love in unhealthy Twos is not love, but sanctimonious claptrap used to manipulate others. While they still use the vocabulary of love, their words are self-serving, designed to get something from others without appearing to do so directly. Manipulation is the name of the game.

Manipulative Twos are the maestros of guilt; they can play others like an orchestra, upping the level of guilt into a disturbing crescendo or damping it down to a whisper, as needed. They play people against each other, and worse, they are able to play others against themselves. It is shocking to people to realize how much the unhealthy Two's manipulations pull them off their own center. Grown men and women, heads of households and corporations, are reduced to so much emotional wreckage by being manipulated into enlisting part of themselves against themselves. But by casting others into self-doubt and making them feel guilty and confused, unhealthy Twos throw others off the scent of their own manipulations.

They undermine others while presenting themselves as "helpers" who can heal the pain they have subtly caused. They insidiously prick at tender spots with one hand while soothing the hurt with the other; they put you down and then bolster your self-confidence with left-handed compliments; they never let you forget your problems, making your future seem hopeless while promising to remain with you forever; they reopen old wounds, then rush to your side to stitch them up. They become your best friend and, unwittingly, your worst enemy.

Naturally, unhealthy Twos are absolutely maddening to deal with. They put themselves in a morally superior position, no matter what they have said or done. And by insisting on the absolute purity of their motives, they call those of others into question. No one can question their behavior or motives without Twos' ascribing evil-mindedness to them. Even tangible evidence has no effect on them since it can be dismissed as irrelevant to their good intentions. Unhealthy Twos can always be depended on to defend themselves by appealing to good intentions and the laws of the heart to sanction anything they do. They use religious rationalizations to extricate themselves from guilt or responsibility for their actions; they make another's attempt at an objective analysis of a situation seem niggling and petty by comparison to their superior ethics, which follow a higher morality. They have turned the dictum "love, and do what you will" into a license to do whatever they want in the name of "love."

Self-deception is the defense mechanism which allows unhealthy Twos to avoid seeing the discrepancy between the virtues they think they possess and their actual behavior. No matter how destructive they are, unhealthy Twos are able, through self-deception, to interpret whatever they do as good. In their minds, they always remain well-intentioned, loving human beings. Their consciences are always clear.

It is important to understand that unhealthy Twos are at peace with being manipulative because they do not have to rationalize individual acts. With the help of self-deception, they have managed to rationalize their entire lives. Once they have defined themselves as "good," they are able to justify whatever they say or do without feeling guilty, and without feeling that they are no longer good.

Freeing yourself from a manipulative Two can be an extremely difficult and wrenching experience, especially since the Two does not want it to happen. If unhealthy Twos were to remain mildly manipulative, they would perhaps be only an annoying drain on others. Unfortunately, their behavior may get markedly worse.

THE COERCIVE DOMINATOR

The possessiveness we saw in average Twos has deteriorated into coercively demanding love from others on their own terms — and neurotic terms at that. What emerges is a delusional sense of entitlement, the feeling that they have an absolute right to get whatever they want from others. From their viewpoint, everyone else owes them whatever they want because of the self-sacrifices neurotic Twos insist they have made in the past.

For saints, neurotic Twos are extraordinarily difficult to deal with — and hell to live with. They are tired of being selfless. They now insist that others put their needs first. Their egos, whose needs were formerly met indirectly through various kinds of service to others, are thrust into the foreground, making demands on others with a vengeance.

They have the unnerving and frustrating knack of belittling everyone else in the name of love. Neurotic Twos can make the most derogatory remarks about others, both behind their backs and to their faces, if need be, "for their own good." They punish others by withdrawing their love. ("Well, you can just try to get along without me!") They do not hesitate to make dire predictions about your possibilities without them. ("You're not going to be happy; you're going to fall right on your face without me.") By denying that they take any personal satisfaction in telling people what they think of them, or in having any ulterior motives whatsoever, they are free to do and say anything they please.

They are furious with others and it shows. The veneer of love drops away, and neurotic Twos let loose a torrent of bitter complaints about how they have been treated, how their health has suffered, and how unappreciated they are. They endlessly dredge up things from the past, harping on how much they have helped you, how hopeless you are without them, and how they made you who you are today. ("Remember what I did for you? Is this the thanks I get?")

While their incessant complaints and disparaging remarks bring them attention, it is the wrong kind of attention — the resentment and anger of others. Of course, unhealthy Twos are aware of this and it becomes a source of fresh complaints. The vicious circle of recrimination continues. However, they feel that anything offensive or hurtful they may do to others does not reflect on them, as deeply loving human beings, but is justified by the unloving treatment they have received. Hence, they can do the most awful things to people without a qualm of conscience. ("If one judges love by most of its results, it is closer to hatred than friendship." — La Rochefoucauld)

Indeed, neurotic Twos want to be loved so much that they may attempt to coerce others to love them in the most damaging ways. It is possible that some forms of pedophilia and child molestation have their roots here, and that Twos, as a group, figure disproportionately in this kind of destructive behavior. It is worth remembering that Twos typically enjoy the trust and admiration of family and friends. They may be teachers, clergymen, day-care workers, or nurses — those whose word and integrity are usually not suspected by anyone. And, at this stage, since Twos are neurotic and in all probability lack satisfactory intimate relationships with their peers, it is possible that they will turn to children to fulfill their emotional and sexual needs.

Moreover, since they are already extremely manipulative and self-deceptive, neurotic Twos are more than capable of taking advantage of the powerlessness of children. Indeed, their helplessness is one of the qualities which attracts Twos to children; they can comfort the very child they have terrorized, playing the role of savior once again.

THE PSYCHOSOMATIC VICTIM

If demanding love from others has gotten them nowhere, unhealthy Twos unconsciously try another avenue. They want to be loved, to be shown concern, and to be appreciated more desperately than ever. Physical illness seems to be a reliable way of ensuring that they receive the appreciation they have been seeking. Becoming an invalid is the solution: others will have no choice but to take care of them. While being cared for is not the same as being loved, it may be as close to love as they are going to get.

Neurotic Twos try to obtain the love of others, which has always been their fundamental desire, by unconsciously desiring to go to pieces. They fear being held responsible for their words and deeds. They also fear that their aggressions have revealed some hypocrisy about themselves which would make them unlovable, their greatest fear. They therefore unconsciously attempt to escape responsibility for past destructive behavior by having a physical breakdown which will, in a sense, exempt them from further punishment. And, in their minds at least, physical suffering will conclusively prove many of the most important claims they have made about themselves: that they have been selfless, that they have been victimized by the ingratitude of others, that they have worn themselves out for others, and so on.

Their health falls apart because, as formidable and willful as neurotic Twos are, the strain of living under enormous contradictions becomes unbearable. The stress of trying to control and justify their hatred of others finally takes its toll physically.

Psychosomatic illnesses are the result of the process known as hysterical conversion reactions. In psychological terms, neurotic Twos are hysterics who convert anxiety into physical symptoms. They usually fall victim to a wide array of mysterious illnesses, including skin eruptions, gastrointestinal problems, arthritis, and high blood pressure — all diseases in which stress plays an important role. (Even average Twos may develop mysterious illnesses; however, by the time a Two is fully neurotic, the list of diseases has become long, and being an invalid has become a way of life.) Because Twos are ill so often, others may suspect a masochistic enjoyment of their sufferings, but, strictly speaking, this is not the case. They do not actually enjoy suffering because the suffering is real; instead, they enjoy the benefits suffering affords them. Horney describes it vividly.

> Suffering is unconsciously put into the service of asserting claims, which not only checks the incentive to overcome it but also leads to inadvertent exaggerations of suffering. This does not mean that his suffering is merely "put on" for demonstrative purposes. It affects him in a much deeper way because he must primarily prove to himself, to his own satisfaction, that he is entitled to the fulfillment of his needs. He must feel that his suffering is so exceptional and so excessive that it entitles him to help. In other words this process makes a person actually feel his suffering more

intensely than he would without its having acquired an unconscious strategic value. (Karen Horney, *Neurosis and Human Growth*, 229.)

Physical suffering is also a permanent, guilt-instilling rebuke to those who have not provided neurotic Twos with the love and appreciation they have always wanted. It is an unending source of demands for attention, care, concern — for love. The "saint" has become a drain on everyone. The most other-oriented person either drives away family and friends or makes their lives unbearable.

Analyzing the Dynamics of the Two

THE DIRECTION OF DISINTEGRATION: THE TWO GOES TO EIGHT

The essential problem with average to unhealthy Twos is that they have not come to grips with their aggressive feelings. Even in the depths of their illness and suffering, neurotic Twos realize that they are still coercing the attention of others, and this thought continues to enrage them. They may be bedridden or hospitalized because they are physically ill, but they are not deranged or dissociating from reality.

Thus, while unconsciously having a physical breakdown has been adaptive (since illness and physical incapacitation take the possibility of violence against others out of their hands), this form of adaptation may not last for long. After all, they may recover and something else may precipitate a move to Eight, the eruption of their aggressive feelings into seriously destructive behavior.

Because they are still neurotic, however, Twos are in no position to deal constructively with their aggressive impulses. Their bitterness and rancor, their desires for revenge and self-vindication are directed to those who have frustrated their desire to be loved. So, when they move to Eight, neurotic Twos strike out at those who have not responded to them as they have wanted. The hatred they have suppressed comes pouring out, and is openly expressed against those who Twos feel have not loved them sufficiently in the past. Love completely turns into hatred, and smoldering hatred into violence and destruction.

A Two at Eight will probably become physically violent, even murderous. Those in his or her immediate family are usually the people most at risk, the very ones for whom, they are convinced, they had nothing but good intentions and undying love. The invalid, the self-sacrificial martyr, the suffering saint becomes a monster, sacrificing others.

THE DIRECTION OF INTEGRATION: THE TWO GOES TO FOUR

When healthy Twos go to Four, they get in touch with their feelings, especially their aggressive ones, becoming aware of themselves as they really are. They graduate from an unwillingness to examine themselves and their motives, and move toward self-knowledge.

Integrating Twos accept the presence of their negative feelings as fully as they accept their positive feelings. This does *not* mean that they act on their negative feelings when they are at Four, but that they are willing to acknowledge these feelings in themselves. Because Twos at Four become emotionally honest, they are able to express the full range of their emotions — not just their loving side, although it is certainly still present and more genuine than ever before.

For the first time, integrating Twos unconditionally accept themselves, just as they unconditionally accept others. It is therefore possible to give something deeper and more personal to others than they have ever done in the past. And when they are loved by others, it is all the more gratifying because others love the whole of them. Integrating Twos can rightly feel that they are no longer loved just for what they do for others, but for who they are.

There is also the possibility of harnessing their fuller, more authentic feelings into forms of creativity. They become deeper human beings who have intuitions into the depths of the human condition. Whatever they give to others is now all the more valuable because integrating Twos are more genuine as human beings, whether as artists or as parents or as friends.

The Major Subtypes of the Two

THE TWO WITH A ONE-WING

The Two's traits and those of a One-wing tend to conflict with each other: Twos are emotional, interpersonal, and histrionic, while Ones are rational, impersonal, and self-controlled. The empathy and interpersonalism of the Two are counterbalanced by the more objective orientation of the One-wing. There is a strong conscience and a desire to act on principles so that a person of this subtype will try to treat others fairly, no matter what their emotional needs are, although because Two is the basic type, they will probably feel conflicts between the head and the heart. Noteworthy examples of this subtype include Mother Teresa, Mahatma Gandhi, Eleanor Roosevelt, Bishop Desmond Tutu, Danny Thomas, Alan Alda, Bill Cosby, Ann Landers, Florence Nightingale, Lewis Carroll, Melanie Hamilton Wilkes, and Jean Brodie.

Healthy persons of this subtype can do a great deal of good for others, partly because of the One-wing's principles. Teaching others, improving their lives, and working for a cause are noteworthy traits. Many charities and religious and philanthropic organizations are probably begun and staffed by this subtype. They want to give the best possible service to others and they do so with less self-regard and more altruism than the other subtype. They may be particularly fine teachers since they not only have an objective, intellectual orientation to facts and values, but the emotional warmth to bring ideas to life. As teachers and parents, they are also very encouraging and appreciative of those in their charge.

In average persons of this subtype, there is a tension between personalism and idealism. As Twos, they empathize with people, but if they have a strong One-wing, their abstract ideals conflict with their feelings, making it difficult for them to empathize with others wholeheartedly. At least some part of them remains judgmental, ready to make moral pronouncements. Average persons of this subtype can be very controlling, both of others and of themselves. They are egocentric, although this is hidden by their ideals, especially the ideal of love. We see the conflicting tendencies of the two subtypes most clearly in the desire to be important to others versus the desire to be reasonable and objective. Persons of this subtype are also more subject to guilt and to self-condemnation than Twos with a Three-wing, since they tend to be more highly critical of themselves when they fail to live up to their own moral standards.

Unhealthy people of this subtype are self-righteous, inflexible, and moralistic about whatever they think is the right thing to do. Self-righteousness and the desire to justify themselves combine with self-deception and manipulation to produce a strongly entrenched mind-set which is very difficult to change. Persons of this subtype are quick to condemn others and are able to justify themselves on moral grounds. They cannot allow themselves to be proved wrong, nor can they allow themselves to be proved selfish, and they completely deny their aggressive feelings. People of this subtype are subject to hypochondria — obsessions and compulsions focused on their bodies.

THE TWO WITH A THREE-WING

The Two's traits and those of the Three-wing tend to reinforce each other: both types relate easily to people. Noteworthy examples of this subtype include Luciano Pavarotti, Sammy Davis, Jr., Leo Buscaglia, Doug Henning, Tommy Tune, John Denver, Pat Boone, and Lillian Carter.

Healthy people of this subtype are charming, friendly, and outgoing. They enjoy the attention of others, are self-assured, and exude an aura of well-being and wholesome self-enjoyment. There is genuine warmth in people of this subtype, and the ability to communicate that warmth to others. They also tend to be more physically attractive than Twos with a One-wing. Social qualities are valued more than moral or intellectual ones.

In average persons of this subtype, we see elements of competitiveness and the desire for success and prestige mixed with the traits of the Two. Twos use others to validate their goodness, Threes to validate their desirability, particularly their sexual desirability. Hence, we find a calculating self-consciousness in persons of this subtype. They are also highly aware of what others think of them and how they come across to others. Having the right friends, dropping names, and cultivating people is typical. We also find the tendency to be self-important and narcissistic, although the Three's calculation of his or her image and the Two's self-sacrificial persona will mask this to some degree. Persons of this subtype fear being humiliated and losing status rather than feeling guilty over the violation of moral ideals.

If people of this subtype become unhealthy, they can be emotionally devastating to others since they become both manipulative and exploitative, deceptive and self-deceptive, opportunistic and neurotically entitled to get whatever they want from others. Hostility toward others can be extremely strong and all-consuming: beneath their apparent charm lies viciousness. They are potentially psychopathic in the destructiveness they are capable of wreaking on others. In them we find elements of malice and the tendency to ruin what they cannot have, especially relationships. Twos with a Three-wing are capable of pathological jealousy and violent crimes of passion.

Some Final Thoughts

As we look back, we can see that Twos have conflicts between their desire to love and their need to be loved, between their genuine self-esteem and their need to manipulate others to feel good about themselves. What is unfortunate is that, to paraphrase Othello, average to unhealthy Twos have loved neither too wisely nor too well. But at least according to their own lights, they have tried to love others. Therein lies the nobility of their goal and the tragedy of their failure to attain it.

The irony is that neurotic Twos have brought about the very thing they have most feared: they want to be loved, but end up being hated, or at least unwanted by anyone. A second, darkly comic irony lies in the likelihood that the only person who may be attracted to the unenviable position of caring for an invalid, neurotic Two may be another Two. If the second Two is manipulatively self-sacrificial about the help which he or she gives, a pathetic duel of wills may play itself out between these two like-minded, draining souls. The result is a macabre dance of death.

If we draw a lesson from this personality type, it is that Twos can be right in their belief about the value of love, yet wrong in their manner of loving others. If they intrude upon people with "love," Twos unwittingly prove that what they force on others is not love, and, for that very reason, is doomed to failure. As soon as ego masquerades behind "love," love becomes tainted and eventually corrupt — with all the consequences we have seen in this personality type.

Chapter 5

Type Three: The Status Seeker

The Three in Profile

Healthy: Inner-directed and authentic, everything he or she seems to be. Self-assured, energetic, adaptable, often physically attractive and popular. Ambitious to improve self, becoming outstanding, a kind of human ideal, embodying widely admired qualities. Others are often motivated to want to be like him in some positive way.

Average: Competitively concerned with prestige and status: career and success are very important. Becomes image-conscious, highly concerned with how he or she appears to others. Pragmatic, goal-oriented, efficient. Calculating and affectless beneath the facade. Constantly promoting himself, making himself sound better than he is. Narcissistic, arrogant, exhibitionistic, pretentious. Hostility and contempt for others surface.

Unhealthy: Can be exploitative and opportunistic, out for himself. A pathological liar, devious and deceptive, maliciously betraying people. May become vindictive, attempting to ruin what he or she cannot have. Sadistic, psychopathic tendencies: sabotage, murder, assassination.

Key Motivations: Wants to be affirmed, to distinguish himself from others, to receive attention, to be admired, and to impress others.

Examples: Jimmy Carter, Brooke Shields, Bruce Jenner, Jane Pauley, Mary Lou Retton, Sylvester Stallone, Truman Capote, Ted Bundy, and Iago.

An Overview of the Three

The United States is fast becoming a "Three" culture: narcissistic, image-oriented, emphasizing style over substance, symbols over reality. The pursuit of excellence is being replaced by the celebration of the artificial as everything is treated like a commodity — packaged, advertised, and marketed. Politics is becoming less concerned with principles or the use of power for the common good than with the display of personalities. Politics serves public relations, selling candidates with their calculated positions to a public which can no longer tell a clone from a real person.

The communications media, particularly television, are primarily concerned with attracting attention so that the public can be sold something. The shallow values and the beguiling glitter of show biz have become the norms by which everything is measured. The only guideline is the ability to gain attention: what is noticed and in demand has value. People are so seduced by the slick package that they often do not realize that there is nothing in it. To paraphrase McLuhan, the package is the message. Calculated images successfully masquerade as reality, from the programmed friendliness of television personalities to the rehearsed sincerity of beauty contestants to the hard fluff of "evening magazine" shows.

Exhibitionism and self-promotion are becoming acceptable as people do whatever it takes to be noticed in an increasingly competitive marketplace. The ideal is to be a winner — to be successful, famous, and celebrated. The quest for success and prestige is everywhere. Every day, a new book tells us how to dress for success, eat for success, or network for success. We are being sold a narcissistic fantasy: that we will be "somebody" if we are like everybody else, only better. If you manage your image properly, you, too, can become a star — or a god.

The personality type Three exemplifies the search for the affirmation of the self, a self which becomes more empty as its apparent perfection bids for more attention.

IN THE FEELING TRIAD

Threes, the primary personality type in the Feeling Triad, are most seriously out of touch with their emotional lives. As a result, Threes have a fundamental problem with their identities. There is a profound split between who they seem to be and who they are, between the image they project to others and the reality behind it. In time, their image becomes their only reality. What average Threes appear to be, from person to person and from moment to moment, is who they are. The great problem for people of this personality type is to become inner-directed, to develop themselves as persons according to their genuine feelings and within their own realistic limitations.

If they are healthy, Threes are worthy of the admiration of others because they have taken pains to acquire the qualities and skills they seem to embody virtually to an ideal degree. The overwhelmingly positive self-esteem of healthy Threes has a basis in fact, and they are often highly regarded by others, both in their personal lives and in their careers. Healthy Threes are outstanding, human nature's stars.

However, average Threes become intensely competitive with others for all forms of success and prestige, since they want to maintain what they have come to regard as their natural superiority over others. Instead of developing themselves, they resort to projecting images that are meant to make a favorable impression on others. Pragmatic and calculating, they are able to change their image to get what they want, showing off and hyping themselves to attract admiration.

If they become unhealthy, Threes exploit others so they can maintain what has become a spurious superiority. They are extremely devious if they are in danger of losing the competition between themselves and others in which they see themselves as always engaged. They become so jealous that they maliciously try to ruin others to achieve the triumph their narcissistic superiority requires.

PROBLEMS WITH HOSTILITY AND NARCISSISM

Like the other personality types of this Triad, Threes have a problem with hostility, which manifests itself as vindictive malice toward anyone who is more successful than they. While Twos and Fours are indirectly hostile, average to unhealthy Threes are more openly hostile in a wide variety of ways, from putting others down to sabotaging them to betraying people. Sensing the viciousness of which unhealthy Threes are capable, others usually give them their way or steer clear of them as much as possible. What is truly frightening about the hostility of unhealthy Threes is how psychopathic they can become if they do not remain on top of others. As others find to their horror, unhealthy Threes can get very nasty if they do not get the limitless admiration they seek.

Average Threes are the most narcissistic of the personality types. While healthy Threes justly possess high self-esteem, average Threes build their identities around an increasingly inflated self-regard: they appear to be utterly in love with themselves. But, more precisely, they are in love with their inflated image rather than their actual selves. Instead of loving themselves as they really are, including a realistic acceptance of their limitations, they love a false facade which bears little resemblance to the undeveloped person beneath.

Narcissists care principally about themselves — and about others only to the degree that they reflect well upon themselves. They remain intensely self-centered, with a limited ability to empathize with anyone else's feelings or needs. This is why they have little capacity for love and why — once they have become narcissistic — average Threes have little capacity to form lasting, mutually satisfying relationships. Relationships are one-sided because both parties are in love with the same person: the Three.

Of course, their narcissism puts them in constant conflict with people. Because they believe so much in their superiority, average Threes are competitive with the very people from whom they want admiration. They show off as if others were no more than an adoring audience endlessly ready to applaud their every move; if others do not applaud, Threes tell them off or humiliate them. Worse, narcissistic Threes add insult to injury by demanding that people admire them even when they are contemptuous of the people whose admiration they want.

The problem is that narcissism is not the same thing as genuine self-esteem. Although average Threes seem to be coolly self-contained, they are not really secure with themselves because their self-esteem is based not on the development of their real capacities but on their ability to capture the attention of others. Threes are finely attuned to people's reactions to them and can respond by projecting whatever image they need at the moment. But since their repertoire of images does not have a corresponding measure of reality behind it, everything they do is done for show, not because they are personally committed to, or deeply involved with, anything outside themselves.

The irony is that behind the facade is a deeply hidden dependency on others, a dependency they cannot acknowledge because of the demands of their narcissism. Once narcissism takes over, Threes cannot live with people and they cannot live without them, because they are hostile toward the people on whom they depend, and because they are "nobody" without the attention of others.

CHILDHOOD ORIGINS

Threes develop the way they do because of their early childhood relationship with their mothers: they identified positively with their mothers or a mother substitute. Threes learned from this relationship to approach every subsequent relationship with the same unconscious expectations they had when their mothers freely lavished attention on them. They expect the world to admire them as unconditionally as their mothers did. Because of their mothers' high regard, they learned to regard themselves as superior beings, expecting that life will ask little more of them than that they merely present themselves to others to receive admiration and reinforcement of their value.

The admiring gaze with which their mothers made them feel important is, in one form or another, the look they are always seeking in the eyes of others. Admiration makes them feel alive and worthwhile; without it, they feel empty and hostile because their sense of self is dangerously threatened. Unfortunately, however, by learning to relate to people in this way, Threes were not encouraged to develop realistically.

Because affirmation of their worth came so effortlessly, Threes did not learn to see themselves as limited in any way. They did not develop a superego (or a conscience). Rather, the faculties which are extraordinarily developed in Threes are their ids and their personas — the energy they are able to invest in themselves and the image which results from that self-investment. They see themselves as people of virtually limitless potential, and as a result, it is easy for them to have grandiose expectations about themselves. Precisely because of their enormous faith in their value, they may actually go far; but because they tend to allow their expectations to become inflated, they are also subject to the comeuppances of reality, with all the unfortunate results we will see.

Indeed, their psychological development is a mixed blessing: on the one hand, it enables healthy to average Threes to pour their energies into achieving their goals to a degree unrivaled by the other personality types. But, on the other hand, their lack of conscience and their inflated notions about themselves enable unhealthy Threes to exploit others without remorse because nothing inside them restrains them from doing so. They use people shamelessly because they do not see them as real or as having any value other than for their own narcissistic fulfillment.

Ironically, average to unhealthy Threes, while seeming to be so superior to everyone else, are in reality severely limited. Unless they develop themselves without regard for the applause of others, they will never know what it really is to be themselves, nor will they be able to relate to, much less love, anyone else. Appearances to the contrary, far from being superior, average Threes are empty: they impress because their package has been designed to impress. They know how to push the right buttons to be admired. But by endlessly seeking admiration, they create idols out of themselves, worshipping themselves and demanding that others do likewise. If others do not, Threes strike out viciously, revealing their true colors, not as gods, but as devils.

Analyzing the Healthy Three

THE AUTHENTIC PERSON

At their best, very healthy Threes transcend their desire to be affirmed by others and accept themselves as they are. They are no longer motivated by a concern for what others think of them or by a desire to obtain applause or admiration. Rather, very healthy Threes shift their center of gravity to become inner-directed and self-generating; in so doing, they plant the seeds of their own interiority, their own feelings, their own identities.

Self-acceptance allows them to know and live within their limits. Healthy Threes are neither discouraged by their limitations nor tempted to deny them; they do not think that they are superior to others or that they have special qualities if, in fact, they do not possess them.

Self-acceptance is a starting point in life which makes other things possible. Unlike what we read in some self-help books, accepting ourselves does not mean embracing our neuroses and bad habits, celebrating them as if they were virtues. On the contrary, self-acceptance involves accepting painful truths about ourselves. It helps us to abjure the world of grandiose fantasies and to cease to listen to the temptation to be false about ourselves in any way. Self-acceptance is, at its simplest, an acknowledgment that one is a limited human being. By accepting themselves, very healthy Threes take responsibility for developing themselves as they are, within the limitations of their talents.

At this stage, healthy Threes are modest and direct about themselves because their energy is invested in being only who they are. They are genuine and authentic, nothing more and nothing less than what they seem to be. Their reality and their image converge, giving them a firm foundation upon which to develop as persons. Their feelings originate from within instead of being simulated during interactions with others. Others become real to them because healthy Threes are becoming real to themselves. They value other people rather than seeing them as ciphers to be exploited for their own glorification.

If there are fewer traits to mention about very healthy Threes than there are about the other personality types at a corresponding degree of health, it is because Threes begin to develop themselves as genuine persons only when they have accepted themselves. They are just beginning to bring the whole of themselves into being. Their development is interior and personal, a matter of changing attitudes and deepening values rather than outward behavior. In a way, very healthy Threes can be characterized by what they are *not* rather than by what they are: they are not image-oriented, not narcissistic, not exploitative, and not hostile. They are, however, individuals who are still in potential, about to make something valuable of themselves.

THE SELF-ASSURED PERSON

Even healthy Threes are not always this healthy. Instead of being inner-directed, they more typically interact with others to defend themselves against the anxiety of being rejected. Aware of how others regard them, healthy Threes go out of their way to assure themselves of affirmation by adapting to others' expectations.

Since they possess the most exquisite social instincts, healthy Threes are extraordinarily well adapted to other people, effortlessly responding to attention the way leaves turn their faces to catch sunlight. Every shift of emotion, every variation of warmth or cooling by others registers immediately in the Three's psyche, in the same way that a sunbather can tell when the thinnest cloud comes between him and the sun. When Threes bask in the attention of others, they positively glow. The affirmation and attention of others makes them feel alive and good about themselves.

Their psychic dynamics are difficult to describe precisely because there is a subtle interaction continually taking place between Threes and other people. The affirming attention of others makes Threes feel desirable, and they respond to people by imitating the values they see in others. Others, seeing themselves reflected in Threes, continue to shower them with attention — and the interaction is sustained.

This subtle interaction began in childhood when, endowed with high self-esteem by the affirmation of their mothers, Threes learned to believe in their own special value as persons. Even at an early age, they were self-assured, convinced of their own worth, as if always saying to themselves, "I am a valuable, significant person." Their self-assurance and feelings of desirability make healthy Threes extremely attractive, which encourages more interactions and more affirmation of themselves. Other people are also attracted to Threes because, as a group, they are more physically attractive than any other personality type — often they were beautiful children whose mothers virtually adored them. They may grow up to be beautiful, athletic, or otherwise endowed with outstanding physical qualities which attract the attention of others. Their physical attractiveness gives them added reason for high self-esteem and self-assurance. Furthermore, others seek out Threes because they enjoy being in their presence: their physical beauty is exciting, stimulating an aesthetic interest in them and frequently a sexual interest as well.

Desirability and attractiveness (both physically and personally) are important qualities for human beings because, on a biological level, we must attract others for the propagation of the species. But we are also social creatures and, to a certain degree, we all need the good regard of others if we are to feel good about ourselves. And people of no other personality type feel better about themselves or are more suited to attracting favorable attention to themselves than healthy Threes.

THE OUTSTANDING PARAGON

Just as negative feelings about oneself reinforce each other, so do positive feelings. Because healthy Threes feel good about themselves, they do things to increase their self-esteem. Having become accustomed to receiving affirmation, they begin to fear being ordinary. As a result, healthy Threes invest time and energy developing themselves, making themselves into outstanding individuals in some way.

Healthy Threes are ambitious and eager to improve themselves in any number of ways — academically, physically, culturally, professionally, and intellectually. They are not ambitious for money or fame or social standing, but to make more of *themselves*. There is much to admire in healthy Threes because they really do embody something excellent. They are worthy of the admiration of others because they are outstanding, frequently model persons in whatever sphere of activity they enter, be it the Olympics, West Point, or medical school. They are all-American boys and girls, men and women who embody the values that the culture admires. (Of course, a particular Three may not embody the values you personally admire or would like to possess, but what he or she always embodies are those values which are affirmed by the culture as a whole.) Thus, Threes are living models of the culture's values, the paragons by which we see and judge ourselves.

Because they possess outstanding qualities, healthy Threes are also able to motivate other people to develop themselves. Others see in Threes what they could be like if they made the effort to develop their potential as Threes have. Moreover, healthy Threes are willing to help others attain the qualities that they embody. If they are terrific dancers, they will teach you how to dance; if they are bodybuilders, they will work out with you at the gym; if they have made a killing on the stock market, they will help you get into the market too.

Not every moment is geared toward self-development. Healthy Threes are extremely charming and lively; they are highly energetic, youthful, and rambunctious, like healthy animals frisking in the sunlight. Their sense of humor admits of a degree of self-mockery, an enjoyment of their own foibles and minor pretentions, which is as disarming as it is charming. These traits, added to their physical attractiveness and other admirable qualities, result in healthy Threes' being in great social demand, because they are so stimulating to be around.

Almost everyone would like to be like a healthy Three, at least in some way. Who would not like to be attractive and at ease with themselves and with others? Who would not like to be self-assured and endowed with the energy and motivation to make the most of their potential? Who would not like to enjoy being themselves as healthy Threes so evidently do? When they are healthy, Threes are truly stars. When you are in their presence, you are aware of something special about them.

Analyzing the Average Three

THE COMPETITIVE STATUS SEEKER

A shift in attitude now takes place: Threes begin to want to distinguish themselves from others. The difference between healthy Threes and average Threes is that average Threes want to establish their superiority over others through competition. Rising above others reinforces their self-esteem, making Threes feel more desirable and more worthy of attention and admiration.

For example, they may be good swimmers or tennis players, but they begin to feel that this is not enough, that they must outdo everyone else. Average Threes therefore create rivalries where none existed. Everything is turned into a contest — their looks, their professional accomplishments, their salaries, their careers, the desirability of their spouses, as if they were always saying "My so-and-so is better than yours." Unfortunately, creating competitions puts all their relationships on an entirely new footing because they begin to compare themselves constantly with others.

One of the most important consequences of this is that their activities all become geared toward winning the competition which is always in the backs of their minds. Average Threes are not concerned with what they have or do because they enjoy it, but because it makes them feel superior to someone else.

Conflicts with others also begin, and get progressively worse, as a result of their competitiveness. Because it is difficult for average Threes to have positive feelings for anyone with whom they compete, they begin to have problems making friends with their peers. Competitiveness makes average Threes see others as threats and obstacles to their own success. They feel comfortable around people only if they feel superior to them in some way, either because others have less status than they do, or because Threes have beaten them in some kind of open or covert contest.

Average Threes pursue success with an efficiency unrivaled by any other personality type. (We can characterize average Threes in a nutshell by the three things they value most highly: success, prestige, and status.) Success to Threes means being number one, a winner. To be sure, average Threes work hard to get and stay on top. They value professional competence and aim at being the best at what they do, mainly for the prestige of being at the top of their profession. The ultimate mark of success for average Threes is to become rich and famous, especially famous. Fame has a deep appeal to them because it means being known by a large number of people. With fame, their existence is affirmed: they are not nobodies.

At this stage, they are careerists, since professional success is the gauge by which they measure their value as persons. Plotting career moves relentlessly, they want to advance as quickly as possible and are willing to do whatever it takes to achieve the success they seek. They get on the fast track at any cost, even if it means sacrificing a marriage, family, or friends. Having a prestigious title or profession is important to average Threes because it reinforces their sense of themselves as successful. (For the same reason, their self-esteem is highly threatened if they do not have a prestigious career, and doubly so if they are unemployed.)

Quintessential status seekers, average Threes are upwardly mobile social climbers for whom having the right friends and associates is critical. They are forever making contacts and cultivating people to further their careers and add to their social luster. They size up others quickly according to their prestige value, as if to ask, "How much status do you have? Are you worth pursuing?"

They are also typically the promoters of status symbols, by creating new social values. Average Threes give possessions their status by adopting them, then using them as the basis for competition with others. Furthermore, exclusivity is a very important adjunct to competitiveness because by excluding less desirable people from their social circle, average Threes make themselves arbiters of who is "in" and who is "out." Status is thus the game of oneupmanship played by those who idolize success. As self-styled arbiters of status, Threes need to ensure that whoever else plays the game will fail, yet still come back for more.

THE IMAGE-ORIENTED PRAGMATIST

Fearful of what others may think about their status and prestige, average Threes at this stage increase the competition with others not by improving themselves, but by improving their self-presentation, their image. They want to make a favorable impression, whether or not the image they project reflects who they actually are. Style over substance — how one comes across to others — becomes supremely important.

The result is that average Threes become less desirable as genuine human beings and more desirable as commodities. Image-oriented Threes correspond (in part) to the personality type described by Erich Fromm as the "marketing orientation."

> The character orientation which is rooted in the experience of oneself as a commodity and of one's value as exchange value. . . .
>
> Success depends largely on how well a person sells himself on the market, how well he gets his personality across, how nice a "package" he is. . . . A stockbroker, a salesman, a secretary, a railroad executive, a college professor, or a hotel manager must each offer different kinds of personality that, regardless of their differences, must fulfill one condition: to be in demand. . . .
>
> The marketing orientation . . . does not develop something which is potentially in the person (unless we make the absurd assertion that "nothing" is also part of the human equipment); its very nature is that no specific and permanent kind of relatedness is developed, but that the very changeability of attitudes is the only permanent quality of such orientation. In this orientation, those qualities are developed which can best be sold. Not one particular attitude is predominant, but the emptiness which can be filled most quickly with the desired quality. This quality, however, ceases to be one in the proper sense of the word; it is only a role, the pretense of a quality, to be readily exchanged if another one is more desirable. (Fromm, *Man for Himself*, 76–77, 84.)

Because average Threes see themselves as commodities, how others perceive them and their image becomes everything. There is, according to this view, no such thing as intrinsic value either in themselves or in others or in the world — only the image whose perfection they seek. Thus, everything is cheapened because the only value anything or anyone has is whether or not it is in demand.

The problem is that they act according to the needs of the image they are projecting, not because they sincerely believe in what they are saying or doing. They can project one synthesized emotional state after another, each equally convincing. They may appear to be sincere, friendly, modest, kindly, repentant, virtuous, and truthful, although they may not be. They may have only adjusted their image to meet the demands of the moment. What they appear to be and what they actually are begin to be quite different. Thus, there is an element of phoniness about average Threes because much of what they say and do is not a true reflection of who they are. "Who they are" is becoming ever more difficult to identify.

Average Threes know how to package themselves. Like the changing coloration of a chameleon, an image is useful to the degree that it allows one to fit into the environment perfectly. Their image allows them to do just that, only one better: they do not merely fit into the environment, the perfect image they project becomes the standard by which others judge themselves. The image assumes a reality of its own once others accept it as desirable.

It is important to stress how subtle average Threes can be in projecting a believable image, and how difficult it is for others to detect whatever degree of falsity is involved, especially if a particular Three is intelligent and well educated. This personality type is by no means limited to vacuous television game show hosts, beauty contestants, or cloned yuppies. Average Threes can be found everywhere, in every profession, from MBA's to White House operatives, from sports figures to politicians, from artists to network anchorpersons.

The clue that others are dealing with an image rather than a person is the average Three's apparent perfection. Threes come across extremely well (the cool, composed Mr. Nice Guy is typical), although in a rehearsed, synthetic way. They are extremely smooth or slick, able to act whatever role they are playing to perfection. Moreover, they are constantly aware of whether others are buying their performance.

It is precisely because their behavior is so perfect that it is difficult for others to put their finger on what Threes lack. If, however, others look deeply enough, they will find nothing essential about average Threes — no genuine feelings, no deeply held personal opinions, no idiosyncrasies, and no passion beneath the smoothly polished surface. Although everything about them seems perfect, the various images do not add up to a whole person. What is missing is a personal sense of engagement and commitment. Average Threes are not connected with themselves, with their own feelings. They are like perfectly engineered machines which perform precisely as expected and therefore continue to be in demand.

As you might expect, there are difficulties with this orientation. Average Threes fear genuine intimacy lest anyone discover their inner emptiness. However, with their considerable charm and ability to adapt to people, they know how to simulate the impression of intimacy, seemingly revealing more of themselves than they really do. This is why average Threes are typically concerned about credibility, with whether people believe the image which they are projecting.

They also fear intimacy because, beneath the image, whatever it is, average Threes are cold and calculating. What they say and do, their opinions and apparent beliefs, are all pragmatically premeditated for effect. Having lived this way all their lives, average Threes are extremely convincing.

On the other hand, there are benefits. Being affectless allows Threes to be extremely efficient at work, unusually able to focus their energy on attaining professional goals. Like every personality type, average Threes make a virtue of necessity: because they are unemotional, they have no strong feelings to tie them down to anything or anyone. Expedient and goal-oriented, they are good at practical problem solving because their pragmatism allows them to respond to situations without being constrained by abstract principles or feelings. They can take either side of an issue — and switch to the opposite side with incredible ease — because they are unfettered by personal convictions or loyalty to anything beyond themselves.

They are essentially technicians who search for a precise technique which they can turn into a formula for success, whether in their careers or their personal lives. Average Threes are masters of jargon, supreme manipulators of symbols to effect their ends, whether to elect a president, sell a toothpaste, or promote themselves. But, despite their charm and perfect behavior, there is something reptilian about them: their cold-bloodedness has an edge of menace about it.

Without a moral system to direct them, the only source of guidance for Threes at this Level is "what works." While they are well suited to mastering technical problems, average Threes are usually not good leaders because they have no personal vision, few genuine values, and no real concern for others. Unfortunately, however, Threes are attracted to positions of leadership because prestige is involved. The upshot is that they lead by following, by telling people what they want to hear rather than what they need to do. Once the image becomes the reality, it takes on a false life of its own.

THE SELF-PROMOTING NARCISSIST

If, despite the excellence of their image, average Threes do not receive the affirmation they want, they shift into an overdrive of self-promotion to impress others. They want others to admire and envy them, to make others think that they are absolutely outstanding in every way, that they have it all, that they are nothing less than perfect.

Impressing people with their complete superiority is the keynote here. They begin to advertise themselves relentlessly, bragging about their accomplishments, pretentiously dropping important-sounding names, "hyping" their achievements, making themselves sound incredibly wonderful, and making whatever they do seem better than whatever anyone else does — and better than it actually is.

Everything they do at this stage is for show, to get people to notice and admire them. Their self-displays all have the subtext "Look at me!" They become shameless braggarts, showing off their culture, their education, their status, their bodies, their intelligence, their careers, their spouses, their sexual conquests, their wit — whatever they think will garner admiration. Their only subject of conversation is themselves, their first, last, and only love. They act as if others were, or should be, enthralled by everything they say and do: others should be honored to know them.

It goes without saying that narcissistic Threes are arrogant, cocky, and highly impressed with themselves. They see themselves as innately superior to others, as if they were always saying, "I am better than you." Feeling superior to others ensures that they will not be rejected by anyone, and if for some reason they are, the rejection will not bother them, since they feel that those who reject them are inferior and do not count anyway. In short, they look at others only to see if others are looking at them.

At this stage, average Threes begin to oversell themselves, making extraordinary claims about themselves. Narcissistic self-inflation marks a degree of dissociation from their actual selves, with all their real limitations, to claims about a glorious self which does not exist. There is actually less than meets the eye here, although this is difficult to perceive because their sales pitch is usually quite convincing. Nevertheless, although they seem to be outstanding, others may begin to sense that they are too good to be true: much of what they say about themselves just does not add up.

Looking good, literally and figuratively, has always been extremely important to Threes, but physical attractiveness is never more important than when they are openly narcissistic. They strike poses, displaying "attitude" both as a way of being exclusive (and unapproachably better than anyone else) and of drawing attention to themselves (without seeming to do so constantly). Male or female, Threes at this Level are exhibitionistic and seductive, using their sex appeal to increase their desirability. Hypermasculine or hyperfeminine sexual displays — being a hunk or stud or beauty queen — are typical. Of course, not all Threes are physically attractive. Nevertheless, physical qualities are important to them, and those who are not attractive may substitute such narcissistically self-enhancing traits as a reliance on intelligence and cleverness, money and success, fame and prestige to impress others.

Narcissism is essentially passive, and the sexuality of Threes has a passive element to it as well: their egos are gratified when they are admired. Narcissistic Threes want others to desire them, although they are not concerned with gratifying anyone else, either sexually or psychologically.

Narcissistic passivity shows up in other ways. Having won others over, narcissistic Threes become arrogantly complacent. As God's gift, they do not have to make an effort toward real goals. They can coast through life, relying on sex appeal and charm. Whatever energy they may have put into cultivating relationships stops: having charmed or seduced others, Threes can now take them for granted. Or they lose interest in others altogether: having made a conquest, they drop people once they receive the boost to their narcissism they were after. They also enjoy frustrating those who attempt to get close to them, as if to say, "You can look, but you can't touch. You can worship me, but you can't have me."

Conflicts with others also result from their pretensions because Threes begin to believe their own hype, puffing up their achievements to ludicrous extremes. ("My discovery will win the Nobel Prize." "My first art exhibit will sell out on opening day.") The trouble is that the more pretentious they are, the more easily offended they are by anyone's pointing out how unrealistic their evaluations of themselves or their expectations for success have become. The irony is that, because of their grandiose expectations, they actually set themselves up for disappointments. And the more narcissistic they are, the quicker Threes are to feel slighted by others. They are very touchy about their self-worth precisely when their narcissism is most inflated, a sure sign that narcissism is not the same thing as genuine self-esteem.

Indeed, if their narcissism is not constantly reinforced, average Threes begin to get hostile, quickly losing whatever sense of humor about themselves they may have once had. They become contemptuous and sarcastic about everyone else. Under the guise of being honest with others, Threes put people down to stay on top, at least in their own minds. Those few friends they still have come in for shabby treatment; they are ignored, stood up on dates or for appointments without apology, and made to feel inadequate and inferior in many different ways. An arrogant smirk says it all.

Analyzing the Unhealthy Three

THE EXPLOITATIVE OPPORTUNIST

Failure is one of the most humiliating prospects for Threes. If they continue to overextend themselves and cannot make good on their claims, they will attempt to maintain their inflated self-esteem by exploiting others.

As unhealthy Threes see it, exploitation of some sort is necessary to continue to project a superior self-image. Ironically, they have become superior not only to everyone else, but also to themselves by overshooting the limits of their talents. Either they must come down to earth and recognize their limitations, or they must take what they need from others to maintain their superiority.

Their fear of failure, and thus of humiliation, makes unhealthy Threes more than willing to be dishonest to get what they need to maintain at least the illusion of superiority. We have already seen that they are pragmatists and have no principles other than what works for them. Now we see the consequences: they lie on their résumés, take credit for the work of others, or plagiarize to make themselves seem more outstanding than they are. Unhealthy Threes are determined not to be losers, no matter who must pay the price for their success.

They are ready to sell out, lie, change their "loyalties," or take advantage of others to come out on top. Because they have never developed a conscience, they do not feel guilty exploiting others. In colloquial terms, unhealthy Threes are hustlers, people "on the make," opportunists taking advantage of situations — always to the detriment of others. Their lack of affect is also particularly valuable now: they can callously use people without the slightest thought for their welfare. ("What's in it for me? How can I use this for myself?")

Others, who may sometimes be aware of their opportunism, are usually afraid of confronting them about it. Unhealthy Threes count on the fact that others dare not say or do anything about their behavior for fear of retaliation. Their lack of decency makes it difficult for others to defend themselves against Threes because they sense that unhealthy Threes will go lower than they are willing to descend.

Exploiting people reveals the contempt in which unhealthy Threes hold others. Because they do not see other people as real or as having value without reference to themselves, using people is not a moral problem for them — because they have no morals. Others are merely providers of attention and admiration, what are called "narcissistic supplies," as objects to be used to aggrandize themselves. This is why there is absolutely nothing reciprocal about a relationship with unhealthy Threes. They will keep a relationship going as long as they get what they want, but will drop someone without a second thought, particularly if someone more desirable comes along. One of the tip-offs that, despite appearances, there is something wrong with unhealthy Threes is precisely their lack of long-term relationships. They run through a staggering number of friends and acquaintances, exploiting people and dropping them once they have gotten what they want.

Yet why are others so often taken advantage of by unhealthy Threes? The answer lies in the strength of the narcissistic desires Threes awaken in others. Others unwittingly give Threes power over them to the degree that they lack true self-esteem themselves. They mistakenly think that Threes will somehow endow them with what appears to be their limitless self-esteem. This never happens. Unhealthy Threes take whatever others have to offer and leave them disappointed and rejected. The sad fact is that Threes would have no power over others if people did not give it to them.

Unfortunately, Threes remain highly functional even when they are unhealthy. (It is axiomatic that Threes always seem to be healthier than they really are.) Even a neurotic Three does not seem to be neurotic. Threes do not become depressed, anxious, emotionally conflicted, incapacitated, or self-destructive. On the contrary, they depress others, make others feel anxious and conflicted, incapacitate others, and drive others to self-destructive acts. It is always others who suffer, not they. Threes are able to walk away from relationships as if nothing has happened, and as far as they are concerned, nothing has. Like sharks, they are extraordinarily well adapted to their environment. And like sharks, they injure and kill cold-bloodedly, and keep moving.

THE MALICIOUS TRAITOR

Unhealthy Threes want to exploit others without having their opportunism exposed. Otherwise, they would no longer appear to be superior since they would have to acknowledge their debts and dependencies. They would be humiliated if others knew their limitations. Furthermore, they would likely be punished for exploiting others opportunistically. As a result, unhealthy Threes cover their tracks, becoming cunning and devious, concealing their true motives and actions as much as possible.

The ability to project an image, which we saw in average Threes, is relied upon more than ever. Unhealthy Threes now become completely deceptive so they can sustain whatever dishonesty they are guilty of while not appearing to be dishonest. ("False face must hide what false heart doth know." — *Macbeth*, I, vii, 82) The image they now project is still convincing, but beneath it, they have become extremely treacherous. Others almost always find out what kind of people neurotic Threes are only after they have already done their damage.

Sneaky and two-faced, neurotic Threes will stab people in the back without a second thought. They do not hesitate to ruin reputations, stir up trouble, double-cross friends, or otherwise betray the trust others have given them. They do not keep secrets, they spread false rumors about others, and they play one person off against another. They sabotage what others have worked for and hurt those who love them because seeing the downfall of others gives them pleasure. ("It is not enough that I succeed, but that others must fail." — Oscar Wilde)

It goes without saying that neurotic Threes are pathological liars. They enjoy lying even if nothing significant depends on it because it gives them a narcissistic boost. They may lie merely to amuse themselves by contemptuously toying with people. Successful lies prove their superiority and the stupidity of others. Many times, however, their lies are far from insignificant, causing others enormous harm, financial loss, or emotional torment. No matter — unhealthy Threes like to cause trouble. Seeing people squirm makes them feel good.

While moments of hostility have erupted from time to time in the past, their hostility has grown into an irrational malice, the result of the extreme jealousy they feel toward anyone who has anything they want. Despite their contempt for people, neurotic Threes are secretly intensely jealous of others precisely because others have attained worthwhile goals instead of chasing after narcissistic illusions. Therefore anyone who is authentic or capable of feeling or who loves and is loved — in short, anyone who is a normal human being — is a threat to their superiority and an object of their malice. Maliciousness may reach delusional proportions as neurotic Threes become obsessed with ruining others so they can be triumphant. It is the dark, hidden side of themselves which they cannot show others.

THE VINDICTIVE PSYCHOPATH

Neurotic Threes secretly fear that others are, and always will be, superior to them. At this stage, they move beyond deception into unmitigated vindictiveness, in effect saying, "I will triumph over you no matter what it takes!" And, if they have nothing to lose, neurotic Threes will stop at nothing. Since they have no capacity to empathize with anyone, nothing restrains them from seriously harming others. Indeed, harming others is essential if they are to continue to feel superior.

> The need for a vindictive triumph then manifests itself mainly in often irresistible, mostly unconscious impulses to frustrate, outwit, or defeat others in personal relations. . . .
> Much more frequently the drive toward a vindictive triumph is hidden. Indeed, because of its destructive nature, it is the most hidden element in the search for glory. It may be that only a rather frantic ambition will be apparent. In analysis alone are we able to see that the driving power behind it is the need to defeat and humiliate others by rising above them. (Karen Horney, *Neurosis and Human Growth*, 27–28.)

At this stage, they are sadistic, diabolically so. They sink to the inhuman level of the psychopath, ignoring the normal limits of behavior, acting out their cruelest fantasies of revenge. Having no internal brakes on their behavior, they do whatever they can until their fury is spent, others are ruined, or someone stops them.

In addition to crimes like assault, arson, and sabotage, psychopathic Threes are entirely capable of murder. Threes are probably the predominant personality type which becomes mass murderers or terrorists who strike out randomly at people. They are capable of killing with as little remorse as normal people have in crushing a paper cup. Their psychopathic behavior may seem unmotivated because of the randomness of their violence, as in the case of a sniper shooting at people on a street below. But from the psychopath's point of view, the crime is motivated by the constant need to regain superiority by destroying others.

It is also worth noting that male psychopaths' victims are frequently women, and since Threes identified with their mothers, this fits the pattern. Their mothers' high regard inadvertently trained them to be narcissistic, and if their narcissism is frustrated, their rage is turned against their mothers or mother substitutes. Rape, torture, and sexual mutilation are frequent outcomes.

Despite their duplicity and deviousness, psychopathic Threes may trip themselves up because part of their need for vindictive triumph includes the desire for their victims to know who victimized them. Their need for attention and affirmation, which we have seen from stage to stage in different forms, becomes their nemesis. However, psychopathic Threes do not care. Public condemnation and notoriety give them the attention they crave: being feared or despised affirms that they exist as "somebody."

Analyzing the Dynamics of the Three

THE DIRECTION OF DISINTEGRATION: THE THREE GOES TO NINE

The underlying problem with Threes is that they are out of touch with their feelings. A move to Nine thoroughly compounds and intensifies this problem, marking a sudden breakdown of their neurotic defenses. They deteriorate into a psychotic-like condition, into a dreamworld from which Threes think that they will not awake. Everything becomes unreal, including the horrible acts they may have perpetrated on others. They no longer feel enraged or hostile or vindictive. When they go to Nine, neurotic Threes unconsciously dissociate themselves from the only feelings they have, their hostile feelings, so completely that they feel absolutely nothing. They are not depressed, but "dead," flat, without energy or interest in anything, even themselves.

When deteriorated Threes become this depersonalized, the extent of their true alienation from themselves becomes apparent. The inflated illusions with which their narcissism allowed them to maintain their sense of self has collapsed, exposing their emptiness. They stop taking an interest in themselves, may gain weight, and sink into a vegetative state. Deteriorated Threes achieve a kind of unity with themselves, but it is the false unity of psychosis. They may also begin to experience moments of anxiety, possibly for the first time in their lives.

If they cannot escape anxiety by gaining support from others, disintegrated Threes may deteriorate even further, into fragmented multiple personalities. This is a final ironic twist for persons who have relied on projecting multiple images of themselves. Their multiple personalities are probably more real, that is, more accurate, reflections of themselves, than the false images they have previously shown to others.

THE DIRECTION OF INTEGRATION: THE THREE GOES TO SIX

Going to Six is frightening for Threes because in doing so, they commit themselves to someone else, exposing themselves to the fear of being rejected. Genuine intimacy with others is especially threatening to Threes because the other will likely see through their image to the reality beneath, a reality which may still be rather undeveloped.

When healthy Threes go to Six, however, they become committed to something or someone outside themselves, realizing that their value is not diminished by being part of something greater than they. Integrating Threes discover that by their commitment to something outside themselves, they paradoxically begin to grow as persons within themselves. Identifying with others allows solid values to take root.

Their commitment to others also allows Threes to do what they are so afraid of doing: exposing how undeveloped they are to someone else. But because they do so within a committed relationship, they find that they are still accepted and therefore have a firm foundation upon which to begin to develop themselves. (A religious conversion may be extremely helpful in this regard.) What also helps healthy Threes to go to and remain at Six is the experience of falling in love with someone who is clearly their superior. If Threes can admire and feel loved by others with whom they are not competitive, relationships have a real chance of lasting. Once Threes have established a committed relationship, the relationship draws qualities from them which may well help them to remain healthy.

When they move to Six, Threes no longer worry about impressing others with their prestige, success, or status, nor do they aggrandize themselves at the expense of others. They use their talents to affirm the value of others rather than themselves. Last, by recognizing the existence of values beyond themselves, integrating Threes develop their consciences. They recognize limits on their behavior and limits on what they can expect from themselves, from others, and from life.

The Major Subtypes of the Three

THE THREE WITH A TWO-WING

In general, the Three's traits and those of a Two-wing reinforce each other. Threes with a Two-wing have extraordinary social skills: they like to be among people and enjoy being the center of attention; they are often extremely charming, sociable, and highly popular. They are also among the most physically attractive of the types, something which adds considerably to their social desirability, as well as to their stimulating effect on others. Noteworthy examples of the Three with a Two-wing include Burt Reynolds, Elvis Presley, Prince Andrew, Jack Kemp, Brooke Shields, Christopher Reeve, Cybill Shepherd, Vanna White, Mark Spitz, Bruce Jenner, Mary Lou Retton, Jane Pauley, Richard Gere, Philip Michael Thomas, Arnold Schwarzenegger, Ted Bundy, Gary Gilmore, Hedda Gabler, and Lady Macbeth.

Depending on how much Two-wing is operative, healthy Threes of this subtype possess some degree of warmth and positive feelings for people — Threes are not completely affectless, of course. They care about those few people they are close to. They can encourage and appreciate others, and their feelings can be touched and hurt. Threes with a Two-wing usually want a particular kind of affirmation from others: besides receiving attention, they want to be loved. This encourages them to be more responsive to the needs and desires of others.

Average Threes of this subtype are able to project their feelings, or the illusion of feelings, as the case may be. Actors, models, and singers are frequently of this subtype. Besides there being a histrionic quality here, elements of possessiveness, the desire to control others, and self-importance begin to emerge. People of this subtype care a great deal about what others think of them: competitiveness, comparing themselves to others, and success in their relationships are particularly important. They not only desire an enviable relationship with a spouse, they want the spouse to be a catch, sexually and socially desirable, one who reflects well on them. Children are also typically narcissistic extensions of the self, as are the home, hobbies, vacation spots, and other values in their lives. The narcissism of this subtype is more open than that of Threes with a Fourwing. Exhibitionism and seductiveness are also more pronounced in people of this subtype.

Unhealthy Threes of this subtype are not only deceptive about getting what they want from others; they can be self-deceptive as well. They can be manipulative and feel entitled, which whets their appetite for revenge against those who do not give them the attention and love they demand. Both the Three and the Two-wing have a problem with aggression: Twos feel aggressive when others do not appreciate them, and Threes are hostile when there is any slight to their narcissism. The combination produces particularly hostile people if they are not on top. The jealousy we see in unhealthy Threes is also present in unhealthy Twos, motivating these people to coerce others to give them what they want. Threes with a Two-wing become malicious toward others, even psychopathically destructive. They are charming psychopaths, attractive men and women who seem to have had everything going for them until they suddenly become violent, usually toward those with whom they are closest, but who, for whatever reason, have frustrated their narcissistic needs.

THE THREE WITH A FOUR-WING

The traits of the Three and those of a Four-wing produce a complex subtype whose traits often conflict with each other. The Three is essentially an "interpersonal" type, whereas the Four withdraws from contact with others. To the degree that the Four-wing is operative, some persons of this subtype seem more like Fours than Threes: they can be quiet, rather private, subdued in demeanor, and have artistic interests and aesthetic sensibilities. Noteworthy examples of the Three with a Four-wing include Jimmy Carter, Gary

Hart, Bryant Gumbel, Chris Wallace, Sting, Mick Jagger, Sylvester Stallone, Henry Winkler, Michael Tilson Thomas, Dick Cavett, Truman Capote, Andy Warhol, Somerset Maugham, and Iago.

Healthy Threes with a Four-wing have some amount of intuition which they can direct both toward themselves and others. Because some self-awareness is also part of the picture, people of this subtype have more potential for gaining self-knowledge and developing their emotional lives than Threes with a Two-wing. They may have artistic sensibilities, although these will more likely be in service of their personalities than in creativity for its own sake. People of this subtype are self-assured and outstanding in some way, and yet also introspective and sensitive.

Since Three is the basic type, however, average Threes with a Four-wing will still be competitive with others and interested in success and prestige, although in more subtle ways than the other subtype. Their imaginations will play a more active role and their feelings, such as they are, will likely be focused on aesthetic objects rather than persons. Since Threes with a Four-wing are usually less attractive physically than those with a Two-wing, intelligence will typically be emphasized in their self-images and social dealings. People of this subtype tend to be more pretentious than the other subtype, putting great stock in their ideas and demanding that others do likewise. They are also more aloof and conscious of how others treat them. Narcissistic feelings of superiority and arrogance mingle with the Four's feelings of exemption and self-indulgence. They can be subtle show-offs, but show-offs nonetheless.

Unhealthy Threes of this subtype alternate between the narcissism of the Three and the self-doubt of the Four. Since Three is basic, narcissism and grandiose fantasies are the rule. When they are disappointed, persons of this subtype react with the Four's depression and self-contempt, although their periods of self-accusation will be relatively brief. (People of this subtype may be misidentified as manic-depressives since their moods may change rapidly, an element which Threes with Four-wings have in common with the manic-depressive disorder. However, the underlying problem here is not anxiety but narcissism and the lack of fulfillment of their grandiose expectations.) It is possible that people of this subtype will also be self-destructive and suicidal if constantly frustrated by reality.

Some Final Thoughts

Looking back at Threes, we saw that only at their very healthiest do they achieve authentic selfhood. Even in the other healthy areas of the Continuum, Threes develop only a part of themselves, like bodybuilders who focus on the development of only one part of their physiques instead of seeking an overall balance. While the qualities healthy Threes develop are real, they are parts, not the whole, of themselves. In average Threes we saw the overdevelopment of a much more insubstantial part of themselves, their image, which served their narcissistic self-glorification. And we saw that unhealthy Threes exploit and ruin others rather than develop themselves in any real way.

Because Threes are so adept at projecting favorable impressions of themselves, it is not apparent that they are actually very undeveloped human beings. The irony is that they are more and more dependent on others to affirm their value just when there is progressively less and less of value about them to affirm.

The final irony is that unhealthy Threes have unwittingly brought about what they most feared. They fear being rejected, but because of their narcissism, exploitativeness, and malice, they end up being rejected. The person so desirous of being affirmed by others is despised as less than human. So much of what others admired turns out to have been a false front, a facade, which has collapsed, revealing inner emptiness.

Chapter 6

Type Four: The Artist

The Four in Profile

Healthy: Becomes inspired and creative, expressing the universal in the human condition. Intuitive and thoughtfully self-aware. Self-revealing, personal, emotionally honest: serious and funny, sensitive and emotionally strong.

Average: The artist and romantic, taking an imaginative-aesthetic orientation to life, expressing personal feelings through something beautiful. Gets self-absorbed, introverted, moody, and melancholy. Feels different from others, exempt from living as others do. Self-pitying and self-indulgent, fostering illusions about life and self. Decadent, a dreamer: impractical, unproductive, effete, and precious.

Unhealthy: Can become alienated from self and others, self-inhibiting and depressed: blocked and emotionally paralyzed. Self-contemptuous, tormented by self-reproaches, self-hatred, and morbid thoughts. Despairing, feels hopeless and turns self-destructive, possibly abusing alcohol or drugs to escape. In the extreme: emotional breakdown or suicide.

Key Motivations: Wants to understand himself or herself, to express himself in something beautiful, to withdraw to protect his feelings, to take care of emotional needs before attending to anything else.

Examples: Tennessee Williams, Rudolf Nureyev, Maria Callas, Ingmar Bergman, J. D. Salinger, Franz Kafka, Marcel Proust, Virginia Woolf, Blanche DuBois, and Laura Wingfield.

An Overview of the Four

In the artist of all kinds I think one can detect an inherent dilemma, which belongs to the co-existence of two trends, the urgent need to communicate and the still more urgent need not to be found. (D. W. Winnicott, quoted in Anthony Storr, *The Dynamics of Creation,* 58.)

What more fruitful way to redressing the balance than by portraying one's inner world in a work of art and then persuading other people to accept it, if not as real, at least as highly significant? Part of the satisfaction which a creative person obtains from his achievement may be the feeling that, at last, some part of his inner life is being accepted which has never been accorded recognition before. Moreover, since art became an individual matter rather than a task for anonymous craftsmen, creative work is generally recognized as being especially apt for expressing the personal style of an individual (which is of course closely related to his inner world). The value we place upon authenticity is often exaggerated; yet there is a sense in which it is justified. However good a painting or a piece of music may be, taken quite apart from its creator, the fact that it is or is not another expression of the personality of a particular artist is important. For it either is or is not an addition to our knowledge of that artist; a further revelation of that mysterious, indefinable and fascinating thing — his personality. (Anthony Storr, *The Dynamics of Creation,* 58.)

The nature of creativity will probably always remain mysterious because its basis is irrational — in the feelings and unconscious of those who create — and because, as Winnicott notes, part of the motive for creating is to remain concealed, to be unfound by others. Yet the motives given for artistic work — to communicate and to conceal the self — are but two possible motives which any person may have for creating. These two motives are, however, particularly appropriate to the Four, the artistic temperament among the personality types. Of course, members of any other personality type can become artists in the sense of making a livelihood by producing works of art, however that is defined. But only Fours turn to art and creativity as ways of communicating and concealing themselves from other people. Fours are in search of themselves. Art is the foremost means they have of finding themselves, as well as their way of reporting to the world what they have discovered.

IN THE FEELING TRIAD

The Four is the personality type which emphasizes the subjective world of feelings, in creativity and individualism, in introversion and self-absorption, and in self-torment and self-hatred. In this personality type we see creative artists, romantic aesthetes, and withdrawn dreamers, people with powerful feelings who feel different from others because self-awareness blocks them from getting outside themselves.

Fours are the most self-aware of the types, and this is the basis of what is most positive and negative about them. The constant conflict we see in Fours is between their need to be aware of themselves, so they can find themselves, and, at the same time, their need to move beyond self-awareness, so they will not be trapped in self-consciousness. The tension between self-awareness and self-transcendence can be resolved in creativity. In the creative moment, healthy Fours harness their emotions without constricting them, not only producing something beautiful but discovering who they are. In the moment of inspiration, they are, paradoxically, both most themselves and most liberated from themselves. This is why all forms of creativity are so valued by Fours, and why in its inspired state, creativity is so hard to sustain. Fours can be inspired only if they have first transcended themselves, something which is extremely threatening to their self-awareness. In a sense, then, only by learning not to look for themselves will they find themselves and renew themselves in the process.

The problem with average Fours, however, is that they try to understand themselves by introspecting on their feelings. As they move inward in a search for self, they become so acutely self-conscious that their subjective emotional states become the dominant reality for them. And, because even average Fours are so involved with their emotions, they do not usually express their feelings directly. Instead, they communicate their feelings indirectly through art, if they have the talent and training to do so.

The overall direction of their personalities therefore is inward, toward increasing self-absorption, because Fours feel that they are different from other people, and they want to know why they feel this way. Ironically, however, they try to find their place in life by withdrawing from it so they can trace the labyrinth of their emotions. But the result of their withdrawal is that even average Fours have noticeable difficulties coping with life, while unhealthy Fours have some of the most severe emotional difficulties of all the personality types.

In healthy Fours, however, the rich life of the unconscious becomes accessible and is given shape. More than any other personality type, healthy Fours are the bridge between the spiritual and the animal in human nature because they are so aware of these two sides of themselves. They sense in themselves the depths to which human beings can descend, as well as the heights to which they can be swept up. No other personality type is as habitually aware of the potentials and predicaments of human nature: human beings are spiritual animals occupying an uneasy place between two orders of existence. Fours sense both sides of their potentially conflicting natures, and they suffer intensely or are ecstatic because of them. This is why, at their best, healthy Fours create something which can move others deeply because they have been able to get in touch with the hidden depths of human nature by delving deeply into their own. By doing so, they transcend themselves and are able to discover something universal about human nature, fusing personal conflicts and divergent feelings into art.

But, like everyone else, most Fours do not live at the peak of their potential. In response to anxiety, they turn inward, becoming self-conscious, particularly about the negativity they discover in themselves. To offset their negative feelings, they use their imaginations to make their lives more bearable. As a result, average Fours begin to withdraw from ordinary life. They become self-absorbed and do not learn how to relate to people or how to manage in the practical world. They feel like outsiders, somehow flawed and different from others, unable to break through the barrier of self-consciousness that separates them from easy commerce with the world.

And if they are unhealthy, their negative feelings feed upon themselves because Fours have closed themselves off from any other influences. Unhealthy Fours are so completely alienated from others, and ironically, even from themselves, that they despair of ever finding a way out of their excruciating self-consciousness. They realize that their search for self has led them into a world of useless fantasies and illusions. Understanding only too clearly what they have done to themselves, and fearing that it is too late to do anything about it, unhealthy Fours hate and torment themselves, turning against themselves to destroy what they have become.

PROBLEMS WITH IDENTITY

Fours find it difficult to transcend self-consciousness because just the reverse is what they want: to become more conscious of themselves so that they can find themselves and arrive at a firm sense of identity by sorting out their feelings. But as they become more self-conscious, Fours become increasingly drawn into unresolved, contradictory, and irrational feelings which they want to sort out before they dare express them.

Self-discovery is an extremely important motive for Fours because they never feel that their sense of self is strong enough to sustain their identities, particularly if they need to assert themselves. Because their feelings change so readily, their sense of identity is not solid, dependable, in their own hands. They feel undefined and uncertain of themselves, as if they were a gathering cloud which may produce something of great power or merely dissipate in the next breeze. Fours can never tell how the next moment will affect them, so it is difficult for them to count on themselves. Something is missing in the self, something they cannot quite put their fingers on, but which they feel they lack nonetheless.

The difficulty is that average Fours may not know what their feelings are until after they have expressed them personally or artistically. But if they express all that they feel, they fear that they may reveal too much, exposing themselves to shame or punishment. On the other hand, by not expressing their feelings, average

Fours undermine the possibility of discovering themselves by getting caught in endless self-absorption. They become aware of being aware of themselves — their consciousness is filled with little more than fantasies and memories, ultimately leading to illusions, regrets, and a wasted life.

CHILDHOOD ORIGINS

As children, Fours did not identify with either their mothers or their fathers. ("I am not like my mother; I am not like my father.") They usually had either unhappy or solitary childhoods as a result of their parents' marital problems, divorce, illness, or simply because of personality conflicts within the family. Lacking positive role models, Fours, as children, turned inward to their feelings and imaginations as the primary sources of information about themselves from which they could construct their identities.

From childhood, Fours felt essentially alone in life. It seemed to them that, for reasons they could not understand, their parents had rejected them, or at least that their parents did not take much interest in them. Fours therefore felt that there must be something deeply wrong with them, that they were somehow defective because their parents did not give them the kind of nurturing attention which, as children, they needed. As a result, they turned to themselves to discover who they are.

Self-knowledge became their most important goal, the means by which they hoped to fit into the world. Fours felt that if they could discover who they are, they would not feel so different from others in the deep, essential way that they do. However, instead of creating themselves through introspection, Fours ironically become trapped in self-consciousness. Their self-consciousness alienates them, making them feel vulnerable and arousing their aggressions at themselves and others, particularly their parents. But because they also feel powerless to express their aggressions or do anything about their condition, they withdraw from their parents and from others, turning their aggressions against themselves.

PROBLEMS WITH HOSTILITY AND DESPAIR

Like Twos and Threes, the other two personality types of the Feeling Triad, Fours have a problem with hostility. They direct their hostility at themselves because of their unconscious fear that something is fundamentally wrong with them. Because they feel that their parents disregarded them, Fours have learned, in effect, to doubt themselves and their worth. Angry with themselves for being defective, Fours inhibit and punish themselves in the many ways which we will see.

On a deep, unconscious level Fours are also hostile toward their parents because they feel that their parents did not nurture them properly. Fours feel that they were not welcomed into the world; they feel out of place, unwanted — and they are deeply enraged at their parents for doing this to them. However, their rage at their parents is so deep that Fours cannot allow themselves to express it. They fear their own anger, and so withhold it, trying to come to terms with it themselves.

As awareness of their hostility and negative feelings gradually wears them out, average to unhealthy Fours sink ever more deeply into self-doubt, depression, and despair. They spend most of their time searching for the courage to go on living despite the overwhelming sense that the essential flaw in themselves is so deep that it cannot be healed. Indeed, the feeling of hopelessness is the current against which they must constantly swim. And if the undertow of hopelessness is too strong, unhealthy Fours either succumb to an emotional breakdown or commit suicide because they despair of ever breaking free of it.

As soon as Fours devote themselves to a search for self by withdrawing from life, they are going in the wrong direction. No matter how necessary this search may seem to them, they must become convinced that the direct search for self is a temptation which eventually leads to despair.

On the other hand, what makes healthy Fours healthy is not that they have freed themselves once and for all from the turbulence of their emotions, but that they have found a way to ride that current to some further destination. Healthy Fours have learned to sustain their identities without exclusive reference to their feelings. By overcoming the temptation to withdraw from life to search for themselves, they will not only save themselves from their own destructiveness, they will be able to bring something beautiful and good into existence. If they learn to live this way, Fours can be among the most life-enhancing of the personality types, bringing good out of evil, hope from hopelessness, meaning from absurdity, and saving what appeared to be lost.

Analyzing the Healthy Four

THE INSPIRED CREATOR

Of all the personality types, very healthy Fours are most in touch with impulses from their unconscious. They have learned to listen to their inner voices while remaining open to impressions from the environment. Most important, they are able to act without self-consciousness, and if they have the talent and training, are able to give their unconscious impulses an objective form in a work of art worthy of the name.

Having transcended self-consciousness, healthy Fours are free to become creative in the root sense of being able to bring something new into the world. Of course, profoundly creative moments come and go because creativity is difficult to sustain. Nevertheless, at their best, Fours are able to sustain creativity because they have transcended their self-consciousness, opening the way to inspiration. They draw inspiration from the widest variety of sources, filtering the raw material of experience through the unconscious. In doing so, inspired Fours are like oysters, transforming all their experiences, even painful ones, into something beautiful. In their inspired creative work, healthy Fours become wellsprings of revelation for others, as if they were conduits through which the sublime passes into the world.

Their creativity is paradoxical because Fours are able to express the personal universally, in something that has resonance and meaning beyond what they intend when they create. By opening themselves to their hidden depths, Fours are able to express something true about everyone. Yet, it is difficult for them to explain where their creativity has come from. Much of their knowledge about themselves and others has the quality of being an inspiration, something which comes to them spontaneously, completely, mysteriously, and beyond their conscious control.

Being creative is not limited to artists, but is an important quality which everyone should try to awaken within themselves. The most important form of creativity is self-creation — renewing and redeeming the self by transcending the ego. It is the process of turning all your experiences, good and bad, into something more for your growth as a person. ("Be the kind of person on whom nothing is lost." — William James)

> [Otto] Rank did not glorify the artist as such, but rather the creative individual, whose expressions varied with the cultural conditions in which he found himself. . . . In fact, Rank argued, the creative artist is still seeking in art a refuge which it would be better to give up and return to real life. Once he does that, he becomes the new man whom psychoanalysis is seeking to create. (Reuben Fine, *A History of Psychoanalysis*, 271.)

By acting in the moment of inspiration which is not primarily a moment of feeling, Fours paradoxically create and discover themselves in what they bring into the world. The problem with their identities begins to be solved. Fours are "told" who they are not by their parents, but by what they discover in their creativity. This is why Fours at their healthiest are not merely artists, as Rank indicates, but creative, life-enhancing individuals, who may also be artists. To be able to renew the self constantly is the highest form of creativity, a kind of "soul-making," which requires a higher state of integration than making a painting or a book or a dance. This is the state the other personality types can learn from healthy Fours, and the state to which Fours constantly aspire.

THE SELF-AWARE INTUITIVE

Even relatively healthy Fours do not always live at such a high level of consciousness. When they draw back from the inspired, creative moment to reflect upon it, or to enjoy their creativity, they lose the unselfconsciousness necessary to sustain it. Inspired creativity can be maintained only in the act itself, by continuing to transcend self-consciousness. Thus as soon as they become conscious of themselves, Fours lose the spontaneous quality of inspiration, becoming self-aware and introspective.

As we saw in the Overview, one of their basic motivations is to understand who they are, since they were not mirrored adequately by their parents. ("Who am I? What is my life all about?") They pay attention to their feelings, to see what they can find out about themselves from this ever present source of self-knowledge.

However, awareness of their feelings creates the problem of automatically distancing even healthy Fours from their environment. Life becomes a kind of theater in which, for better or worse, they are both spectators and actors. While self-awareness allows healthy Fours to use the distance they sense between themselves and everything else as a framing device to understand themselves more clearly, self-awareness also makes it difficult for them to be self-assertive or sustain practical activities. Moreover, they realize that there is nowhere for them to hide. Fours are forced to acknowledge disquieting realities about themselves, others, and life because self-awareness makes them sensitive both to the world and to their subconscious. Nevertheless, healthy Fours are not afraid of what their feelings are telling them, even though those feelings may be painful and disturbing.

Fours are not only sensitive to themselves, they are sensitive to others because they are intuitive. Intuition gives Fours the ability to understand how others think and feel and see the world. Intuition is not some sort of useless side-show telepathy, but a means of perceiving reality by way of the unconscious. It is like receiving a message in a bottle which has washed up on the shore of consciousness.

Self-awareness is the psychological basis of intuition. Fours are conscious of themselves, the world, and other people by way of the unconscious. And, it is by seeing how their experiences affect them that Fours hope to discover their own dimensions. (Or more poetically, "I note the echo that each thing produces as it strikes my soul." — Stendhal)

Fours correspond to Jung's introverted intuitive type.

Introverted intuition is directed to the inner object, a term that might justly be applied to the contents of the unconscious. . . .

> Although his intuition may be stimulated by external objects,
> it does not concern itself with external possibilities but with
> what the external object has released within him. . . .
> In this way introverted intuition perceives all the background
> processes of consciousness with almost the same distinctness as
> extraverted sensation registers external objects. For intuition,
> therefore, unconscious images acquire the dignity of things.
> (C. G. Jung, *Psychological Types*, 398–399.)

Because the richest part of their conscious life is outside their
control, even healthy Fours are aware that they are not completely
in control of themselves. Their intuitions come and go like ghosts
which cannot be summoned at will. Moreover, their intuitions can
be unsettling, making them aware of feelings which are difficult to
identify or resolve. Intuitions are also difficult for Fours to express
rationally — precisely because intuitions are irrational and have
unconscious roots. For better or worse, their intuitions make them
conscious of an endless stream of positive and negative feelings
about themselves and the world. It therefore takes Fours time to
identify and understand their intuitions, and courage for them to
accept what their intuitions are telling them.

THE SELF-REVEALING INDIVIDUAL

Healthy Fours need to express what they feel so they can know
what their intuitions are telling them about themselves. They are
the most personal of the personality types, revealing themselves to
others with directness and authenticity. They do not put on masks,
hiding their doubts and weaknesses, nor do they deceive themselves about their feelings and impulses no matter how unseemly or
unflattering these are. Healthy Fours willingly reveal their flaws
and irrationalities to others, since they feel that these things are not
merely incidental to who they are, but reflect their essence. It would
be dishonest to communicate themselves to others if they did not
communicate the whole of themselves, the bad along with the good,
doubts along with certainties. There is something very human about
this: theirs is a genuineness and depth of feeling, a willingness to be
touched, even at the expense of pain, if that is the authentic thing
to do.

Healthy Fours are concerned with being true to themselves as individuals, even at the risk of being censured by those who value tradition or convention over self-actualization. The emotional honesty we find in healthy Fours may well antagonize, or at least embarrass, others, who may wish that Fours were not so candid about themselves. But what healthy Fours bring to society is the example of their humanity, the message that everyone is valuable because they are individuals.

Thus, just as healthy Fours want to be true to themselves, they also want others to be true to themselves. ("This above all: to thine own self be true, / And it must follow, as the night the day, / Thou canst not then be false to any man." — *Hamlet* I, iii, 78–80) They are respectful of the individuality of others, sensitive about their feelings, considerate of their privacy and their needs. Fours willingly allow others to find their own way in life without trying to control them, one reason why they make good parents, friends, listeners, and therapists. They see other people as "other," not as functions of themselves or as objects to be used for their own gratification.

Because healthy Fours are aware of themselves as individuals, they have a sharp sense of their unique otherness, as well as the otherness of everything. Although they are not lonely, they understand that they are alone in life, an individual consciousness. From this point of view, healthy Fours are not merely individualists but existentialists, aware of their existence as individuals.

While there is a certain seriousness about all of this, healthy Fours are not serious about everything. They have a rich sense of humor because they see the poignant absurdity of much of human behavior in the light of the larger questions of life. Healthy Fours have a kind of double vision on human nature: at the same time, they can see the devil and the angel, the sordid and the noble in human beings, especially in themselves. The ironic juxtaposition of such opposites is as funny as it is deeply touching. The incongruities of the human condition make healthy Fours shake their heads in amusement, and nowhere are they more aware of human incongruities than in themselves.

Analyzing the Average Four

THE IMAGINATIVE ARTIST

Fearing that they will be misunderstood, or that their feelings will be hurt if they express themselves too personally, Fours seek other ways of dealing with their feelings, relying on artistic expressions of themselves. Artistic activity of some sort gives them a means both of revealing and communicating themselves without exposing themselves directly.

Of course, not all average Fours are artists, and certainly not all artists are Fours. Nevertheless, since revealing their feelings remains essential to their emotional health, any artistic activity average Fours engage in is especially valued because art becomes a substitute for themselves, a means of expressing the self through a kind of proxy to the world.

If they are professional artists, they must have discovered which medium is best suited for their talents; they also must have learned their craft so that they can express themselves adequately. If Fours are not professional artists, or are in professions that do not allow an artistic outlet for self-expression, they will typically regard their work merely as a way of supporting themselves while their real interest lies elsewhere — in beauty and some sort of aesthetic self-expression. If they were given a magic wish, average Fours who are not artists would choose to become painters, singers, ballet dancers, poets, novelists, sculptors, writers, or some other kind of artist.

If they do not have the ability to make works of art, average Fours try to make their environments more beautiful, for example, by decorating their apartments tastefully, by collecting art, or by dressing well. Fours are powerfully attracted to beauty, whether in people or in things, because aesthetic objects stimulate their feelings and reinforce their sense of self. Moreover, aesthetic objects symbolize the perfection and wholeness that Fours would like to find in themselves. Having sensed that something is missing in the self, they attempt to replace this inner loss by heightening the impact of beauty on their emotions. They are romantics, idealizing beauty.

However, average Fours use their imaginations to intensify their emotions, increasingly shifting their attention away from reality as they rework the world in their fantasies. They want to be swept away by grand passions, lyrical longings, and stormy emotions which, by elating, keep the sense of self alive. The romantic imagination may dwell on nature, God, the self, the other, or some combination of these, looking for portents and meanings, fascinated with death and the passing of all things. But because average Fours use them so often, their imaginations become powerful and seductive, an endless source of solace and gratification.

Fours are also strongly attracted to those who stimulate their feelings and sense of beauty. However, they begin to relate to people in their imaginations as if others were aesthetic objects, to be contemplated like works of art rather than as persons in their own right. Fours also easily become infatuated with others, holding long conversations with their lovers and friends in their imaginations. Scenes of love and longing, courtship and romance, possessing the other in sexual ecstasy, and the bitter sorrows of letting go of the beloved play themselves out.

Unfortunately, the greater part of their relationships takes place almost solely in their imaginations, without others ever being aware of their attention or the degree of their ardor. By using their imaginations, average Fours heighten the emotional impact of relationships, making them into something extremely exciting, while sparing themselves the problems of self-exposure and rejection. Naturally, this approach to people is fraught with difficulties, not the least of which is that others inevitably turn out to be different from what Fours imagined them to be.

While there is nothing wrong with being imaginative, once the desire to heighten emotions in fantasy takes root, things start to become imbalanced because average Fours relate to their fantasies instead of to reality. The intuition we saw in healthy Fours has deteriorated into the unlimited use of the imagination as a way of making up to themselves for experiences they do not actually have.

THE SELF-ABSORBED INTROVERT

If for some reason average Fours are unable to express themselves at all, they withdraw from the environment entirely rather than risk the emotional problems involved with communicating anything about themselves to others. They become preoccupied with themselves, wanting to be left alone so that they can cope with their feelings, including those generated by their imaginations, *before* they attempt to express themselves again.

At this stage average Fours are reserved, shy, and extremely private — melancholy outsiders, painfully self-conscious. Since they are confused about their feelings, Fours are not sure of themselves. It is difficult for them to meet people, to make small talk, or to work with anyone else. Their need to withdraw only makes average Fours feel socially inept and uncomfortable around others, not so much because they do not like people — quite the contrary, they long to have intimate, intense relationships — but because they are so self-conscious that they cannot function well.

Naturally, social life becomes a burden to them. Dealing with people threatens their emotional equilibrium. Average Fours typically do not even try to be sociable or friendly, especially with anyone they do not know well. Instead, they project an aura of silence and aloofness. While others may think that they are mysterious, or perhaps mystically profound, Fours at this Level are simply introverted and are attempting to disguise their growing emotional vulnerabilities behind the protective haze of mystery. If someone has hurt their feelings and they have withdrawn to lick their wounds, their withdrawal is as aggressive an act as average Fours allow themselves, a denial of their presence to the other, although it annoys Fours greatly if the offender does not realize that they have done so.

Many of their problems stem from the fact that average Fours take everything personally. They must interiorize their experiences — feel their feelings — for their experiences to have meaning to them. But by interiorizing everything, average Fours become vulnerable and uncomfortably self-conscious — hypersensitive. For example, a nasty reply by a waitress can ruin their day, and a perceptively critical comment from a friend can become a thorn in their sides for months. If anyone should tease them or prick at their defenses, average Fours feel cut to the quick and do not know how to respond. ("What does so-and-so mean by that?") They simply cannot be easygoing or spontaneous, since their increasing self-absorption does not allow it.

Because they internalize all their experiences, everything seems to be connected with everything else. Every new experience affects them, gathering associated meanings until everything becomes overloaded, full of private associations. If they are healthy, this richness of emotional connections feeds their creativity because their internalized and augmented experiences become available as inspirations. But the ironic result of self-absorption is that average Fours lose touch with their emotions. They feel confused, amorphous, unanchored to anything permanent in themselves.

Rather than help to sort out their feelings, withdrawal makes average Fours feel more inadequate. They begin to doubt their ability to sustain contact with the environment, or to defend themselves adequately since they feel so vulnerable and storm tossed. They become extremely conscious of not fitting into the environment as easily as others seem to. It is a short step from "Why do I feel this way?" to "What is wrong with me?" Self-doubts assail them, as do problems with self-esteem.

While healthy Fours can be quite comfortable when they are alone, average Fours often feel lonely. They feel that, at best, they are only tolerated by others (seldom really liked), and any problems in their relationships will invariably result in rejection, something which will only confirm their worst fears about themselves. Their assessment of their social situation may or may not be accurate, but average Fours give themselves few opportunities to find out.

Instead, they brood about themselves. And because they are emotionally vulnerable to real or imagined slights, they become extremely moody and temperamental. Moods become the precondition for every action because average Fours constantly introspect on their feelings to see how they feel before they do anything. They put off writing letters, going to the grocery, or looking for a job until they are in the right mood. But since Fours never know when they are going to be in the right mood, things either do not get done, or they are done against internal resistance, producing no pleasure.

This is not a satisfying way to live, even for Fours. Nevertheless, they continue to withdraw because they feel they are being called away from the environment by something inside themselves, although they are not sure by what. It is as if they have been physically wounded and were bleeding to death. Before they can do anything else, Fours feel they must obtain the first aid they need. Some inner disorder must be attended to before they can give their attention to anything else.

Unfortunately, the longer they are absorbed in themselves, the less average Fours are able to grasp the essential self or discover what is causing their pain, which only tantalizes them to continue their search for self. They do not see that by withdrawing from the world, they have lost perspective on themselves. They go around in self-enclosed circles, becoming more aware of who they are *not* than who they are — an irony for the personality type whose agenda in life has been to understand itself.

THE SELF-INDULGENT AESTHETE

The longer they remain self-absorbed, the more practical and emotional difficulties Fours unwittingly create for themselves. They have not developed their social and professional skills, and their self-esteem has suffered from constant self-questioning. They feel vulnerable and unsure of themselves. In a word, average Fours feel different from others because by withdrawing from the environment, they have become different. And because they are different, they feel they have needs that must be satisfied in unusual ways. They therefore want to compensate themselves for what they lack by indulging their desires. They feel they are exceptions to the rule, exempt from expectations, totally free to "be themselves." The result is that they become completely undisciplined, luxuriating in whatever emotional and material pleasures they can afford.

Average Fours may once have attracted interest, and even some sympathy, from those who found their reserve and self-consciousness endearing, or at least intriguing. Others may have been touched by their shyness and vulnerability. But now the picture has changed. Self-indulgent Fours antagonize others because they are so perversely willful. They have no sense of social responsibility; they cannot be counted on for anything; and they resist all obligations, becoming petulant if anything is forced upon them either by events or by people. They take a special pride in maintaining the freedom to do things their own way, in their own time, or not at all. ("I do what I want to do when I want to do it.")

Because they feel different from others, they feel special and exempt from living as everyone else does, free from any obligation to follow the ordinary conventions of social life. ("*I* can't work in a factory!") They feel that everything is permissible because of their emotional needs: their time is their own, and they resent any intrusion whatsoever. They resist everything, from having a job to employing healthy self-discipline to cooperating with others, if they think that doing something else will make them feel better about themselves. But rather than being strengthened by their self-indulgences, average Fours are further weakened by them. By definition, self-indulgence does not satisfy real needs, only transient desires. However, since self-indulgent Fours often live alone, they do not have to worry about anyone's knowing the full extent of their indulgences or calling them to task for them.

By insisting on the freedom to do as they please, they become increasingly precious and totally impractical, manifesting an effete disdain for reality. Affectations and mannerisms substitute for genuine self-expression, giving some Fours a certain dramatic effeminacy. If they are still artists, their art becomes as self-indulgent and self-referential as they are. And because they are self-indulgent, they usually do not work seriously at much of anything, lapsing instead into eroticism and languorous, overwrought fantasies. Brilliant poetry, heart-rending music, and portentous winter novels pour from their imaginations — as long as they never try to write them down.

At this stage, average Fours are still self-aware enough to know that they are missing out on many important aspects of life, particularly relationships. Consequently, they feel sorry for themselves. They may become minor hypochondriacs, worrying about themselves — since no one else does. Self-pity is among the least attractive of traits, yet average Fours indulge in it excessively because it allows them to rationalize whatever they want. It allows them to feel that life owes them something. They can revel in their tragic existence without trying to change or say no to themselves.

Wallowing in their feelings gives self-indulgent Fours something to do, a way of occupying their time. The problem is, however, that their imaginary pleasures can never be satisfying because they are always unreal. The imagination is enticing nonetheless because it keeps their feelings at a fever pitch. By indulging their imaginations, their sense of self is kept alive, even as the life is being drained out of it.

To make up for their lack of achievement, Fours at this stage typically give themselves over to sensuality as a way of deadening the too-sensitive self to its growing unhappiness. They may become sexually licentious, engaging in anonymous sexual activities for release, for fleeting human contact, and for excitement. Or they may lose themselves in sexual fantasies, sinking into erotic daydreams rather than making any real efforts at anything. They may masturbate frequently, virtually a symbol for their self-referential, ingrown way of life. They may become obsessed with those with whom they have fallen in love in their imaginations, providing themselves with an endless source of pain and pleasure, desire and frustration, violent and wasteful feelings. Or they may sleep excessively or abuse food, drugs, and alcohol.

Their dependency on their imaginations has brought Fours to an overripe, unsavory state. Their emotions are too lush, as if they were rare orchids that have been kept in a hothouse all their lives — the hothouse of self-absorption. At this stage, average Fours are decadent, at least in the estimation of others. Naturally, Fours do not see themselves that way — they are simply making up for their many deprivations.

Of course, they cannot admit that they are deprived because they have deprived themselves of contact with reality. The sad fact is that by now they have abandoned the search for self, and have substituted self-gratification for the discovery of an identity which is growing ever more nebulous.

Analyzing the Unhealthy Four

THE ALIENATED DEPRESSIVE

As we have just seen, self-indulgent Fours consider themselves exempt, free to live in a world of self-gratification. In time this creates a new source of anxiety: the fear that they may lose the possibility of attaining their hopes and dreams, especially their hope of self-actualization. Actualizing themselves is what Fours have always wanted, but if something happens to make them feel that that dream has been lost, they suddenly feel cut off from themselves. Something they have done or failed to do now comes home to roost, and suddenly they "spiral in" to some core of themselves, both in shock and to protect themselves from even more loss.

Unhealthy Fours are angry at themselves for what they have done to themselves. They realize that they have wasted precious time, missed opportunities, and have fallen behind others in almost every way — personally, socially, and professionally — and they feel acutely ashamed. They envy others — everyone else seems to be happy, accomplished, and successful in the many ways in which Fours feel they are not. They see, much to their sorrow, that withdrawal into self-absorption has not turned out to be a way of finding themselves. Instead, things have gone wrong: they are wasting their lives, and they know it. They feel terribly confused and racked with self-doubt. They feel like failures — they have not accomplished anything worthwhile and fear that they never will.

Unhealthy Fours unconsciously inhibit themselves from having any kind of meaningful desires because they do not want to be hurt anymore, especially by having desires and expectations for themselves. The result is a sudden total blockage of all feelings, as if life had suddenly been drained from them. Whatever fulfillment they may once have found in their creative work, whatever hopes they may have had, suddenly vanish. They instantaneously become fatigued, apathetic, alienated from themselves and others, sinking into emotional paralysis, unable to function at all.

Exerting themselves in any way is extraordinarily difficult. They cannot bring themselves to sit in front of an easel or a typewriter until their creative juices begin to flow again; nor can they call friends or go to a movie. Looking for work or finding a therapist is out of the question. They feel like staying in bed all day, and often do. Ironically, unhealthy Fours can no longer be self-indulgent even if they wanted to because they simply cannot bring themselves to get involved with anything.

As angry at themselves as they are, unhealthy Fours fear expressing their anger lest it make things worse. If they are angry at someone else — a failed romance, for example — for disappointing their expectations, unhealthy Fours are so enraged that they cannot stand being in the same room with the former beloved, the object of such recent erotic obsessions. They are so angry that they hold themselves back from showing reactions of any kind, insofar as is possible. (Others, however, can see that they look desolate, sigh deeply, and are close to tears.)

Unhealthy Fours are still self-aware, and they realize that they are depressed and on the verge of becoming even more depressed. They know that only with the greatest difficulty will they be able to keep themselves from going under emotionally. An inner light is going out, one which they fear may never be rekindled. Everything seems to be futile and dying.

THE EMOTIONALLY TORMENTED PERSON

Depressed and alienated from themselves and others, unhealthy Fours go from bad to worse. They fear that because of their depression and inability to function, they are doomed. Their disappointment with themselves intensifies into a consuming self-hatred.

Neurotic Fours turn against themselves with an absolutely withering self-contempt, seeing only the worst in themselves. They excoriate themselves about everything: the mistakes they have made, the time they have wasted, their unworthiness to be loved by anyone, their worthlessness as human beings. They are caught in the grip of obsessionally negative thoughts, and their relentless self-reproaches become a form of delusional thinking into which no ray of hope can intrude.

Morbid fantasies become obsessions. They are convinced that they are outcasts in life, sacrificial victims, endlessly suffering for what their parents have done to them and what they have done to themselves. They feel pathetic, rightly rejected by everyone. They also feel guilty for existing: they have contributed nothing, and people would be better off without them. Their self-hatred is like an electron accelerator whipping incidents of virtually no significance into formidable forces, smashing them into what little self-esteem remains.

Not only are unhealthy Fours convinced that they are utterly and permanently defective, they are also convinced that others regard them as contemptuously as they regard themselves. They have absolutely no self-confidence, and no reason to hope that they will ever be able to acquire any. A chasm of inner darkness has opened inside them, like a black hole draining whatever life they have. They are extremely distraught, yet unable to shake themselves free of the self-accusations and feelings of hopelessness plaguing them. They may sit alone for hours, barely breathing and yet violently tormented. They may burst into tears and uncontrollable sobbing, then retreat into silence and intense inner suffering once again.

Everything becomes a source of torment to them: the whole of life becomes an unbearable reminder of their alienation from it. If they were once artists, their unfinished work mocks them; if they were once in love with someone, their failure in love mocks them; if they once had a family or a job, their failures mock them as well.

Unfortunately, many of their self-accusations have a basis in fact. Because of their self-absorption and self-indulgences, Fours have missed many opportunities to do something positive with their lives. To a real extent, they are responsible for bringing their anguish upon themselves, and they know it — which is why their self-accusations cut so deeply. But rather than truly expiate for guilt by punishing themselves, their self-hatred only destroys whatever inner resources they still possess. The only way out is to do away with their tormented consciousness altogether.

THE SELF-DESTRUCTIVE PERSON

If conditions do not change for the better, their despair becomes so deep that neurotic Fours will attempt to destroy themselves, one way or another. When they become hopeless, what remains to be seen is the form their despair will take — whether they will kill themselves directly or indirectly, through drugs or alcohol or some other means.

It is difficult for other personality types to understand that because of their self-hatred neurotic Fours feel cut off from life itself. Everything in the world — everything positive, beautiful, good, and worth living for — has become a rebuke to them, and they cannot bear the thought of living that way for the rest of their lives. They must do something to escape from their crushingly negative self-consciousness. In essence, neurotic Fours must rid themselves of themselves, since they feel defeated by life and see no way of coming to life again.

Neurotic Fours truly believe that they are utterly hopeless, so a suicide attempt is meant to work. It is not a cry for help: it is a way out. Despairing Fours embrace death as a final solution to the ongoing problem of their life. Death is a welcome chance to merge with nothingness, a hoped-for annihilation of their painful self-consciousness.

Suicide is not only a way of escaping from their intense mental suffering, it is a rebuke to others for not helping them enough, for not understanding their needs, for not caring about them. From the Four's point of view, others' lack of love and understanding has driven them to take their own life. Suicide is the ultimate act of withdrawal, an aggressive act by which Fours inflict suffering on others without having to be aggressive or guilty or having to face the consequences.

Suicide also holds another attraction: it is the one thing in life over which despairing Fours still feel they have any control. By contemplating suicide, they feel that they remain the masters of something, even if it is only the possibility of saying no to life, of refusing to go on being tormented. The mere thought that, if they wished, they could put an end to themselves is a source of comfort.

Before they have reached this stage, Fours have doubtless thought about suicide many times. The danger is that the more they think about it, the more they may become infatuated with death as a solution to their problems. When they are in despair, having rehearsed suicide so often in their imaginations, they may act without any more consideration or warning to others.

The Dynamics of the Four

THE DIRECTION OF DISINTEGRATION: THE FOUR GOES TO TWO

If neurotic Fours do not commit suicide, they will probably try to free themselves from their crushing self-hatred in another way. Their movement to Two is a metaphor for their desire to escape from themselves by becoming dependent on someone who will provide the love and understanding they have missed.

Although they are usually withdrawn from people, average, and particularly unhealthy, Fours have always wanted and needed peo-

ple, and their move to Two is an ironic, unintended acknowledgment of this. Fours are drawn to Two because they need to overcome
their alienation from themselves and others by finding someone
who will love them. By so doing, unhealthy Fours hope that they
will, in time, be able to love themselves and actualize the good that
is in them. Unfortunately, however, neurotic Fours are almost completely incapable of entering into and sustaining a genuine relationship with anyone. They are too emotionally disturbed and self-
contemptuous to function, much less to be able to truly love anyone else.

Instead, when neurotic Fours go to Two they may well have some
sort of nervous breakdown, indirectly coercing someone to take
care of them, but not necessarily the beloved of their imaginations.
Eliciting pity from others substitutes for being loved. They may
also be without financial resources, and therefore expect to live off
someone else in what is little more than a parasitic existence and an
extension of the feeling of exemption which we have already seen.
Furthermore, since they are broken down, deteriorated Fours also
feel exempt from having any expectations placed on them, even the
expectation that they get well.

Ironically, Fours at Two will likely begin to hate the very person
they have become dependent upon, since their dependency is a
constant reminder of their defects and lack of self-esteem. Conflicts
will escalate as Fours alternate between intense feelings of aggression toward themselves and aggression toward the other. Others
will no doubt also be infuriated with deteriorated Fours because
many of their problems were either caused or greatly exacerbated by
their own actions. They have brought much upon themselves, and
now, others feel, it is they who are being forced to help undo what
Fours have so perversely done to themselves.

Deteriorated Fours cannot escape the fact that it is futile to attempt to find themselves through someone else, since they still
hate themselves. They will therefore probably destroy the very relationship they so desperately depend on. The prognosis for deteriorated Fours is bleak indeed: if they do not receive adequate
professional help, they may well eventually go mad, commit suicide, or both.

THE DIRECTION OF INTEGRATION: THE FOUR GOES TO ONE

Healthy Fours actualize themselves by focusing on something ob jective, something beyond their feelings and their imaginations. When healthy Fours go to One, they move from the world of subjectivity to the world of objectivity, from self-absorption to principled action. They have found the courage to act without reference to their feelings and have thus freed themselves from the relentless tug of self-absorption. They are no longer controlled by their feelings, but by their convictions, acting on principles rather than moods.

Fours at One acknowledge that there are values to which it is necessary to submit. They willingly become self-disciplined, working consistently toward actualizing their potential so they can contribute to the world. Ironically, integrating Fours find the freedom they have sought by desiring to do what they ought to do instead of doing whatever they please in a misguided search for self. By being part of the world, they find a context in which to discover themselves.

And since they receive satisfaction from reality, they are no longer tempted to be self-indulgent, nor do they think of themselves as different from others. Instead, integrating Fours submit both to reality and to the dictates of conscience, willingly putting limits on themselves, thereby overcoming the tendency to exempt themselves from social and moral obligations. Like healthy Ones, integrating Fours are exceptional teachers, objective about themselves and yet, because they are Fours, they are able to bring the riches of the subjective world to the light of day. Their intuition is reinforced by excellent judgment, personal insight by reason.

Finally, because integrating Fours have transcended themselves, what they create is objective, something from which they can learn what is true about themselves. Integrating Fours are able to contemplate their creation, whether it is a work of art, an act of kindness, or a successful relationship, not only learning who they are, but giving themselves reasons for genuine self-esteem. They learn that to the extent that their creation is good, the person who created it must also be good.

The Major Subtypes of the Four

THE FOUR WITH A THREE-WING

The traits of the Four are in some degree of conflict with the traits of the Three-wing: Fours are introverted, withdrawn, vulnerable, and self-aware, whereas Threes are extroverted, popular, well defended, and lack self-awareness. The Four's search for self is in marked contrast to the Three's ability to project simulated images to others without regard to the real self. The Four's fear of exposing itself (in a sense, a fear of success) is the opposite of the Three's self-display and competitive desire for success. The Four's introverted self-consciousness contrasts with the Three's charm and other extroverted social skills.

As conflicting as these two component types are, both are nevertheless concerned with self-esteem issues: the Four tends to have low self-esteem, the Three high self-esteem. Both opposing sets of traits can coexist in the same person, although uneasily. Noteworthy examples of the Four with a Three-wing include Tennessee Williams, Maria Callas, Rudolf Nureyev, Frédéric Chopin, Marcel Proust, Martha Graham, Paul Simon, Harold Pinter, Lawrence Olivier, Robert DeNiro, Walt Whitman, Albert Camus, E. M. Forster, Gustav Mahler, Peter Ilich Tchaikovsky, Charles Ryder, and Blanche DuBois.

Because of the Three-wing, healthy people of this subtype can be sociable, ambitious, and accomplished, particularly in the arts. They are in touch with who they are and who they are becoming, but with a more extroverted, energetic dimension to them. People of this subtype are also usually ambitious, physically attractive, and possess a certain social sense, which counterbalances the Four's tendency to withdraw from others. They are adaptable, sensitive to others, and have a good sense of humor.

Average people of this subtype may be helped out of their self-absorption by a concern for what others think of them. Since people of this subtype have the ability to project a favorable image, they are able to conceal their real emotional condition more effectively than the other subtype: others may not realize how vulnerable or emotionally troubled they may be. Fours with a Three-wing are competitive and interested in making something of themselves in the world, but they fear success, self-exposure, and possible humiliation. However, to the degree that the Three-wing is operative, this subtype also has narcissistic tendencies (exhibitionistic desires for attention and admiration) which may serve as partial motives for their behavior. And, to the degree that their narcissistic needs are unfulfilled in reality, their desires for triumph can both play a part in their fantasy life and become a focal point for disappointments.

Since unhealthy persons of this subtype are still fundamentally Fours, they take out their aggressions principally on themselves. They are self-inhibited and alienated from others, depressed, self-contemptuous, and so forth. However, to the degree that the Three-wing plays a part in the overall personality, there will be moments when they act like unhealthy Threes. People of this subtype can be hostile and malicious; their secret envy of others will be reinforced by the Three-wing's jealousy. Exploitativeness, opportunism, and duplicity may also be present, although these traits increase their shame and guilt if they should succumb to them. The vindictive malice which we find in Threes is rarely acted upon by this subtype. If it ever is, however, neurotics of this subtype will punish themselves even more severely than they inflict pain on anyone else. Crimes of passion and suicide are possible.

THE FOUR WITH A FIVE-WING

The traits of Fours and of Fives tend to reinforce each other. Both are withdrawn types: Fours withdraw to protect their feelings, Fives to protect their security. Fours with a Five-wing will be markedly more observant of the environment, particularly of other people. There is an intellectual depth and intensity here which is not found in the other subtype, but also a corresponding social insecurity. Noteworthy examples of the Four with a Five-wing include Virginia Woolf, Franz Kafka, Ingmar Bergman, Saul Steinberg, J. D. Salinger, Bob Dylan, Søren Kierkegaard, Hermann Hesse, William Blake, and Hamlet.

Healthy, gifted individuals of this subtype are probably the most profoundly creative of all the types because they combine intuition with insight, emotional sensitivity with intellectual comprehension, frequently with stunningly original, even prophetic, results. Fours with a Five-wing burn brighter than Fours with a Three-wing, but at the risk of burning themselves out faster.

Average persons of this subtype are given not merely to self-absorption, but to philosophical and religious speculation. Their emotional world is the dominant reality, but with a strong intellectual cast. People of this subtype tend to be extreme loners, more lacking in social connectedness than the other subtype. Thus, their artistic expressions more completely substitute for the person than in Fours with a Three-wing. These people also frequently have an otherworldly, ethereal quality about them; they are extremely independent and unconventional to the point of eccentricity. They also tend to be secretive, intensely preoccupied with their thoughts, and purposely enigmatic in their self-expressions. Their creative ideas may also be somewhat unusual, possibly even surreal. Members of this subtype care little for communicating with those who cannot understand them. Rather, they are interested in expressing their inner vision, whether sublime or terrifying, bleak or lyrical.

Unhealthy persons of this subtype inhabit a particularly barren and terrifying inner world. There is a self-denying, even life-denying, element of inner resistance to everything outside the self, throwing all of the Four's existential problems into sharper relief. Since Four is the fundamental personality type, Fours with a Five-wing are assailed by self-doubt, depression, alienation from others, inhibitions in their work, and self-contempt. To the degree that the Five-wing plays a part in the overall personality, unhealthy Fours of this subtype will also resist being helped by anyone, thus increasing their alienation from others. They also tend to project their fears into the environment, resulting in distorted thinking patterns which may include elements of suspicion, paranoia, and phobias. Not only are people of this subtype subject to torment from their self-hatred, they can see very little that is positive outside themselves, and they become very pessimistic about the apparent meaninglessness of life. Of all the personality types, people of this subtype are potentially the most isolated from themselves and from reality. They are prone to the depressive forms of schizophrenia.

Some Final Thoughts

Looking back on their deterioration, we can see that neurotic Fours have ironically brought about their own worst fear — that they are defective in some permanent way. The pity is that they may not always have been nearly so defective as they feel they are, but that they have become profoundly defective because they hate themselves. They have created a self-fulfilling prophecy and suffer the consequences.

From our present perspective, we can also see that one of the most important mistakes Fours make is to equate themselves with their feelings. The fallacy is that to understand themselves they must understand their feelings, particularly their negative ones, before acting. Fours do not see that the self is not the same as its feelings or that the presence of negative feelings does not preclude the presence of good in themselves. However, as they deteriorate, the bad drives out the good: their negative feelings about themselves gradually obliterate any positive ones they might have developed.

Fours must make a leap of faith that, despite their lack of a clear sense of themselves, they will discover themselves most surely by acting positively toward others. They must love others even if they do not feel that they have been loved adequately. When they love others, Fours will begin to discover who they are, and self-esteem will follow. They will also discover that because they can love, they must have learned to love from somewhere. What they have been given has perhaps been enough after all.

Chapter 7

Type Five: The Thinker

The Five in Profile

Healthy: Becomes a visionary, profoundly comprehending the world, discovering something new; possibly a genius. Observes everything with extraordinary perceptiveness and insight. Able to concentrate and get mentally involved: becomes knowledgeable, an expert. Innovative, produces extremely valuable, original ideas.

Average: The intellectual, becomes analytic, specialized, making a science of things: into research and scholarship. Detached, enjoys speculating about abstract ideas and spinning out complicated interpretations of reality. Begins to interpret everything according to a pet theory, becoming reductionistic, farfetched, eccentric, imposing ideas on the facts. Iconoclastic, extremist, radical interpretations.

Unhealthy: Can get very reclusive and isolated from reality. Cynical and antagonistic, repulsing attachments with others. Obsessed by strange, threatening ideas, becoming paranoid and prey to gross distortions and phobias. Insanity with schizophrenic tendencies common.

Key Motivations: Wants to understand the environment, to gain more knowledge, to interpret everything as a way of defending the self from threats from the environment.

Examples: Albert Einstein, Sigmund Freud, Friedrich Nietzsche, D. H. Lawrence, Emily Dickinson, Simone Weil, Jean-Paul Sartre, Jacob Bronowski, James Joyce, Charles Ives, Bobby Fischer, and Ezra Pound.

An Overview of the Five

The connection between genius and madness has long been debated. These two states are really poles apart, the opposite ends of the personality spectrum. The genius is someone who fuses knowledge with insight into the nature of the world, someone who has the ability to see things with utter clarity and awe-inspiring comprehension. What separates the genius from the madman is that the genius, in addition to extraordinary insights, has the ability to see them correctly, within their context. The genius perceives patterns which are actually present — whereas the madman imposes patterns, projecting an erroneous idea onto every circumstance. The genius may sometimes seem to be out of touch with reality, but only because he or she operates at a more profound level. The madman, however, is truly out of touch with reality, having nothing but delusions to substitute for it.

The Five is the personality type which most exemplifies these extremes. In the Five we see the genius and the madman, the intellectual and the scholar, the mildly eccentric crackpot and the deeply disturbed delusional paranoid. To understand how these widely diverse states are part of the same personality type is to understand the Five.

IN THE DOING TRIAD

Fives are members of the Doing Triad. Their potential problem with doing results from the fact that they emphasize thinking over doing, becoming intensely involved with their thoughts. Fives think so much that their mental world becomes all engrossing, virtually to the exclusion of everything else. This is not to say that Fives do nothing at all, but that they are more at home in their minds, abstractly analyzing their environment, than they are in the world of action.

All three members of the Doing Triad — Fives, Sixes, and Sevens — focus their attention on the world outside themselves. This may seem to contradict the statement that Fives are engrossed in their thoughts, but it actually does not. Fives focus their attention on the external world for a variety of reasons, one of the most important of which is that the material they think about comes through their sense perceptions — the accuracy of which they can never be completely sure of because they are not certain about what lies outside themselves. The only thing they know with certainty is their own thoughts. Hence, the focus of their attention is outward, on the environment. The source of many of their problems is their need to find out how their perceptions of the world square with reality so that they can act in it — and *do* things with certainty.

PROBLEMS WITH SECURITY AND ANXIETY

Like the other two members of the Doing Triad, average Fives tend to have problems with security because they fear that the environment is unpredictable and potentially threatening. Fives protect themselves by being extraordinarily observant so that they can anticipate problems in the environment, particularly problems with other people. Their curiosity, their insight, their need to make sense of their perceptions — and eventually, their paranoid tendencies — are all attempts to defend themselves from real or imagined dangers.

When Fives are healthy, they observe reality as it is and are able to comprehend complex phenomena at a glance. In their search for security, however, the perceptions of even average Fives tend to become skewed. They come to premature conclusions about the environment by projecting their faulty interpretations on it. They begin to reduce the complexity of reality to a single, all-embracing idea so that they can defend themselves by having everything figured out. And if they become unhealthy, Fives are the type of persons who take their eccentric ideas to such absurd extremes that they become obsessed with completely distorted notions about re-

ality. Ultimately, unhealthy Fives become paranoid, utterly terrified by the threatening visions which they have created in their
minds.

Their problem with anxiety, one of the issues common to the
personality types of the Doing Triad, is related to their difficulty
with perceiving reality objectively. They are afraid of allowing anyone or anything to influence them or their thoughts. They fear
being controlled or possessed by someone else. Ironically, however,
even average Fives are not unwilling to be possessed by an idea, as
long as the idea has originated with them. Nothing must be allowed
to influence their thinking lest their sense of self be diminished,
although by relying solely on their own ideas, without testing them
in the real world, Fives eventually become out of touch with reality.

The upshot of this is that average to unhealthy Fives are uncertain whether or not their perceptions of the environment are valid.
They do not know what is real and what is the product of their
minds. They project their anxiety-ridden thoughts and their aggressive impulses into the environment, becoming fearful of the antagonistic forces which seem to be arrayed against them. They gradually
become convinced that their peculiar, and increasingly paranoid,
interpretation of reality is the way things really are. In the end, they
become so terrorized that they cannot act even though they are
consumed by anxiety.

The basis of their orientation to the world is thinking; personality type Five corresponds to Jung's introverted thinking type.

> Introverted thinking is primarily oriented by the subjective fac-
> tor. . . . It does not lead from concrete experience back again to
> the object, but always to the subjective content. External facts are
> not the aim and origin of this thinking, though the introvert
> would often like to make his thinking appear so. It begins with
> the subject and leads back to the subject, far though it may range
> into the realm of actual reality. . . . Facts are collected as evidence
> for a theory, never for their own sake. (C. G. Jung, *Psychological
> Types*, 380.)

Although they correspond to Jung's introverted thinking type,
Fives are perhaps more precisely characterized as a subjective
thinking type because the aim of their thought is not introverted
(that is, directed toward themselves); rather, it is directed outward

toward the environment, which Fives want to understand for defensive purposes. The impetus for their thinking comes, as Jung says, from "the subjective factor," from their need to know about what lies outside themselves, as well as from their anxiety when they do not understand the environment. This is why thinking is the method Fives use both to fit into the world and, paradoxically, to defend themselves against it.

One of the results of the way Fives think is that even healthy Fives are not very deeply rooted in experience. They are the type of people who get a great deal of intellectual mileage out of very little experience because they always find something of significance where others see little or nothing. This may lead to great discoveries. However, when they stop observing the world and focus their attention on their interpretations of it, Fives begin to lose touch with reality. Instead of keeping an open mind while they observe the world, they become too involved with their own thoughts. Whatever does not agree with their ideas is simply not perceived or is rejected, with serious consequences for themselves.

CHILDHOOD ORIGINS

As a result of their childhood experiences, these children became ambivalent to both parents. Their parents may have nurtured them erratically, or they may have been emotionally disturbed or alcoholic or caught in a loveless marriage, and therefore not dependable sources of love and reassurance. The result is that these children become ambivalent not only toward both parents, but ambivalent toward the world.

As a result of their ambivalence, Fives learn to live in a state of constant alertness about their environment. Because they fear being controlled by others, they train themselves to observe their parents and the environment in general so that they can foresee events and take protective steps accordingly.

However, the ever present conflict which Fives unwittingly create is that they need to understand the environment and at the same time defend themselves against it. Just as they both love and hate their parents, they love and hate the environment, feeling pulled between their desire to identify with it and be detached from it. Fives attempt to resolve their ambivalence by not identifying with anything other than their thoughts about the world outside themselves. They feel that their thoughts are "good" (that is, correct, and can be safely identified with), while outside reality is "bad" (and must therefore be vigilantly watched), so that it can be repulsed at a moment's notice.

Although they continue to find their parents, the world, and other people fascinating and necessary, Fives also feel that they must keep everything and everyone at a distance lest they be in danger of being possessed by some outside force. Thus, from the very way they think — their cognitive style — Fives set up a strict dualism between themselves and the world: they see everything as essentially split into two fundamental areas — the inner world and the outer world, subjects and objects, the known and the unknown, the dangerous and the safe, and so forth. This sharp split between themselves as subjects and the rest of the world as objects has tremendous ramifications throughout their lives.

PROBLEMS WITH DETACHMENT AND PARANOIA

When they are healthy, Fives do not have to detach themselves from the environment because they feel secure enough to observe reality as it is. But as they deteriorate down the Continuum toward unhealth, their perceptions become more intensely focused on what seems to be threatening and dangerous in the environment. As a result of their hyperalertness to threats, their mental world becomes filled with anxiety. Ironically, however, Fives must have "danger" on their minds to feel safe: the more paranoid they become, the more completely defended they try to be.

In the end, since they invariably focus on what is threatening, Fives turn their terrifying projections into their *only* reality, and in so doing, turn their minds against themselves — literally scaring themselves "out of their minds." They become completely defenseless against the environment, which they find supremely dangerous because their minds have made it so. They become so paranoid that it is extraordinarily difficult for them to turn to anyone for help. Yet, unless paranoid Fives can reach out to someone, they have few ways of getting back in touch with reality.

If they live like this for long, their thought processes become so delusional and terrifying that they must separate themselves not just from the world but even from their own thoughts. Neurotic Fives become schizoid, unconsciously splitting themselves off from their teeming minds so that they can continue to live. Recoiling in horror, they retreat into emptiness — and yet more horror.

Analyzing the Healthy Five

THE PIONEERING VISIONARY

At their healthiest, Fives have the paradoxical ability to penetrate reality profoundly while comprehending it broadly. They are able to take things in whole, perceiving patterns where others see nothing but confusion. They are able to synthesize existing knowledge, making connections between phenomena which no one previously knew were related, such as time and space, the structures of the DNA molecule, or the relationship between brain chemistry and behavior.

The healthiest Fives do not cling to their own ideas about how the world works. Instead, they encompass reality so profoundly that they are able to discover unanticipated truths they could not have arrived at by mere theorizing. They make discoveries precisely because they are willing not to know the answers for a while, keeping an open mind while they observe reality.

Because they do not impose their thoughts on reality, healthy Fives are able to discover the internal logic, the structure, and interrelated patterns of whatever they observe. As a result, they have clear thoughts into obscure matters, and are able to predict events, often far in advance of the ability of others to verify them. Fives operating at the peak of their gifts may seem to be prophets and visionaries, although the explanation is simpler. They possess foresight because they see the world with extraordinary clarity, like a weaver who knows the pattern of a tapestry before it is completed.

The result is that they transcend rational thought to reveal objective reality, and in so doing they move toward the ineffable, to a level of comprehension where words, theories, and symbols are left behind. They perceive the world in all its complexity and simplicity with a vision that seems to come from beyond themselves. They are closer to contemplatives than thinkers.

Very healthy, gifted Fives so perfectly describe reality that their discoveries seem simple, even obvious, as if anyone could have thought of them. But the genius's insights are obvious only in hindsight. To have made the leap from the known to the unknown, and to describe the unknown so clearly and accurately that the discovery accords perfectly with what is already known, is a great achievement.

Thus, very healthy Fives are intellectual pioneers who open up new domains of knowledge. An individual Five, if sufficiently gifted, may well be a genius of historical dimensions, able to make staggering intellectual breakthroughs for mankind. A genius of the highest caliber may understand the way the world works for the first time in history. Less gifted individuals may have a sense of the genius's excitement when they first understand calculus or how to use a computer. Their understanding is new to them and can be thrilling. Others can only imagine how exciting it must be for someone to discover something totally new — when the discovery is new not only to that individual, but to everyone.

THE PERCEPTIVE OBSERVER

Even though Fives are not always this healthy, they are still extraordinarily conscious of the world around them, its glories and horrors, incongruities and inexhaustible complexities. They are the most mentally alert of the personality types, curious about everything. Healthy Fives enjoy thinking for its own sake; possessing knowledge — knowing that they know something, and being able to turn it around in their minds — is extremely pleasurable for them. Knowledge and understanding are exhilarating.

Given sufficient intelligence, healthy Fives penetrate the superficial, getting to profound levels very quickly. Their insights can be brilliant because they have the uncanny ability to see into the heart of things, noticing the anomaly, the curious but heretofore unobserved fact or hidden element which provides a key for understanding the whole. Because they see the world with unfailing insight, they always have something interesting and worthwhile to say. The act of seeing is virtually a symbol of their entire psychological orientation. If something can be seen, that is, apprehended either by the senses or the mind, Fives feel that it can be understood. Once something is understood, it can be mastered. Then Fives can act with the certitude they desire.

Nothing escapes healthy Fives unnoticed because they do not merely observe the world passively, they concentrate on it, noting how things go together to form patterns and bear meaning. People and objects are perceived in detail, as if Fives were training a magnifying glass on the environment. Since their minds are so active and they find everything around them so interesting, Fives are never bored. They like learning what they do not know and understanding what is not obvious. No matter how much they know, they always want to learn more, and since the world is, for all intents and purposes, infinite in its complexity, there is always more to know.

Healthy Fives are also able to perceive far more than others because they have the ability to sustain concentration; they are not easily distracted. They quickly become deeply involved in the object of their scrutiny so that they can understand how it works — why something is as it is. Their intellectual curiosity leads them to expend considerable effort to find out more about those things which have caught their attention. They are incredibly hard workers who will attack a problem for years until they solve it, or until it becomes clear that the problem is insoluble. They are also very good conceptualizers, asking the right fundamental questions and defining the proper intellectual boundaries for the problems with which they are involved. They do not attempt to do the impossible, only to understand what they have understood before.

Healthy Fives want to possess knowledge of the objective world, and yet, the very act of inquiring into things immediately adds a subjective element to the process. (Physics has taught a psychological truth — that the presence of the observer changes what is being observed.) Furthermore, even though the need to understand the environment is healthy, the desire to possess as much knowledge as possible reflects a disposition to fear the unknown. Even at this stage, healthy Fives are subject to a certain amount of anxiety about the environment if they do not understand it. (And, of course, because they cannot understand it until they deal with it, they are caught in a conundrum.) Therefore the habit of observation reflects not simply a dispassionate curiosity but a deeply personal need.

THE KNOWLEDGEABLE EXPERT

By observing the world and having insight into it, healthy Fives accumulate knowledge. Now they want to apply their ideas in the environment. More than any other personality type, healthy Fives enjoy using their knowledge to see how it corresponds with reality and how it can affect reality.

People of this personality type possess expert knowledge in various intellectual disciplines, whether in the arts (for example, French opera of the seventeenth century or Egyptian hieroglyphics), or in the sciences (how to build a computer or put a satellite into space). Healthy Fives are usually polymaths, possessors of knowledge in a wide range of intellectual disciplines, and expert in them all. Healthy Fives know what they are talking about and share their knowledge with others, enriching the whole of society with their learning. It is precisely because their insights are so on target that both healthy Fives and their ideas are especially valuable to the rest of society. Where would we be without the computers and antibiotics, the sophisticated communications media and the technological innovations of all sorts which make up the modern world?

Sometimes the results of their expertise are ingenious inventions and technological marvels which yield highly practical results. At other times, few things may result from their original ideas, although in time those ideas, too, may have practical applications. What is impractical in one era often becomes the underpinnings of an entirely new branch of knowledge or technology in another, such as the physics which made television and radar possible.

Because Fives understand things so perceptively, their profound knowledge enables them to get to the heart of difficulties so that they can explain problems, and possible solutions, clearly to others. Healthy Fives like sharing their knowledge because they often learn more when they discuss their ideas with someone else. This is why healthy Fives make exciting teachers, colleagues, and friends. Their enthusiasm for ideas is infectious, and they enjoy fertilizing their own areas of expertise with those of other intellectuals and thinkers, or really, with anyone who is as interesting, curious, and intelligent as they are.

As much as they like being among those who can understand and appreciate their insights, healthy Fives are nevertheless extremely independent. For the most part, learning and thinking are solitary adventures best embarked on alone. Because they never know where their discoveries will lead, Fives value their independence very highly; they are willing to be as unorthodox as their inquiries require, pursuing their interests and discoveries regardless of the sanctions of others or of society. They are not afraid to challenge existing dogmas, if need be.

Their innovations can be revolutionary, overturning previous ways of thinking. Owing to the nature of their interests and the scope of their intellects, healthy Fives give us powerful ideas which can literally change the course of history.

Analyzing the Average Five

THE ANALYTIC SPECIALIST

The essential difference between average Fives and healthy Fives is that average Fives begin to fear that they do not know enough to act or to make their ideas or discoveries public. They feel that they have to study more, to do more research and experimentation, to involve themselves even more deeply with their subject. ("The more you know, the more you know you don't know.") They therefore become highly analytic and specialized, dissecting reality into ever simpler parts so that it can be studied in more depth. In a word, healthy Fives possess knowledge, whereas average Fives are in pursuit of it.

Average Fives analyze everything in great detail, taking things apart, literally or intellectually, to find out how things work. They take an empirical approach, quantifying things, attempting to be objective so they can arrive at certain knowledge. But in so doing, they unwittingly begin to take things out of context, no longer looking at the whole.

By quantifying and analyzing everything, average Fives tend to make a science of whatever they are interested in, whether history, linguistics, stereo equipment, jogging shoes, or the sociology of ape families. It is here that we see the beginning of their tendency to abstract from reality, concerning themselves with only those aspects of reality which capture their attention. They are by no means out of touch with reality in any unhealthy sense yet. They are, however, narrowing the focus of their perceptions so they can pursue their intellectual interests in more depth.

Of course, many things in the physical world can be measured precisely: the distance to the moon, the velocity of a bullet, the varying depths of the ocean. The problem with the empirical approach, however, is that it eliminates anything which the tools of a particular analysis cannot measure. What cannot be measured objectively is not verifiable, and therefore not scientific, and therefore not certain. (However, many of the most valuable things in life cannot be measured empirically. Love, for example, cannot be calibrated or weighed on a scale. Instead, if average Fives study love scientifically, they measure things like eye contact, pulse rate, and brain chemistry, which may be quantified.)

In their pursuit of knowledge, average Fives tend to become specialists in some field, delving into a body of technical knowledge not understood by most. (As specialists, they take pride and pleasure in their ability to say, in effect, "I know something that you don't know.") Some Fives may become specialists within an academic discipline, analyzing genetic structures or the mathematics of snowflake formation or the migration patterns of birds in the Amazon Delta. Others may specialize in less academic areas, becoming specialists in antiques, stamp collecting, or jazz. In any event, their approach is the same: collecting and analyzing data to acquire more knowledge.

Average Fives are typically bookish. They haunt bookstores, libraries, and coffeehouses catering to intellectuals who discuss politics, films, and literature far into the night. They love scholarship and are fascinated with the technical appurtenances by which they acquire knowledge. And while they will spend money to obtain whatever tools they need to pursue their intellectual interests, be they medieval manuscripts or computer equipment, average Fives are usually loath to spend money on themselves or their own comfort because they identify with their minds, not with their bodies.

Even those Fives who are not scientists usually like to think of their approach to reality as scientific, or at least rigorously intellectual. Every personality type deals from its strongest suit, and the intellect is what Fives are gifted with and what they favor in their development. As a group, Fives are the most intelligent of the personality types, filling the rosters of Mensa, engineering schools, and Nobel Prize laureates. Since being a Five is a psychological orientation to life and not solely a matter of possessing intellectual prowess, there are Fives who are not unusually intelligent. Nevertheless, using the mind is how Fives find their place in the world and thereby obtain security and self-esteem. (Intellectual pursuits may also have been fostered by an "ugly-duckling" child to compensate for physical and social handicaps.) In any case, average Fives consider themselves thinkers and intellectuals because they live in their minds more than in the world of action or practicality.

THE INTENSELY INVOLVED THEORIST

If their scientific and analytic methods fail or do not yield answers quickly enough to satisfy their emotional needs, average Fives become uncertain of what their ideas mean even as their need for certainty increases. New questions arise, the answers to which Fives do not know. As a result, they resort to speculation and interpretation rather than observation and investigation, becoming more intensely involved with their ideas and less with reality.

This is a turning point in their development. Rather than investigate the objective world, average Fives at this stage begin to become preoccupied with their own interpretations of it, mentally detaching themselves from the environment by becoming more intensely involved with one small aspect of it.

More than any other personality type, average Fives personify Descartes's famous dictum, "I think, therefore I am." They can be characterized in a nutshell as disembodied minds because, as far as they are concerned, the body is merely the vehicle for the mind. At this level, they do not pay much attention to their physical conditions except when they get in the way of their thinking. They become so deeply involved in projects that they forget to eat or sleep or change their clothes. They frequently look like the proverbial absent-minded professor, or the disheveled German metaphysician. No matter. To them the life of the mind, the excitement of pursuing and possessing knowledge, is what counts.

They plunge into complex intellectual puzzles and labyrinthine systems — elaborate, impenetrable mazes by which they can insulate themselves from the world while dealing with it intellectually. They get involved in highly detailed, complicated systems of thought, immersing themselves in obscure theories, whether these have to do with the abstruse regions of such traditional academic studies as astronomy, mathematics, or philosophy, or with esoteric topics such as the Cabala, astrology, and the occult. They are endlessly fascinated with intellectual games (such as chess or Dungeons and Dragons) making areas of study into a kind of game and games into an area of study.

The problem is that as Fives speculate and theorize, turning their ideas around in their minds, examining them from every angle, endlessly producing new interpretations, they lose the forest for the trees. With every new conjecture, they have no sense of certitude that their speculations are final: everything remains hanging in the air, in a cloud of possibilities. For example, the more they write, the more complex the exposition becomes until it is virtually incomprehensible. As brilliant as they may be, average Fives do not easily publish their ideas because they cannot bring them to a conclusion.

Furthermore, all ideas seem equally plausible to Fives, since they can make a convincing case for almost anything they think of. Anything thinkable seems possible. Anything thinkable seems real. They are intellectually and emotionally capable of entertaining any new thought, even horrifying or outlandish ones, since speculating on new possibilities is virtually all they do. Their ideas, however, begin to have no direct connection with the outside world. (The problems of epistemology not only fascinate them; average Fives unwittingly live them out.) But establishing a relationship between their ideas and reality is no longer the primary function of the thinking of average Fives. Instead, speculation maintains the sense of self by keeping the mind active.

Moreover, for all the time they spend thinking, average Fives do not communicate to others clearly because their thought processes are so complex and convoluted. They get into too much detail; their ideas become highly condensed. The stream of consciousness floods out in elaborate monologues, making it difficult for others to follow their train of thought. They go off on tangents, jumping from one point to another without indicating the intervening steps in their logic. A perceptive observation about Beethoven's Ninth Symphony may be followed by a disquisition on deafness and the need for further miniaturization of electronics if Star Wars is going to work. Their monologues may well be fascinating, and possibly breathtaking in the sweep of their intellectual range; however, their monologues may also be strange and tedious because the mental exertion required to follow them is exhausting. Nor is it always clear that the trip will be worth the effort, although average Fives think that whatever they have to say is as interesting to others as it is to them.

Both for better and for worse, they are extremely high-strung individuals, as if their nervous systems were tuned to a higher pitch than those of the other personality types. Fives seem to lack the ability to repress the unconscious impulses which erupt into their minds, fueling their intense involvement in their perceptions, their work, and their relations with others.

This is why, as they become ever more preoccupied with their speculations, average Fives become increasingly detached from everything around them by the all-consuming intensity of their mental processes. They become more involved with their ideas than with objective reality. Theories are ceaselessly generated both to detach themselves from the world and to stay engaged with it. Thus, as Fives shift down the Levels toward unhealth, they ironically move contrary to their genuine capacity for observation, living ever more completely in their minds — and to that extent, out of touch with reality. They lose perspective, finding hidden meanings and causes everywhere.

Because they see ominous implications in almost everything, average Fives are typically fascinated with power. They feel that knowledge is power and that by possessing knowledge, they will be secure because they perceive more than others do — and hence, can protect themselves. They are attracted by areas of study which deal with some form of power, whether in nature, or in politics, or in human behavior. However, Fives are also ambivalent about power and suspicious of those who have power over them. They feel that whoever has power may use it against them, putting them in the control of others, one of their deepest fears.

The more detached average Fives are, the more ambivalent they are to just about everyone — attracted to people, yet suspicious about them. They want to figure out what makes other people tick, just as they analyze other objects of intellectual interest. ("What you just said was *so* revealing — you're incredibly angry at women, aren't you?") Yet they usually try to avoid getting deeply involved with others because people are unpredictable. Emotional involvements arouse strong feelings which average Fives find difficult to control: the passions flood too easily into their minds. But because Fives also have strong sexual impulses, they cannot avoid involvements altogether, as much as they would like to. Thus, Fives find people and relationships endlessly fascinating, yet remain wary.

It is therefore typical of average Fives either to be unmarried or to have stormy relationships with most people. Intimacy with others gets so involved, so complex and exhausting, that they stop trying to make contact with others and become reclusive, burying themselves ever more completely in their work and ideas. They want no one to be close enough to them to gain control over their thoughts, their sole domain.

For this reason, average Fives are also the natural agnostics and atheists among the personality types, because God, as an omniscient, omnipotent person, is an intolerable idea. They cannot bring themselves to believe in something or someone whom they cannot understand. Nor do they want God to have access to their minds. Fives want to be omniscient — they do not like the idea that God might be. Moreover, the problem of evil is an enormous stumbling block: the horror and uncertainty of the world is so apparent to Fives that any God who allowed the world to be as it is must be sadistic, an evil god, a God they refuse to become involved with.

THE EXTREME REDUCTIONIST

In time, the complexities Fives create in their minds cause new, and more complicated, problems for them. Nothing is clear or certain; anxiety increases.

To have certitude so that they can act if they have to, average Fives begin to force their conclusions. The mind seeks order, and if after much speculation, average Fives do not perceive it, their minds impose an order of their own. As a result, they unwittingly project their perceptions into the environment, becoming totally convinced of the truth of one particular idea which seems to hold the key to all understanding. They move from "What if?" to "It is!"

Thus, they read into things more than is actually there, becoming reductionistic, eliminating all complexity by settling upon an all-encompassing explanation. At this stage, Fives reduce everything to a lower common denominator than is necessary, explaining everything as nothing but a variation of something else. This way, their theories are always confirmed. Uncertainty ceases.

Reductionists are thinkers who cannot wait to find the right answer. Because they focus so intensely on one thing, everything else goes out of focus, especially how that "one thing" fits into a larger picture. Ironically for those so given to complex thought, reductionistic Fives oversimplify reality. For example, dismissing the flower, reductionistic Fives focus on the ooze from which it sprang, as if the brightest blossom were "nothing but" mud in some insignificantly altered state; painting is nothing but the desire to smear feces; God is nothing but a projection of the father into the cosmos; because human beings have some things in common with machines, they are nothing but biological machines, and so forth. The result is that their ideas mix legitimate insights with extreme interpretations, while Fives themselves have no way of knowing which is which.

A certain extremism is as typical of their social style as it is of their intellectual viewpoint. In political or artistic matters, reductionistic Fives are usually radicals, populating the avant-garde. They love to take ideas to their furthest limits — for their shock value, to defy what has conventionally been thought or done, or to puncture and demolish popular opinions. (And even if they are not as correct as Fives think they are, their provocative ideas virtually force others to react to them, stirring up debate.) As dyed-in-the-wool nonconformists and dissenters, they rebel against all social conventions, rules, and expectations, whether these involve feminism, politics, child rearing, sexual liberation, or all of them in some peculiar combination. They have an ax to grind. Understanding has been abandoned for polemics.

The subjective nature of their introverted thinking is now evident as their ideas become farfetched and outlandish. No matter, Fives at this Level always find corroboration for whatever they think, even though the plain facts do not bear them out.

An irrational element — a kind of perverse resistance to reality — has tainted their thought processes. Reductionistic Fives are not crazy, even though their ideas are strange and extremely unorthodox. Healthy originality, however, has deteriorated into quirky eccentricity; the genius has become little more than a crank. (They may believe that coeducation causes moral degeneracy or that the height of the Great Pyramid has healing powers.) Yet their extreme ideas are so much a part of their sense of self that Fives will defend their ideas at all costs, asserting them vigorously, and attempting to demolish all counterarguments. Contentious and quarrelsome, they also worry about establishing their intellectual priority and protecting their ideas, threatening lawsuits if they think that someone has stolen one of their brilliant theories.

Even so, as radically extreme and reductionistic as many of their ideas are, average Fives are not necessarily completely off the mark. They are usually too intelligent not to have something interesting to say. The problem is knowing which of their ideas are valuable and which are not.

Analyzing the Unhealthy Five

THE ISOLATED NIHILIST

The need to maintain certitude about their interpretation of reality sets the stage for Fives to become extremely antagonistic toward anyone who disagrees with them. Their aggressions are aroused when people question their ideas — or worse, if their ideas are ridiculed or dismissed. To maintain their identities, which are so wedded to their ideas, unhealthy Fives go on the offensive: individuals must be discredited, their ideas shown to be worthless, their solutions to problems an illusion, their world a fool's paradise. Thus, unhealthy Fives unwittingly provoke others into rejecting them, and then become antagonistic and nihilistic about the value of all relationships. But in so doing, they become profoundly isolated and extremely cynical about the value of ever relating to anyone.

Indeed, their need to reject what others believe is so strong that they take pleasure in debunking whatever is positive in life, trying to prove the virtual impossibility of human relationships and the complete rottenness at the core of human nature. Unhealthy Fives take delight in deflating what they see as the bourgeois illusions by which others get through life so comfortably and to which they have not fallen prey because of their greater intellectual honesty.

As usual, there is a half truth operating here. While others may well be living too comfortably for their own good, while some people may be self-deceptive, while some families and some relationships may be tainted by hypocrisy, jealousy, and struggles for power, it does not necessarily follow that cynicism is the best response. Unhealthy Fives throw out the baby with the bathwater: faith, hope, love, kindness, friendship — all are extraordinarily difficult for them to believe in because of their fear of involvement with others. Attachment to others is too threatening at this stage, so unhealthy Fives must justify their isolation by becoming nihilistic and cynical about all relationships — indeed, about the value of humanity itself.

Just as an intense stream of water from a fire hose can hold back a crowd, the intensity of their minds, overheated by their erupting aggressive impulses, repels everything that might influence them. Their scathing antagonisms are directed particularly toward people because unhealthy Fives must maintain their isolation so that they will not be influenced by anyone. While usually not violent, unhealthy Fives may rant and rave, write long diatribes and denunciations, or suddenly withdraw into a glowering, hateful silence. Since most people are repulsed by this kind of behavior, their isolation rapidly deepens, which is exactly what unhealthy Fives want. Yet, for that reason, they are prey to ever worsening distortions in their thought processes. Of course, other people react to their excoriating contempt, and either dismiss them as sick or else counterattack. Aggressions — and fear — continue to escalate.

Unhealthy Fives stew in their feelings of contempt for everything. Unfortunately, while antagonism keeps the sense of self alive, it fills their minds with hatred. And by devaluing everything and rejecting all their attachments to the environment, unhealthy Fives are worse than merely isolated; they are filled with aggressions which cannot be discharged because they do not want to get into violent conflicts with others. Unhealthy Fives are thus in a terrible dilemma: they are obsessed with their aggressions yet unable to act on them because they fear the consequences. The result is they do not act; they seethe instead.

THE DELUSIONAL PARANOID

Unhealthy Fives would like to destroy everything, so detestable has the world become in their eyes. The irony is that they begin to think that everyone hates *them* and wants to destroy *them* instead. The result is that neurotic Fives become paranoid, projecting their antagonistic feelings into the environment.

As a result of projecting their fears and aggressions onto others, neurotic Fives become terrorized by what they find. Everyone and everything seem dangerous. Mere coincidence becomes conclusive fact for them. Even the most innocent remarks confirm their paranoia. They think a stranger walking toward them on the street is a policeman come to arrest them, or a spy who has them under surveillance, or a madman about to attack. Mental connections go haywire; they relate things which have no basis in fact, yet neurotic Fives are absolutely convinced that they are related. Unfortunately, their delusions only succeed in making their fears all the more consuming. Mere eccentricity has deteriorated into true craziness — insane paranoid delusions.

Paranoid delusions of persecution may alternate with compensating delusions of grandeur and delusions of reference, the notion that they are being watched by someone important — God or extraterrestrials, for example — providing neurotic Fives with a sense of importance. They may think that they are great inventors or Napoleon or Joan of Arc. Paranoid elements may also be mixed with the grandiose delusions: the FBI is out to get them because they alone know about research into a nuclear antigravity device. Or the paranoid elements alone may dominate their delusional thinking: they become convinced that the telephone is bugged, their mail is being read by the CIA, their food is poisoned, their friends are secretly plotting against them. However, more than ever, paranoid Fives think that they are in greater touch with reality than anyone else. They alone see what is really going on.

What begins to frighten even neurotic Fives is that their thoughts seem to have a life of their own. Their thoughts are uncontrollable, scaring them when they do not want to be scared. Their minds race wildly and they become terrified by fears from which they cannot possibly escape since, after all, their fears originate in themselves.

Like Dr. Frankenstein, they are in danger of being destroyed by processes to which they themselves have given life.

As their fears spread and grow in intensity, they encompass and distort more of reality until doing anything becomes impossible because everything is charged with terrifying implications. Thus, neurotic Fives may begin to be incapacitated by phobias. Inanimate objects take on a sinister appearance — the ceiling is about to collapse on them, their armchair may swallow them up, the television is giving them brain cancer. They may also experience hallucinations — hearing voices or having grossly distorted visual perceptions. They begin to experience their bodies as alien, turning against them just as the environment has seemed to turn against them. Neurotic Fives cannot rest or sleep or distract themselves because they must be vigilant and because they cannot turn off their minds. As a result, they become physically exhausted, only compounding their problems.

Life becomes unbearable: they seem to see too much, as if their eyelids had been removed. But the truth is that their minds are devouring them. The world becomes filled with terrors because their minds are filled with terrors.

THE EMPTY SCHIZOID

Ultimately, neurotic Fives unconsciously "solve" the problem of how to control their minds, especially the anxiety produced by their consuming paranoia, by unconsciously splitting consciousness into two parts. Neurotic Fives retreat into that part of themselves which seems safe, regressing into an autistic-like state which resembles psychosis.

At this final Level, neurotic Fives defend themselves from reality by unconsciously cutting themselves off from every connection with it. To put this another way, neurotic Fives are so terrorized by their thoughts that they must get rid of them somehow. They do so by identifying with the emptiness which is made within themselves when they negate their remaining identifications. In effect, they detach themselves from themselves, like parents who, to stop being tormented by the memories of a dead child, throw away everything that reminds them of the child. The result is that neurotic Fives live in a totally empty house — the self which has been purged of everything that reminds them of their terrifying and painful attachments to the world.

Thus, neurotic Fives deteriorate into a state of inner emptiness and, if they continue to live this way, in all probability into a form of schizophrenia.* All their former intellectual intensity and capacity for involvement is gone. Neurotic Fives at this stage are utterly isolated from their environment, from other people, and from their inner life — from their ability to think, to feel, and to do.

Neurotic Fives have finally succeeded in putting distance between themselves and the environment, although at the price of completely removing themselves from it. The irony is, however, that what they have removed themselves from is not actually reality, but the projection of their anxieties about reality. They have succeeded only in removing themselves from their thoughts and feelings. Once neurotic Fives have done this, they become unable to cry out to anyone from the void they have created within themselves. All is emptiness within the abyss of the purged self.

---

* Because of the importance of schizophrenia, we should consider the hypothetical links between this disease and the Five. It seems likely that schizophrenia is one of the possible outcomes of a neurotic Five's way of coping with the world. The stress caused by social isolation and the physical exhaustion brought about by a hyperactive mind may eventually cause a change in the chemical balance in the brain, resulting in the thought disorders of schizophrenia. Of course, not every unhealthy Five is schizophrenic, and not every schizophrenic is a Five. But this personality type does seem to be more prone to schizophrenia than any other.

A way of conceptualizing a possible relationship between the Five and schizophrenia is to think of these two entities as if they were on parallel mental tracks. At some point when the brain can no longer function within the neurotic Five's life situation, it skips tracks from neurosis to schizophrenia. From a mainly psychological maladjustment, the person jumps into a different realm: into a chemical and physical disease which, of course, has psychological ramifications. This might explain why some neurotic Fives remain neurotic while others develop into schizophrenics and why some schizophrenics become ill without being either Fives or neurotic.

The Dynamics of the Five

THE DIRECTION OF DISINTEGRATION: THE FIVE GOES TO SEVEN

The main problem for Fives is to move from thinking to doing, from knowledge to experience. They must find a source of security within themselves to enable them to act with a reasonable degree of certitude. Schizoid Fives need to reestablish contact with reality (particularly the positive aspects of it), although they are completely incapable of doing so now. When neurotic Fives deteriorate further to Seven, they act impulsively, erratically, and hysterically. They act out anxiety, like a neurotic, manic-depressive Seven.

Neurotic Fives lurch from an isolated, paranoid state in which they are immobilized by their terrors to one of wildly manic activity. They lunge into literally mindless actions, by which they succeed only in getting themselves into worse trouble and more serious conflicts with the environment. Such a development cannot satisfy their real needs because, since they are still neurotic, they are virtually incapable of learning anything from their new experiences. They are irrational, have extremely poor judgment, and make poor choices about which actions to take. And since they still cannot identify with anything or anyone, they cannot make any useful contact with the environment. Throwing themselves into new experiences does not help at all.

One further result of a move to Seven is that deteriorated Fives go totally out of control. Some of the terrible things they have feared may actually happen as a result of their erratic and irresponsible behavior. For example, they may be killed — not because they are assassinated by the CIA or by Martians, but because, not watching where they are going, they get run over by a truck. Out-of-control Fives are reckless and accident prone: they may be poisoned, not by the KGB but because they may mistakenly eat something they should not. Fearing that they have reached some sort of horrible dead end in their lives, they may impulsively do permanent harm to themselves or someone else. As anxiety reaches an ever new pitch, they may do something irrevocable, such as kill someone or commit suicide.

THE DIRECTION OF INTEGRATION: THE FIVE GOES TO EIGHT

Fives typically do not feel that they know enough to act: there is always more to know. They will always feel insecure until they have mastered the real world and are not simply masters of their own minds. From a psychoanalytic point of view, their egos are typically too weak for their ids — their aggressions and other impulses tend to overpower their minds.

This no longer happens to healthy, integrating Fives because they have incorporated their perceptions of the world into themselves by identifying with them instead of merely observing them. They no longer identify just with their thoughts, but also with the objects of their thoughts. Thus, integrating Fives have overcome their fear of the environment to learn to trust it. Hence their self-confidence grows, after the manner of healthy Eights.

When they go to Eight, Fives also realize that, as little as they think they know, it is still more than almost anyone else. They also realize that they do not have to know absolutely everything before they can act. They will learn more as they do more; they will be able to solve new problems as they arise. Absolute certitude is an illusion; it cannot be achieved.

Integrating Fives act from a realization of their own genuine mastery. While they do not know everything, they know enough to lead others with confidence. The correctness of their ideas has been so well confirmed by reality that they no longer fear acting. They acquire the courage it takes to put their ideas, and consequently *themselves*, on the line. Thus, integrating Fives realize that they are able to contribute something worthwhile to others. As a result, their thoughts are finally given expression in action and possibly in leadership. Integrating Fives show others how to do what only they know how to do. And, as we have seen, the practical value of their ideas may be incalculable.

The Major Subtypes of the Five

THE FIVE WITH A FOUR-WING

The traits of the Five and those of the Four-wing are often in conflict with each other: Fives are cerebral, holding experience at arm's length, while Fours internalize everything to intensify their feelings. Despite these differences — or because of them — these two personality types make one of the richest subtypes, combining possibilities for outstanding artistic as well as intellectual achievement. Noteworthy examples of this subtype include Albert Einstein, D. H. Lawrence, Friedrich Nietzsche, Oriana Fallaci, Hannah Arendt, Emily Dickinson, Italo Calvino, Jean-Paul Sartre, Jacob Bronowski, Glenn Gould, Peter Serkin, Klaus Tennstedt, Elvis Costello, and Stanley Kubrick.

In healthy people of this subtype, we find the union of intuition and knowledge, sensitivity and insight, aesthetic appreciation and intellectual endowments. This subtype is particularly aware of — and on the outlook for — the beautiful in a mathematical formula, for example. For this subtype, beauty is one of the indications of truth because the order which beauty represents is a confirmation of the objective rightness of an idea. One of the foremost strengths of healthy Fives with a Four-wing lies precisely in their intuition, since intuition helps them uncover areas of knowledge where their conscious thoughts have not yet ventured. For them, inspiration is the handmaiden of discovery. Fives with a Four-wing are also more humanistic, artistic, personal, and emotional than the other subtype.

In average persons of this subtype, there can be an off-putting detachment from the environment both because they are involved in their thoughts and because they are introverted and emotionally self-absorbed. Analytic powers may be used to keep people at arm's length rather than to understand them more deeply. Emotionally delicate, people of this subtype are moody and hypersensitive to criticism, particularly regarding the value of their work or ideas, since this impinges directly on self-esteem. Both component types tend to withdraw from people and be reclusive. Since Five is the basic type, persons of this subtype are intense, able to concentrate on their work and their ideas. But to the degree that the Four-wing is operative, they also feel emotionally vulnerable, which hinders their ability to work. One typical solution is to find emotional solace in various forms of self-indulgence — in alcohol, drugs, or sexual escapades.

Unhealthy persons of this subtype may fall prey to debilitating depressions yet be disturbed by aggressive impulses. Envy of others mixes with contempt for them; the desire to isolate the self from the world mixes with regret that it must be so. Intellectual conflicts make their emotional lives seem hopeless, while their emotional conflicts make intellectual work difficult to sustain. Moreover, if this subtype becomes neurotic, it is one of the most alienated of all of the personality types: profoundly hopeless, nihilistic, self-inhibiting, isolated from others, and full of self-hatred. Suicide is a real possibility.

THE FIVE WITH A SIX-WING

The traits of the Five and those of the Six-wing reinforce each other, combining to produce one of the most difficult of the personality types to contact intimately or to sustain a relationship with. Persons of this subtype have problems trusting others both because they are essentially Fives and because the Six-wing reinforces anxiety, making any kind of risk taking in relationships difficult. Hence, their interpersonal relations are erratic and, in general, are not an important part of their lives. Noteworthy examples of this subtype include Sigmund Freud, Simone Weil, James Joyce, Charles Darwin, Karl Marx, James Watson, Doris Lessing, Cynthia Ozick, Bobby Fischer, B. F. Skinner, Isaac Asimov, Ezra Pound, and Stephen Hawking.

Healthy people of this subtype are loyal and committed to their families and beliefs. They are extraordinarily hard workers, caring little for their own comfort and much more for their work and the fulfillment of their duties. In them we find an intellectual playfulness, a good sense of humor, as well as other attractive, lovable qualities. If others have been tested and permitted to come closer, they discover that people of this subtype have a deep capacity for friendship and commitment. There is also an endearing element in their desire to be accepted by others, and even if they are sometimes socially clumsy, others cannot help but be touched by their eagerness to reach out to people.

However, average persons of this subtype generally have problems with relationships. They do not seem to know what to do with their feelings, much less how to express them directly. Hence we find an insensitivity to their own feelings and emotional needs, as well as to the feelings and emotional needs of others. They have no awareness about how they communicate themselves to others. (They are the classical intellectual nerd, the socially inept oddball.) They are totally wrapped up with intellectual pursuits and live completely in their minds, immersing themselves in their work to the exclusion of everything else. When interpersonal conflicts arise, average Fives with a Six-wing avoid resolving problems by burying themselves even more deeply in their intellectual work and by employing passive-aggressive techniques, putting off people and problems rather than dealing with them directly. They can be rebellious and argumentative for no apparent reason, although something may have touched off unconscious emotional associations.

Neurotics of this subtype have a tendency to be suspicious of others and extremely fearful of intimacy of any sort. The isolation and paranoia we see in unhealthy Fives are reinforced by the Six-wing's suspicion, inferiority feelings, and conviction of being persecuted. We also find the tendency to overreact, and hence to act irrationally and in masochistic, self-defeating ways.

Some Final Thoughts

Taking an overall view of the Five, we can see that there has been a struggle between various pairs of polar opposites: between thinking and doing, between a fascination with the world and a fear of the world, between identification with others and a rejection of them, between love and hate. This process of attraction to and repulsion from the environment as a whole began with their ambivalence toward their parents. But unfortunately, what has happened is that Fives gradually become so obsessed with defending themselves from potential threats from the environment — that is, from whatever they see as evil — that they also exclude the good. Eventually, there is nothing in the world with which Fives can identify, nothing true or valuable in which they can believe. The final result is nihilism: there is nothing left to which they can attach themselves.

Like every other personality type which becomes gripped in the downward spiral of neurosis, Fives bring about the very thing they most fear: that the world is threatening, unpredictable, and ultimately meaningless. The irony is that they have brought about meaninglessness themselves since they have rejected attachment to everything. And by intensifying their involvement with their mental processes, instead of finding security or power, Fives have brought about their own insecurity and powerlessness.

It is a tragic end. If there is something perverse and dark — even demonic — about Fives, it is that to protect themselves they have relentlessly repulsed the world and other human beings. What then is left? Only a fascination with — and a terrifying attraction to — the darkness.

Chapter 8

Type Six: The Loyalist

The Six in Profile

Healthy: Becomes self-affirming, trusting of self and others, independent yet symbiotically interdependent and cooperative as an equal. Appealing, endearing, and lovable, eliciting strong emotional responses from others. Committed and loyal to those with whom he or she has identified; family and friends important. Reliable, responsible, and trustworthy.

Average: Identifies with an authority figure, becoming obedient to it. The traditionalist and "organization man": dutiful, but also tends to react against the authority. Ambivalent, passive-aggressive, indecisive, evasive, and cautious. Reacts to ambivalence by becoming defensive, taking a "tough guy" stance: authoritarian, highly partisan, blaming and scapegoating others to overcompensate for his or her fears.

Unhealthy: Can be insecure, clingingly dependent, self-disparaging, feeling inferior. Extremely anxious, overreacting to anxiety. Paranoid, feels persecuted. Acts irrationally, bringing about what he or she most fears. Self-defeating, humiliating self to be rescued from the consequences of his actions and from anxiety: masochistic tendencies.

Key Motivations: Wants security, to be liked and have the approval of others, to test the attitudes of others toward him, to fight against anxiety and insecurity.

Examples: Robert F. Kennedy, Walter Mondale, Phil Donahue, Marilyn Monroe, Diane Keaton, Johnny Carson, Ted Turner, J. Edgar Hoover, Jerry Falwell, Richard Nixon, G. Gordon Liddy, Joseph McCarthy, and Archie Bunker.

An Overview of the Six

Sixes are full of contradictions. They are emotionally dependent on others, yet do not reveal much of themselves. They want to be close to others, yet test them first to see if they can be trusted. They worship authority, yet fear it. They are obedient, yet disobedient; fearful of aggression, yet sometimes highly aggressive themselves. They search for security, yet feel insecure. They are likable and endearing, yet can be mean and hateful. They believe in traditional values, yet may subvert those values. They want to escape punishment, yet may bring it on themselves. Sixes are full of contradictions because anxiety makes them ricochet from one psychological state to another. And in response to anxiety, Sixes look to an authority to put their anxiety to rest.

> Our system of education teaches us to put our faith in something else — a corporation, a marriage, a trade, a profession, a religion, politics, something, one might almost say *anything*, which offers us a set of rules we can obey and rewards us for obedience to them. It's safer to be a domestic animal than a wild one. (Michael Korda, *POWER!*, 254.)

For Sixes, security comes from a rock-of-ages allegiance to an authority outside the self which they can obey. Sixes want to feel protected and secure by having something bigger and more powerful than they guiding them. IBM will do, but so will the Communist party or the Republican party or the church. The doctrines Sixes believe are important to them, but not as important as having someone to believe in.

IN THE DOING TRIAD

Sixes are the primary personality type in the Doing Triad. They are the most out of touch with the ability to make decisions and act on their own without reference to someone else, particularly an authority figure in the form of a person, an institution, or a belief system. Sixes look to an authority to supply them with a direction in life, to tell them what they can and cannot do, to put limits on them — in a word, for security, especially emotional security. Of course, in one way or another, all nine personality types have some kind of relationship with authority figures, but Sixes are the most affected by this need.

Sixes are among the most puzzling of the nine personality types because they are reactive, fluctuating from one state to another — usually the virtual opposite — very quickly. Sixes can be baffling and frustrating because they reverse themselves so frequently: they can be lovable and endearing, then cranky and negative; they can be decisive and self-assertive, then, almost in the next moment, indecisive and clinging. While they seek the approval of those who are important to them, they resist being in a position of inferiority. They may be obedient, and then openly disobedient, deviating from what the authority has told them to do. As a result, because Sixes are the most contradictory of the personality types, they are one of the most difficult to understand. They often remain so enigmatic, even to those closest to them, that the most others can say about them is that they are "easy to like but hard to get to know."

The key to understanding Sixes is that they are ambivalent: the two distinct sides of their personalities oscillate between aggressive and dependent tendencies. They feel both strong and weak, dependent and independent, passive and aggressive. As with Dr. Jekyll and Mr. Hyde, it is difficult to predict the state Sixes will be in from moment to moment. At each Level, they display a personality substantially different from what has gone before and what will follow.

To make matters more complicated, Sixes are not only ambivalent toward others, they are ambivalent toward themselves. They like themselves and then disparage themselves, feeling inferior to others. They have confidence and then seem hopeless, as if they could not do anything without help from someone else. They feel weak-kneed and cowardly, then suddenly fill with rage and strike out at others. A double set of dependent and aggressive impulses operates in them, continuously interacting in various complex combinations because Sixes react ambivalently not only to the external authority, but to the internal authority, their superego.

The result is that Sixes oscillate from one emotional state to another. As they shift first one way, then another, there seems to them to be little emotional stability or interpersonal security they can call their own. This is why it is so apt to identify Sixes as the personality type which has "the most trouble with doing" — not only because they look outside themselves for direction to act from an authority, but because the actions they actually take are often indecisive and circuitous.

It is impossible to understand Sixes without understanding their oscillating nature. Maintaining their sense of self requires that *both* sides of their psyches interact with each other. Sixes cannot emphasize one side of themselves and ignore the other — for instance, they cannot become independent by suppressing their dependent side. For better or worse, they are an amalgam of both sides of themselves. When they are healthy, both sides work hand in hand with each other. However, if tension between their two sides increases, so does anxiety, and therein lies the source of many of their problems.

PROBLEMS WITH ANXIETY AND INSECURITY

All three personality types of the Doing Triad have a problem with anxiety, but Sixes, as the primary type, have the greatest problem with it. They are the type which is most conscious of anxiety — "anxious that they are anxious" — unlike other personality types, who are either unaware of their anxiety or who unconsciously convert it into other symptoms. Fives, for example, displace anxiety into intellectual pursuits; Sevens repress it through constant activity. On the other hand, Sixes are aware that they are anxious: sometimes they are able to resist it, and sometimes they succumb to it. Because of their psychological dynamics, however, even average Sixes may not always show how anxious they actually are. There are times when they may not seem to be anxious at all since when they react to anxiety, average Sixes can be highly aggressive and belligerent. Nevertheless, anxiety underlies everything, either as an expression of it, or as a reaction to it.

Along with anxiety, average to unhealthy Sixes feel insecure because their feelings are ambivalent: they do not know how they feel about other people. Sixes want people to like them, but they become suspicious of others, fearing that they do not. Moreover, average Sixes also do not know how others feel about them. As a result, they test others to discover the attitude of others toward them, constantly looking for evidence of approval or disapproval. And if average Sixes deteriorate into neurosis, they become so suspicious of others that they become paranoid, anxiety ridden, and so insecure that they cannot function.

Sixes correspond to Jung's introverted feeling type. Even though they belong to the Doing Triad, Sixes are emotional because their feelings are affected by anxiety. Unfortunately, Jung's description of this type is not one of his clearest. Possibly to explain his difficulty in describing this type, Jung says,

> It is extremely difficult to give an intellectual account of the introverted feeling process, or even an approximate description of it, although the peculiar nature of this kind of feeling is very noticeable once one has become aware of it. (C. G. Jung, *Psychological Types*, 387.)

As we have just seen, it is difficult to describe this personality type in simple terms because its psyche continually changes. It may be helpful to think of Sixes as "ambiverts," a mixture of extroverted and introverted feelings. This is why they react to whatever they have done, especially if anxiety has been aroused, by doing the opposite to compensate. They then react to this new state, and then to the next, ad infinitum. For example, they may be affectionate toward someone; then, fearing that they will be taken advantage of, they become suspicious of the very person who has just been the object of their warmth. But, becoming anxious about their suspicions, they seek reassurance that the relationship is still all right. As soon as they receive reassurance from the other, Sixes wonder if they have not been too ingratiating, so they overcompensate by becoming defensive, acting as if they did not need the other person.

And on it goes. If you have difficulty understanding someone who is a mass of contradictions, you are probably dealing with a Six.

It is also important to understand that while Sixes are emotional, they do not show their emotions directly — as Twos do, for example — even to those they are closest to. Ambivalence toward both themselves and others causes them to give mixed signals. Or, to put this another way, Sixes react to their feelings — particularly anxiety — and communicate their reactions rather than their feelings. Except when Sixes are very healthy, others can rarely be certain of what is really on their minds.

This is why achieving independence and emotional stability, especially freedom from anxiety, is so important to them. If they are too compliant, their self-esteem suffers: they feel inferior to others, like someone who can be pushed around. On the other hand, if they are too aggressive in their search for independence, they fear that they will alienate the very people who provide them with security and will be punished in some terrible way. The challenge Sixes face is to find a way of maintaining both sides of their personalities, gradually reducing the tensions between their conflicting sides until they form a reciprocal unit — themselves as healthy persons.

CHILDHOOD ORIGINS

As the result of their childhood experiences, Sixes identify positively with their fathers or a father figure, such as a grandfather or teacher. As children, Sixes wanted the security of being approved by their fathers and felt anxious if they did not receive it. As they grew up, their positive identification with their fathers shifted to an identification with more abstract father figures, such as civil authorities or belief systems from which they could obtain security.

As children, Sixes learned to feel secure by trying to please their fathers in whatever ways were demanded. They learned to follow the rules of the home and to become responsible members of society by being obedient, approved members of their first group, their families. But in doing so, they learned that value exists outside themselves in the authority who will reward them if they do what they are told. If they do not comply with the authority, Sixes fear retribution both from the authority and from what they have internalized of it, a strong and active superego. Of course, individual

Sixes may or may not rebel against their authority figures in later life, but the pattern of orienting themselves to life by obtaining the approval of others (who, in one way or another, function as authority figures) is one which has become ingrained in their nature.

Of all the personality types, Sixes can be the most engaging and lovable people imaginable when they are healthy. The reactive quality of their psyches makes them delightfully playful and unpredictable. They want to be liked, and they have endearing, childlike qualities which we find in no other personality type. If they trust you, they can be the most loyal of friends. If you enjoy their loyalty, they will fight for you as they would for themselves — indeed, even better. Average Sixes, however, can be too dependent on the authority figure, while at the same time reacting against their dependence and displaying the passive-aggressive ambivalence we have seen. When their aggressive side gets the upper hand, average Sixes can be the most petty and mean-spirited of people — bigoted, authoritarian, and prejudiced — not at all lovable or endearing, as they were when they were healthy. And if they become unhealthy, Sixes feel painfully insecure and extremely anxious, overreacting to everything as their wildly fluctuating emotions create severe problems for themselves and others. If they cannot resolve their anxieties and conflicts, Sixes become self-defeating, bringing on themselves the very punishments they so fear.

Analyzing the Healthy Six

THE SELF-AFFIRMING PERSON

At their best, very healthy Sixes learn to affirm themselves. They thus have a positive basis for forming balanced relationships with others and, paradoxically, with themselves. They feel secure, accepted, and comfortable with themselves.

Self-affirmation is internal, an act of belief in oneself. It is emphatically not the same thing as narcissistic bragging about oneself. The self-affirmation of very healthy Sixes is an act of self-confidence arising from a realization of their own value without reference to anyone else. Their self-affirmation marks a shift from seeing all good residing in others, especially in an authority figure, to having a realistic faith in themselves. Very healthy Sixes are no longer reactive, but mature, their own persons. They are noticeably more adult than they have ever been, so much so that others are able to depend upon them as fully as Sixes have probably depended on others.

In their relationships, very healthy Sixes achieve a dynamic interdependence, a true reciprocity, which brings out the best in both parties. No one dominates the relationship, and no one is inferior in it. Healthy Sixes are able to support others and be supported by them, to love and be loved, to work by themselves and with others. They are fully cooperative, coequal partners, able to interact with others without anxiety. For the first time in their lives, they feel genuinely secure because they trust themselves and are consequently able to trust those who are worthy of it.

Their deepest feelings are free to emerge because they have tapped the inner springs of courage — faith in themselves. They no longer react to their feelings and so are able to express themselves effectively both personally and in their work. If they have the talent and training, they may become outstanding artists or leaders because they have acquired the necessary emotional equipment. Very healthy Sixes are particularly effective leaders because they know what it is like to feel insecure and to look to someone else for help. They are able to help create genuine security for others. Becoming courageous is a high achievement for Sixes, which is why we see it only in their healthiest state. The courage of very healthy Sixes is all the more praiseworthy because it has been won not merely against external difficulties but against inner doubt. ("The only security is courage." — La Rochefoucauld)

Because anxiety is part of the human condition, it is useful for even very healthy Sixes to remember that they will never be entirely relieved of it. Of course, the more integrated Sixes are, the less anxious they feel. But they cannot expect that they will never feel anxious. Human beings cannot insure themselves against disease, loss, or any of the thousand mishaps of fate. Healthy, self-affirming Sixes therefore must not demand that they will always feel absolutely secure since this is an impossible goal. Rather, they must learn to harness the inevitable degree of anxiety which goes with the territory of being human to achieve higher goals.

THE ENGAGING PERSON

Even relatively healthy Sixes do not always affirm themselves; nor do they feel quite the equal of others. They begin to look for security outside themselves because, for one reason or another, they fear being abandoned and alone in life. They feel they need other people and that their well-being depends on establishing and maintaining positive relationships.

Trust is an important issue. Sixes want to find someone they can trust completely so they can form permanent emotional bonds which will give them the security they want. They want to be liked so they can have the emotional security which comes from being accepted by others. To this end, healthy Sixes develop the capacity to engage others emotionally.

Even adult healthy Sixes have an unmistakably endearing quality which unconsciously appeals to people. This quality was doubtless what Jung was referring to when he wrote of the difficulty involved in describing the introverted feeling process.

While healthy Sixes are extremely endearing, it is sometimes difficult to say what makes them so because this is a subjective quality: what appeals to one person may not appeal to another. What is always the case, however, is that healthy Sixes know how to arouse strong emotional responses in others, engaging their emotions unconsciously. They have the capacity to get people to respond to them partly because Sixes, along with Threes, are among the most physically attractive of the personality types. Some of their appeal may well have a sexual, seductive element to it. ("I wanted to become famous so that everybody would like me and I'd be surrounded by love and affection." — Marilyn Monroe)

But it is more than that. The answer to what makes healthy Sixes so appealing and lovable, and what makes others want to give them the emotional security they seek, is that this kind of interaction has been primed by Sixes themselves. Their desire to be accepted by others leads Sixes to behave in a way which encourages others to offer love to them. They have an inviting, ingratiating quality which stimulates relationships. Even so, their appeal is not always easy to identify precisely since it can be very subtle — a matter of eye contact, of smiling a lot, and of subliminal body cues — nor is it necessarily overtly seductive or ingratiating in a fawning way.

We might understand their appeal better by observing the same process in children: the qualities of trust, expectation, and love which children display to their parents are the qualities with which healthy Sixes engage others. They are able to communicate the nonverbal message, "There is nothing to fear here — you can get close to me, if you let me get close to you."

Some people are, of course, impervious to this; they find the ingratiation of even healthy Sixes childish, although it is not necessarily immature. While there are those who dismiss them, there are many who are susceptible to their appeal, and there is much to like about Sixes since they intentionally try to be liked. They can be extremely winsome, playful, even silly, with a rather cute "little boy" or "little girl" mischievousness about them. They have an infectious smile and a droll, self-deprecating sense of humor, teasing those with whom they want to form a relationship. Good-natured bantering is a sign of affection from Sixes, a sign that they want to become closer to you.

Naturally, their attempt to create a relationship with someone else is flattering. Others are asked, more by deed than by word, for their friendship, and are offered trust and affection in return. A relationship with a healthy Six can be delightful and emotionally rewarding for both parties. Note, however, that the desire to engage the other automatically puts the other person in the superior position, something which will have significant consequences later on.

THE COMMITTED LOYALIST

The very act of engaging someone else at least raises the possibility that the attempt will be rejected or that the relationship will not go well. Having to engage others is sure to raise at least a glimmer of anxiety, even in healthy Sixes. They cannot help but realize that, by seeking security outside themselves in the good will and acceptance of others, they are bound to feel some insecurity. As a result, healthy Sixes do not want just to elicit protective feelings from others, but to form permanent alliances. To stimulate this, they become committed to others, extremely loyal, and very dependable.

Healthy Sixes are able to commit themselves deeply to those with whom they have formed special emotional bonds. They give themselves to others and want to have others respond to them in kind. This is why being part of a family of some sort is so important to them. The family is virtually a symbol of the kind of emotional support and stability Sixes seek. They want to have people they can depend on, to have unconditional acceptance, to have a place where they belong. Having close ties with family and friends makes them feel that they are not alone. Being committed to others diminishes the fear of being abandoned.

Sixes find it almost impossible to break their emotional bonds, even should they desire to do so. ("Once a friend, always a friend.") If Sixes have given their hearts away, their love may, in time, turn to hatred but never to indifference. For better or worse, they are never entirely free of their attachments, whether to an individual, a football team, a country, or a belief. Their commitments last because they are not superficial choices but deep identifications which become important parts of who they are.

Healthy Sixes express their commitment to others by being extremely loyal, never hesitating to defend their friends and their relationships. Whether others are right or wrong, Sixes can be counted on to be there for them. They are the kind of people others know they can absolutely depend on. In the business world, healthy Sixes are highly valued because they are prodigiously hard workers, diligent, trustworthy, and able to assume responsibility. Healthy Sixes are industrious workers in whom we find no "problem with doing." They are highly valued for their reliability whether they work alone or with others. For these reasons, and because they are so likable, healthy Sixes, if they are intellectually gifted, frequently rise in their professions. They succeed like the tenacious tortoise who beats the faster, flightier hare.

Some of the virtues of healthy Sixes are not in vogue in today's "Me first!" "Looking out for number one" society. However, the assets of this personality type — commitment, perseverance, faithfulness to communal values, belief in loyalty, family, religion, friends, and the welfare of the group as a whole — speak for themselves and need no apology.

Analyzing the Average Six

THE OBEDIENT TRADITIONALIST

Once Sixes become committed to a person or a group, they may begin to fear taking responsibility for themselves. They want to feel secure by adhering to the rules of the group and to have the approval of others, especially of an authority figure, before they act in any important way. Average Sixes are not independent, nor do they care to be. They want boundaries set for them by an authority, whether the authority is a person (as it often is) or an impersonal set of rules or beliefs.

Healthy loyalty to those they are committed to has deteriorated into dependency. Average Sixes feel comfortable being told what to do, and more than any other personality type, they attempt to find security by being obedient to an all-encompassing authority which gives them guidance in every important area of their lives. They do not question the authority since doing so would make them feel on their own and anxious, feelings they would rather avoid.

In distinction to what we saw in healthy Sixes, average Sixes are more likely to be followers than leaders. Instead of making decisions themselves, they look for precedents and answers in documents or in rules and regulations — "scriptures" of one sort or another. (Average Sixes who function as leaders most likely do so by forming committees and governing through consensus rather than making decisions independently.) The rules average Sixes follow are always subject to the interpretation of an authority figure, from a drill sergeant who interprets the army's rules to a priest who interprets the church's rules to the law itself, which interprets society's rules. Sixes feel that if they follow the rules, no one can criticize them or punish them, no matter what those rules tell them to do. ("I was just following orders," "The priest said it was all right," and "I don't ask questions, I just do what I am told" are typical of their attitude at this stage.) But while obedience frees average Sixes from much anxiety, it tends to jeopardize their own maturity since they depend upon someone else to take responsibility for making decisions.

This does not mean that average Sixes cannot make decisions in some matters, but that they find it difficult to make such major decisions as whom to marry or which job to take on their own. They would rather have someone else tell them what to do. In a marriage, for example, the burden is on the spouse to make decisions. This is not to say that the dependency which we find in average Sixes is a clinging helplessness, but that average Sixes want security and are willing to subordinate themselves to someone else to obtain it.

Moreover, average Sixes are not spineless Milquetoasts. They are true believers who, from their point of view, are merely obeying legitimate precepts which should be obeyed because they have the weight of authority and time-tested traditional values on their side. Average Sixes therefore do not mind getting some form of "permission" before doing things, nor do they mind following rules and official procedures. (Indeed, average Sixes are adept at making the rules and regulations laid down by the authority work for them: having the law or the organization on their side can frequently be very convenient.)

Thus, average Sixes are satisfied with being traditionalists, organization men, and team players, the main personality type which populates most institutions and bureaucracies — the backbone of groups of all sorts. Instead of being oppressed by authority, average Sixes feel strengthened by it. Belonging to a group of some sort makes them feel they are not alone but that they are stronger and more secure precisely because they are members of a group. (A fraternity or club or large corporation has this appeal, as do political parties, unions, and religious affiliations.) The strength of the group far exceeds the strength of any individual member, and groups are able to achieve many things which individuals alone cannot. Also, close friendships arise ("bonding" on sports teams or among women in an office, for example) which are emotionally satisfying to average Sixes. There are, however, two major drawbacks. First, average Sixes tend to do things because they have been ordered to. Blind obedience may well not be in the best interests of either the individual or, ultimately, the group itself.

Second, possessing a group identity encourages a parochial way of looking at the world, in which everyone is divided into "them" versus "us" groups. Of course, the world is greatly simplified when people know who thinks the same as they do, who has the same values, who believes the same about religion, country, and politics. But parochialism also creates unnecessary divisions between people. And even within their own group, average Sixes make it their business to find out who is pulling his or her weight and who is not. They do not like it when others do not take the authority figure or the rules as seriously as they do. If others are not as loyal or obedient, it not only makes them angry — it threatens them.

THE AMBIVALENT PERSON

If they are too obedient, average Sixes begin to wonder what others in their group think of them. Maintaining their self-esteem requires that Sixes react *against* people (including the authority), at least occasionally. Average Sixes do not want to feel that they are being taken advantage of or that others do not respect them. So they react against people, becoming evasive and unpredictable, sometimes in small ways, sometimes by being guarded and openly defensive.

Remember that Sixes can be quite different from Level to Level along the Continuum. We are now beginning to see their oscillations more clearly, from the obedience we have just seen to ambivalence, from doing as they are told to reacting against it. At this stage, Sixes test others (including the authority) to find out how others feel about them. But they also test others because average Sixes are unsure of their own feelings and want to find out how they themselves feel. They are anxious about themselves and anxious about others, sometimes reacting aggressively toward others, sometimes compliantly. Sometimes, it seems, both ways at the same time. In short, their feelings are confused and contradictory.

Because of these opposing tensions in themselves and their relationships, average Sixes are deeply ambivalent. As the opposing sides of their alternating psyches surface, average Sixes fluctuate between compliant and aggressive impulses, feeling that others like them and then do not. Or Sixes feel that they like others and then that they do not. Knowing their ambivalence toward others, they cannot help but feel that others are ambivalent toward them. And knowing how quickly they can turn on someone else, Sixes feel that others may well turn on them. So they become guarded and evasive.

Because they are also not in touch with their desires, average Sixes now have difficulty doing things on their own, making decisions by themselves, or leading others if they are called upon to do so. They go around in circles, unable to make up their minds, unsure of themselves and what they really want to do, dithering around and procrastinating. If they must act, they are extremely cautious, making decisions timidly, covering all bases with legalisms and precedents which both guide and protect them. When something must get done, they wait until the last moment to get started, and then work under great pressure to meet their obligations.

Ambivalence has been described by psychologists, probably because indecision and anxiety bring a lot of patients into therapy.

> The ambivalence of passive-aggressives intrudes constantly into their everyday life, resulting in indecisiveness, fluctuating attitudes, oppositional behaviors and emotions, and a general erraticism and unpredictability. They cannot decide whether to adhere to the desires of others as a means of gaining comfort and security *or* to turn to themselves for these gains, whether to be obediently dependent on others *or* defiantly resistant and independent of them, whether to take the initiative in mastering their world *or* to sit idly by, passively awaiting the leadership of others; they vacillate, then, like the proverbial donkey, moving first one way and then the other, never quite settling on which bale of hay is best. (Theodore Millon, *Disorders of Personality*, 244.)

While ambivalence allows Sixes to evade responsibility for their behavior, it also generates a great deal of emotional stress, causing them to become tense and tired. It is as if they simultaneously had one foot on the accelerator and the other on the brake. Whenever they are under tension of any sort, they complain a lot, and get grumpy and negativistic. They may also be frigid or impotent whenever anxiety or tension gets in the way of sexual performance. Drugs and alcohol, in particular, may be used to ease tensions. However, if Sixes overuse either as a solution to their anxieties, they risk becoming dependent, ironically trading dependency on the authority for dependency on something else, perhaps much worse.

Sixes become extremely frustrating to deal with because they force others to take responsibility for decisions while sending out mixed signals about their own desires. One result is that no one can get a straight answer from them: yes means no, and vice versa. They may say that they would like to meet someone for dinner, for example, but never agree on a date. They seem to be friendly but are defensive, holding on to people with one hand while putting them off with the other. Their evasiveness forces others to take the lead in everything, while average Sixes merely react unpredictably, either by going along with or by rejecting what has been decided. If something goes amiss, they complain loudly about it, while avoiding any responsibility for the poor decision.

By being aggressive to others indirectly, average Sixes express the aggressive side of their passive-aggressive nature. For example, a Six who is angry at someone may put that person on "hold" on the telephone and "forget" to come back. A passive-aggressive employee may frustrate the boss by "forgetting" a deadline or by losing materials. Because of their indirection, passive-aggressive aggressions are never open, so Sixes can avoid responsibility for them.

Passive-aggressive indirection shows up in all their social interactions, even in their humor, which now has an edgy, sarcastic note. Passive-aggressive humor allows Sixes to get in a jab at people indirectly, by saying the opposite of what they mean. ("Of course I respect you — I treat you with all the respect you deserve.") People may not understand how caustic their jokes are until the aggressive subtext sinks in sometime later on.

This Level is a turning point in the deterioration of average Sixes. For the first time they realize that their attitudes toward themselves and others are complex and confused. They begin to be suspicious of others and of themselves. They are not sure of the authority or how the authority feels about them. They do not know either their thoughts or their feelings; they are not sure what to do or not do. In short, all kinds of doubts and anxieties enter their minds, and once they do, they are difficult to put to rest.

THE OVERCOMPENSATING TOUGH GUY

Rather than attempt to resolve their doubts and anxieties, average Sixes react against them, shifting to another reversal of behavior. They overcompensate for ambivalence and indecision by becoming very aggressive toward themselves and others in an effort to prove that they are not anxious, indecisive, or dependent. They strongly assert the aggressive side of their passive-aggressive ambivalence in an attempt to repress the passive side.

At this stage, Sixes employ the defense mechanism of "counter-phobia," trying to master their growing anxieties by striking out at whatever seems to have aroused them. In its innocent forms, counterphobia is well employed by people to master their fears — for example, by children who are afraid of the dark purposely going into a dark room to overcome their fear. But at this Level, average Sixes are far from innocent. Counterphobia makes them overcompensate: they strike out too aggressively at whatever threatens them. They become boastful, swaggering "tough guys," rebellious and belligerent, harassing and obstructing others however they can to prove that they cannot be pushed around.

Their overcompensated aggressions are not a sign of true strength, but are more a way of feeling superior to others by frustrating or harming them in some way. Instead of becoming strong, average Sixes at this stage merely make life difficult for people since they are mean-spirited and occasionally violent. They are caricatures of authority, martinets and petty tyrants, full of bombast and bluster, dangerous but weak — and therefore especially dangerous.

We have already seen that average Sixes identify with groups, but now they are extremely partisan and authoritarian, strictly dividing people according to those who are "for us" and those who are "against us." Everyone is reduced to bare dichotomies of them against us, outsiders versus insiders, friends versus enemies. The loyalty we saw in healthy Sixes has deteriorated into rank, militant partisanship. Their attitude is "My country (my authority, my leader, my beliefs) right or wrong." Should their group be challenged, average Sixes see it as an attack not only on their authority and belief systems, but on their way of life. While anxiety is still their underlying problem, at this stage hatred of others is its manifestation.

Authoritarian Sixes are extremely prejudiced in the defense of their own group, reacting with a siege mentality to all outsiders, whom they look on with suspicion as potential enemies. Like vigilantes, they will fight, sometimes quite viciously, against outsiders — and even against members of their own group who seem to them not to be completely on their side. But because of the dynamics of overcompensation, ironically Sixes often deviate from the very rules they have been taught. Sixes who so firmly believe in democracy become rabid bigots, eager to deny civil rights to fellow citizens. Christians hate, thereby contradicting their beliefs as Christians. The law-and-order person becomes a lawbreaker in the name of the law.

Sixes who are leaders are particularly dangerous at this stage. They may have been sought after as leaders precisely because of their apparent aggressiveness and willingness to go to any length to uphold the group's "traditional values." Unfortunately, they usually turn out to be demagogues, inciting insecurities in others so they can acquire the strength of a mob behind them. Insecurity, hatred, not courage, is the impetus here.

If there is no clearly defined enemy, overcompensating Sixes will find one, settling on a scapegoat of some sort as the focus for their aggressions. One of the uglier aspects of Sixes at this stage is their need to have a person or group on whom they can release aggressions. Their scapegoats are always assigned the basest motives so that bigoted Sixes will feel justified in dealing with them in whatever way satisfies their emotional needs. Ironically, the people they typically hate — blacks, Jews, homosexuals, foreigners, "outsiders" of all sorts — often embody the very weaknesses and insecurities Sixes fear in themselves.

It would be difficult to persuade others who did not know them before they became so prejudiced and authoritarian that they are, or once were, capable of being lovable and endearing people. They are so mean and petty now that they are anything but lovable. Moreover, since the strength of their authoritarian belligerence is built on a shifting psychic foundation, it is not a permanent state. But, unfortunately, because their aggressions are real, they may last long enough for Sixes to do serious mischief, or worse harm, to others.

Analyzing the Unhealthy Six

THE INSECURE PERSON

If they act too aggressively, Sixes may begin to fear that they have jeopardized their relationship with the authority and will suffer some sort of serious punishment as a result. Although they may not have actually run afoul of the authority, they fear that they have. As a result, they become prey to intense anxiety, seeking reassurances that, no matter what they have done in the past, their relationship with the authority is still intact. (Beneath the armor of the tough authoritarian is a frightened, insecure child.)

Average Sixes who once exhibited a blustering toughness, at moments even feeling that they no longer needed the authority, have shifted abruptly. Tearful and obsequious, they are disgusted with themselves for not having been tough enough to stand on their own two feet, to defend themselves, to be independent. They feel cowardly because they have not been able to sustain their aggressive behavior, not because they have not tried.

Sixes become unhealthy because their self-disparagement and massive insecurity create intense feelings of inferiority and worthlessness. The indecision and evasiveness we saw in average Sixes have deteriorated into terrible insecurity and anxiety. Unhealthy Sixes are convinced that they are incompetent and unable to do anything on their own. They become clingingly dependent on the authority, or, if the original authority has already abandoned or rejected them, on some new authority.

Unhealthy Sixes feel absolutely worthless. They whine and complain and disparage themselves so much that they weaken whatever remaining strength they have and become an emotional drain on everyone. Those around them begin to feel insecure and anxious themselves because Sixes have the uncanny ability to induce their anxieties, as well as other feelings, into others. Their despondency gets people down, virtually forcing others away. Of course, this only makes unhealthy Sixes all the more clinging, more "morbidly dependent" in Karen Horney's phrase, and more difficult to deal with.

They put themselves down constantly and truly feel inferior to everyone else. ("Anyone who likes me must have something wrong with him.") By disparaging themselves, they seem to be saying, "You ought to love me because I am helpless and no good without you." They do not believe in themselves, and they cannot believe that anyone else could, either. If someone should encourage them, unhealthy Sixes immediately discount anything positive said to them. They are not so much looking for a pep talk, although that helps momentarily, but for the promise that someone strong and forceful will take over for them — a father figure.

At work, their colleagues cannot help but notice their insecurity and anxiety. The quality of their performance is poor because they are too anxious to concentrate and are frequently absent from work because of mysterious psychosomatic problems, little physical breakdowns which put them in bed for a day or two, or on the bottle for somewhat longer. (Any previous problem with alcohol now worsens considerably because unhealthy Sixes need alcohol — or some other drug — to deaden anxiety and take the edge off insecurity.)

The longer Sixes remain like this, the more hopeless and insecure they feel, and the more hopeless and insecure they genuinely become. Others may suspect that they are not really interested in solving their problems, since "having problems" and complaining about them function as ways of obtaining reassurances from others. In fact, unhealthy Sixes have a vested interest in maintaining their problems so that someone will come to their aid and give them the security they crave.

THE OVERREACTING HYSTERIC

The oscillating nature of their psyches once again makes itself felt: unhealthy Sixes shift from self-disparagement to become overreacting and hysterically anxious. At the previous stage, unhealthy Sixes were anxious because they disparaged themselves and felt inferior. Now, in addition, neurotic Sixes are anxiety-ridden because they have lost the ability to control their anxiety. They are irrational and hysterical when they think about themselves, suspicious and paranoid when they think about others.

Insecurity has escalated into a state of free-floating anxiety so great that neurotic Sixes irrationally misperceive reality, turning everything into a crisis. Neurotic Sixes unconsciously project their own aggressions onto others, becoming paranoid about the aggressions they find. This marks yet another "reversal" in their deterioration because neurotic Sixes no longer see their own inferiority as the main problem, but the hostility which others apparently have toward them. To put this differently, they shift from fearing themselves to fearing others.

In a sense, the fears of average Sixes are replayed in a more intense form when they become neurotic. Average Sixes want to test others to find out how they feel about them. Neurotic Sixes are positive that the verdict is negative and that others are out to get them. If their boss is gruff, neurotic Sixes irrationally overreact, becoming certain that they are going to be fired. If they get into a conflict with their landlord, they are sure he will evict them or hire a hit man to retaliate. They see conspiracies plotted against them everywhere; they feel persecuted by everyone, especially by the authority who, they are convinced, is trying to punish them for their failures. In fact, neurotic Sixes are in a particularly terrible conflict about authority: because they are so anxious, they need the authority more than ever; yet, because of their paranoia, neurotic Sixes feel the authority hates them.

It is important to understand that neurotic Sixes are bundles of irrational fears looking for reasons to be afraid. They live under a cloud of dread, absolutely certain that something horrible is about to happen to them, blowing the smallest incidents completely out of proportion. It is, of course, impossible to reason with them. Everything seems like the end of the world to them, and since they undoubtedly have genuinely serious problems, they are thrown into a panic about everything. Precisely when their problems and failures are multiplying, they cannot cope.

Their hysterical overreactions can be somewhat adaptive, however. Irrational behavior — the kind of hysterical, exaggerated acting out neurotic Sixes engage in — prevents them from fully confronting their fears. Hysteria is thus a form of manic defense, allowing them to run away from whatever is troubling them. It is also still a means of attempting to elicit help from others because they are so afraid.

THE SELF-DEFEATING MASOCHIST

If overreacting to their fears does not elicit the help they want, neurotic Sixes may provoke punishment from others in order to maintain a relationship with them, even if it is a masochistic one.

They become self-defeating, another reversal. Instead of continuing to be anxiety-ridden, living in dread that something awful will happen to them, neurotic Sixes bring defeat and punishment on themselves. Ironically, just as they may once have scapegoated and persecuted others, they now turn their aggression against themselves with the same hatred and desire for revenge.

Neurotic Sixes bring disaster of some sort on themselves, not to end their relationship with the authority, but to reestablish a protective one. By bringing defeat on themselves, they at least save themselves from being defeated by someone else. As painful and humiliating as whatever they do to themselves is, it expiates guilt and defuses the self condemnations which might push them to suicide. In a sense, then, they defeat and humiliate themselves so that they can be rescued from a worse fate.

It is also important to understand that neurotic Sixes are masochistic not because they take pleasure in suffering as such, but because they hope their suffering will draw to their side someone who will save them. Masochistic suffering seeks union with another, as if to say, "Punish me because I have been bad. Then you can love me again."

> Wilhelm Reich agreed that behind the masochist's behavior lay a desire to provoke authority figures, but he disagreed that this was in order to bribe the superego or to execute a dreaded punishment. Rather, he maintained, this grandiose provocation represented a defense against punishment and anxiety by substituting a milder punishment and by placing the provoked authority figure in such a light as to justify the masochist's reproach, "See how badly you treat me." Behind such a provocation is a deep disappointment in love, a disappointment of the masochist's excessive demand for love based on the fear of being left alone. (Leland E. Hinsie and Robert J. Campbell, *Psychiatric Dictionary*, 452.)

Even if neurotic Sixes succeed in being punished by someone else, they nevertheless retain an element of control. Hence, their self-esteem is not at absolute zero. They have elicited punishment and gotten the reassurance they want from the authority through the act of being punished. For neurotic Sixes, to be punished by the authority is still to be loved. Someone still cares. Thus, masochism avoids the much more threatening problem of being rejected and abandoned, and gives neurotic Sixes a degree of satisfaction —without which they would probably commit suicide.

The Dynamics of the Six

THE DIRECTION OF DISINTEGRATION: THE SIX GOES TO THREE

Sixes who go to Three no longer masochistically turn their aggression against themselves; instead, they turn it against others to see them suffer. Going to Three marks the eruption of their sadistic and aggressive feelings in undiluted form. Aggressions toward others have been building for some time, but except during the Level of belligerent overcompensation, Sixes usually hold their aggressions in check as much as possible so that they can elicit love and protection from others.

Now, whatever inner restraints they previously put on their aggressive behavior are removed, and Sixes become as psychopathic as unhealthy Threes. The authoritarian hatred seen in average Sixes returns in a much more aggressive and dangerous form. Deteriorated Sixes strike out at others violently to overcome their inferiority feelings once and for all. They vindictively hurt others, even though their victims may not have been the actual cause of their suffering.

Sixes who go to Three manifest all the traits of unhealthy Threes. They can be psychopathically sadistic and destructive, consumed with hatred and the desire to destroy those who do not love them. They become pathological liars for the same reason that unhealthy Threes do — to make fools of others and triumph over them. They may rape, torture, and kill their victims.

But Sixes at Three remain fundamentally Sixes, and they are ambivalent about the hated other: their still-divided psyche wants to elicit love from the very person they may be violent toward. Psychopathic violence, at least in deteriorated Sixes, is merely another form of self-defeat, but one which demands the strictest punishment. If they have broken the law, Sixes at Three will not succeed in eliciting a punishment which reconciles them to the other. Instead, they may be imprisoned or executed or themselves become the object of hatred and revenge.

THE DIRECTION OF INTEGRATION: THE SIX GOES TO NINE

In the simplest terms, Sixes need to resolve their ambivalence and their anxiety about themselves and others. This is precisely what happens when they go to Nine.

Sixes at Nine are much more emotionally open, receptive, and sympathetic toward people, and as a result, their emotional spectrum grows much wider. Integrating Sixes are emotionally stable, peaceful, and self-possessed. They fully overcome their tendencies to be dependent, and instead become autonomous and independent, persons on whom others can and do rely. Integrating Sixes are able to reassure and support others rather than seek reassurance and support from others, as we have seen throughout their Continuum.

In fact, Sixes at Nine are quite different from even healthy Sixes. A revolutionary change for the better has taken place in the integrating Six: he or she becomes independent and yet, paradoxically, is closer to others than ever before.

One unexpected payoff of this development is that integrating Sixes develop a greater number of friends than they had when they looked to others for protection, either as authority figures or as members of their in-group. No longer reactive to people, they are able to form a stable union with others. Others seek them out because they are so healthy, mature, and well disposed to people. The playfulness and sense of humor we saw in healthy Sixes has not been left behind, although added to these qualities are the Nine's sunniness of disposition, optimism, and kindheartedness, traits for which Sixes are not usually known, but which they now possess in abundance.

Integrating Sixes at last attain not only security but the ability to trust others, something which has always eluded them. Because they now trust themselves, they can — and do — finally trust others.

The Major Subtypes of the Six

THE SIX WITH A FIVE-WING

The traits of the Six and those of a Five-wing are in some degree of conflict with each other. The general orientation of Sixes is toward dependency on others, while the orientation of Fives is toward detachment from people so that they can avoid being influenced by anyone. Noteworthy examples of this subtype include Richard Nixon, Robert F. Kennedy, Robert Redford, Peter Ueberroth, Rock Hudson, Paul Newman, Billy Graham, Walter Mondale, Alexander Haig, G. Gordon Liddy, Joseph McCarthy, J. Edgar Hoover, Jerry Falwell, Lyndon La Rouche, Meir Kahane, and John Hinckley, Jr.

Healthy people of this subtype are not only endearing, they can also be very interesting individuals. They may have a strong intellectual streak, depending on how much Five-wing is in their overall personality. They frequently have keen insights based either on academic learning or practical knowledge. They are usually shrewd observers of the environment, particularly people, and put a premium on foresight and predicting how others will react. Their perceptions are more original than those of Sixes with a Seven-wing, but because Six is the basic type, they come across not as intellectuals but as extremely competent, knowledgeable individuals.

The anxiety we see in average Sixes also causes people of this subtype to be more intense than Sixes with a Seven-wing. Persons of this subtype tend to be constricted in the expression of their emotions, and are usually more cynical, negativistic, and contentious. The legal and business worlds are typical arenas for their energies. They also see the environment as a threatening place; suspiciousness, secrecy, fanaticism, and membership in organizations for mutual protection are common. They also tend to be the more physically attractive of the two major subtypes of the Six; this group includes some of the most physically attractive individuals of all the personality types, by contemporary American standards. Yet, narcissism (arrogance, brashness) may be an overcompensation for insecurity and inferiority feelings. Sexual conflicts may be a problem, since there is increased suspiciousness of others.

Unhealthy persons of this subtype are extremely suspicious, tending toward either mild or severe paranoia. They may abuse alcohol or drugs as a way of dealing with anxiety and paranoid delusions, as well as of bolstering their inferiority feelings. There may be sadomasochistic tendencies in sexual expressions. The extent and nature of their self-destructiveness will be hidden from others because of their reclusive nature. This is also a very violent subtype. Intense stress will likely lead to outbreaks of rage and extremely destructive behavior accompanied by breaks with reality. Murder is more likely than suicide.

THE SIX WITH A SEVEN-WING

The traits of the Six and the traits of a Seven-wing reinforce each other. This subtype is more clearly extroverted, more interested in having a good time, more sociable, and, for better or worse, is less intensely focused upon either the environment or itself than Sixes with a Five-wing. Noteworthy examples of this subtype include Ted Kennedy, Marilyn Monroe, Johnny Carson, Phil Donahue, Ted Turner, Bruce Springsteen, Sally Field, Diane Keaton, Teri Garr, Elton John, Rob Reiner, Mikhail Baryshnikov, Reggie Jackson, Tom Selleck, Billy Carter, Andy Rooney, Fred Mertz, Archie Bunker, and the Cowardly Lion.

Healthy persons of this subtype desire not only to feel accepted and secure with others, but also happy, particularly with regard to material well-being. People in this subtype are extremely likable and sociable, taking neither themselves nor life that seriously, or at least, not solemnly. If they are intelligent and talented, they may be accomplished in a number of areas, particularly sports, entertainment, politics, or the arts — whatever field brings them into contact with people or the public eye. People of this subtype are usually extremely playful and funny, since a sense of humor is one of their most salient means of coping with life and its tensions.

Average persons of this subtype do not handle anxiety, tension, or pressures well. They react by becoming ambivalent and indecisive, as well as impulsive, grumpy, and peevish. Their sense of humor is used to deflect others, and their passive-aggressiveness to get them out of unpleasant situations. They have a curmudgeonly quality, easily souring on those people and things that have brought them displeasure and aroused their aggressions or anxiety. However, they do more blustering than real damage. When they overcompensate, they are less prone to be destructive of others and more apt to do those things which may eventually become self-destructive.

Unhealthy persons of this subtype are more disposed to becoming dependent on others, and they do not attempt to disguise the depth of their emotional needs. Inferiority feelings combine with the desire to escape from themselves. Unhealthy Sixes with a Seven-wing have few means of dealing with anxiety, and as anxiety gets worse, they become increasingly emotionally erratic. People of this subtype are in a flight from anxiety, tending to become manic rather than paranoid. They act out their unconscious fears, flying into hysterical overreactions much more readily than the other subtype. This subtype is also subject to debilitating panic attacks, since anxiety, rather than aggression, has the upper hand. Suicide attempts, as a way of eliciting help, are likely.

Some Final Thoughts

Looking back on the deterioration of Sixes, we can see that they have ruined their desire for security. Unhealthy Sixes are self-defeating persons who are their own worst enemies. If they persist in masochistic, self-defeating behavior, neurotic Sixes will likely drive away everyone on whom they depend. They will be abandoned and alone, the very things they most fear.

There is nothing wrong with forming alliances with others, but it is crucial for Sixes to be aware of the character of their authority figures, since they have such an important influence on them. Commitment to a good person goes far in helping Sixes to be good themselves; commitment to a person who brings out their aggressions and insecurities will have very bad effects on them indeed..

Sixes fear being abandoned and alone because without at least one other person in their lives they would be completely at the mercy of anxiety. Other people put boundaries on them, governing their fluctuations between anxiety and their response to it, aggression. However, Sixes need some tension in their psyches to maintain their sense of self. Ironically, then, Sixes interact with people both to control anxiety and to stimulate it. But, of course, anxiety is unpleasant and aggression dangerous, so Sixes also look to others to save them from the consequences of both states should they get out of hand. Thus, their psyches present an insoluble conundrum unless Sixes can find a way to completely break out of it. They must learn that they do not have to react to people or depend on them if they trust themselves. Sixes can trust themselves only if they learn that they have an authority within themselves. And by trusting themselves, they truly learn to trust others, transforming their aggressions into sources of constructive power.

Chapter 9

Type Seven: The Generalist

The Seven in Profile

Healthy: Becomes appreciative, grateful, awed by the wonders of life: joyous, ecstatic. Highly responsive, enthusiastic, vivacious, and lively. Practical, productive, an accomplished "achiever": the generalist who does many different things very well. Frequently dazzlingly multitalented.

Average: The worldly sophisticate and connoisseur, constantly amusing himself or herself with new things and experiences. Extroverted, uninhibited, and hyperactive, a "doer," into too many things superficially: a dilettante. Materialistic, into conspicuous consumption, yet greedy for more, never feeling that he has enough. Demanding, self-centered, excessive, yet jaded.

Unhealthy: Can be rudely offensive and insensitive about other's needs while going after what he or she wants. Impulsive, infantile, and obnoxious: does not know when to stop. Debauched, a dissipated escapist. Gets out of control, acting out rather than dealing with anxiety. Addictive, compulsive, manic-depressive defense. "Hysterical" panic reactions when defenses fail.

Key Motivations: Wants to be happy, to have fun and amuse

himself, to do and have more of everything, to escape anxiety.

Examples: Arthur Rubinstein, Leonard Bernstein, Barbra Streisand, Peter Ustinov, Joan Collins, Joan Rivers, Liberace, John Belushi, Auntie Mame, and Martha in *Who's Afraid of Virginia Woolf?*

An Overview of the Seven

It is no great difficulty to see why the life of diverse hedonism is unsatisfactory even on its own terms. Boredom, its ultimate enemy, is unavoidable. . . . A life devoted to the collection of enjoyable or "interesting" experiences is an empty life. It is not a life of spirit, but one in which spirit disappears in the multitude of diversions. . . . When we think of it, we all know that those who are in a position to sample life's sweet diversions are no better off in any fundamental way than those who are not. We know that those who have thrown themselves into lives of self-indulgence are often racked with emptiness, loneliness, self-hatred, nostalgia, and yet are unwilling to change. Knowing all this, however, we would be reluctant ourselves to pass up the opportunity for such a life. Why is this so? Because we convince ourselves that we would be judicious in our use of pleasure. We would practice restraint. . . . The life of superficial diversions has great attraction, as does the pastry table for the child. In the latter case it is, we know, because the child is not serious about his eating habits. So it is, also, with us. . . . To throw oneself into indulgence is to say, "All I am is a potential for pleasure. The more pleasure that exists, the greater I am." No one can believe this in earnest, of course, and this is why such a life must rest upon self-deception. (John Douglas Mullen, *Kierkegaard's Philosophy,* 100–101.)

Some of those blessed with the sweetest pleasures of life are in fact *not* "racked with emptiness, loneliness, [and] self-hatred." Some are truly happy and know how blessed they are. Then there are those who seem to be quite happy — at least, they think they are — but they are merely amused and distracted, grabbing after the pleasures of life rather than experiencing happiness on its deeper levels. Finally, there are those who, despite having everything, are bitter and disappointed. For some reason, the possession of wealth and all the good things of life has not been enough for them. Why the differences among these three kinds of people?

All the personality types are faced with the issue of how to "use" the world to its best advantage, although the Seven is the type which most exemplifies this universal problem. How to enjoy pleasure without living for pleasure? How to possess the good things of life without being insensitive to the needs of others? How to live in the world without getting lost in it? For better or worse, the Seven lives out these questions.

IN THE DOING TRIAD

Sevens are one of the three personality types in the Doing Triad. The nature of their potential problem with doing is that they tend to overdo everything, spinning out of control in a search for happiness. Sevens are excited by the environment: they respond to stimuli strongly, throwing themselves into the world of experience with enormous vitality. Sevens react to everything with such immediacy that whatever they do rapidly leads to more doing.

Experience is their guide to life. Sevens are at home among the tastes, colors, sounds, and textures of the material world. Their identities and self-esteem depend on their obtaining a steady stream of sensations. Their personality traits, their defense mechanisms, and their motivations all reflect the fact that to Sevens everything desirable exists outside themselves in the world of things and experiences. Sevens therefore have very little interest in what they cannot immediately sense. They are neither introspective nor especially person-oriented. Instead, they are experience-oriented — extroverted, practical, and materialistic. They feel that the world exists for their pleasure, and that it is up to them to get what they want for themselves.

When they are healthy, their experiences are a source of immense satisfaction to them, and they learn to do many things well because the focus of their attention is on producing something in the environment. However, the focus of average Sevens shifts away from productivity to the possession and consumption of more goods and experiences. They stay busy to keep their level of stimulation high. However, hyperactivity makes happiness ultimately elude them because they do not appreciate anything they do or have. This is

why, if they become unhealthy, Sevens are little more than dissipated escapists, acting impulsively and increasingly out of control.

Sevens correspond to the extroverted sensation type in the Jungian
typology:

> As sensation is chiefly conditioned by the object, those objects
> that excite the strongest sensations will be decisive for the indi-
> vidual's pyschology. The result is a strong sensuous tie to the
> object. . . . Objects are valued in so far as they excite sensations,
> and, so far as lies within the power of sensation, they are fully
> accepted into consciousness whether they are compatible with
> rational judgments or not. The sole criterion of their value is the
> intensity of the sensation produced by their objective qualities. . . .
>
> No other human type can equal the extraverted sensation type
> in realism. His sense for objective facts is extraordinarily devel-
> oped. His life is an accumulation of actual experiences of concrete
> objects. . . . What he experiences serves at most as a guide to fresh
> sensations. . . . [S]ensation for him is a concrete expression of
> life — it is simply real life lived to the full. His whole aim is
> concrete enjoyment, and his morality is oriented accordingly.
> (C. G. Jung, *Psychological Types,* 362–363.)

Jung's description of the extroverted sensation type applies exceptionally well to Sevens. No personality type is more practical or
more widely accomplished than they are. Their positive, even joyous, orientation to the world produces a great deal of happiness for
themselves and others. But, if their appetites get the better of their
ability to control them, average Sevens consume more than they
need and more than they can possibly appreciate. They begin to
enjoy their experiences less while becoming anxious about obtaining more of everything.

PROBLEMS WITH ANXIETY AND INSECURITY

As enjoyment decreases, average Sevens feel anxious and insecure,
the common problems of the Doing Triad, leading them to overdo
their activities all the more. But as they become hyperactive, average to unhealthy Sevens not only do not enjoy what they do, they
become even more anxious and insecure and are tempted to dissipate themselves even further. They do not realize that it will be-

come increasingly difficult for them to break out of this vicious circle once they become addicted to staying in motion.

Because they are so thoroughly extroverted, Sevens are completely intolerant of anxiety. They do not want to deal with anxiety or examine its causes in their lives because doing so draws them inward, making them anxious; extroversion pulls them outward, toward the environment, automatically repressing anxiety. They discover that the distractions which their activities provide repress anxiety whenever it threatens to erupt into consciousness. They therefore throw themselves into more and more experiences to avoid having to face anxiety or any feeling of unhappiness.

The flaw with this is that the more average to unhealthy Sevens do, the less satisfaction their experiences are able to provide. They do not see that their happiness is precarious and easy to lose, because they neither interiorize their experiences nor control their appetites. Ultimately, if they invest little of themselves in their experiences, Sevens cannot be satisfied by what they do. To their mounting panic, they discover that nothing makes them happy. They then become enraged and terrified because it seems that life has cruelly deprived them of happiness.

CHILDHOOD ORIGINS

Sevens develop as they do because, as children, they had a negative orientation to their mothers or to a mother substitute. For a wide variety of possible reasons, Sevens feel frustrated by their mothers, who did not make them feel secure. As a result, Sevens try to compensate for the nurturance they feel they did not receive by getting things for themselves.

It is probable that, in most cases, their mothers did not intend to frustrate them when they were children. Some other childhood deprivation, such as poverty, war, being orphaned, or a long illness, may have shaken their expectation that the good things of life would be given to them. Poverty, for example, would be enough to instill in them the drive to acquire money so that they will never again experience the deprivations of poverty. Thus, for whatever reasons, the fear of deprivation becomes the fundamental motivation for this personality type. The other side of the psychic coin is that Sevens demand that all their desires be satisfied. Possessing whatever they think will make them happy becomes symbolic of having their mothers' love.

PROBLEMS WITH APPETITES AND AGGRESSIONS

Average Sevens want instant gratification. They place no limits on themselves and deny themselves nothing. If they see something they want, they must have it. If something occurs to them to do, they must do it right away. If something gives them pleasure, they want more of it immediately. Their appetites are strong, and the lengths to which they go to gratify their desires allow us to characterize Sevens as aggressive personalities. However, since they are also insecure, the picture is mixed: they enlist their aggressive impulses to stave off their anxieties and insecurities.

Sevens also typically get into conflicts with people by putting others in the position of having to place limits on them instead of doing it themselves. Whatever self-control average Sevens have must come from outside themselves, either from others who are forced to say no to them, or from reality itself, which may well frustrate their desires. If they are frustrated, Sevens become enraged because it unconsciously raises the memories of their real or imagined childhood deprivations. Those who frustrate average to unhealthy Sevens are not likely to forget the anger they arouse, or the depth of the need Sevens unwittingly display.

When Sevens are healthy, however, they concern themselves with the satisfaction of their genuine needs rather than the gratification of every desire. They are productive, adding to the world instead of merely consuming it. They become accomplished, making the environment yield more of its riches for themselves and for others. They are also unusually happy people because they truly assimilate their experiences, getting in touch with their feelings and with themselves.

But as they deteriorate toward unhealth, Sevens allow their appetites to run amok, and they become greedy, selfish, and insensitive to the needs of others. They care only about their own gratification. The terrible irony is that since unhealthy Sevens interiorize nothing, nothing can satisfy them. They are like drug addicts who need a larger and larger "fix" to maintain their artificial highs. In the end, unhealthy Sevens become so indiscriminate in their search for happiness that they fly totally out of control, both in their actions and their ability to repress their ever-mounting anxiety. Panic overwhelms them because they have nothing solid within to anchor themselves to. The type which affirms life so completely when it is healthy becomes, when it is unhealthy, the type which is most terrified by the very conditions of life itself.

Analyzing the Healthy Seven

THE ECSTATIC APPRECIATOR

At their best, very healthy Sevens have enough faith in reality to allow themselves to contact the environment without attempting to make it supply them with anything. They discover that whatever life holds is enough to satisfy them — if they assimilate it into themselves. Moreover, reality deeply experienced makes them not merely happy but ecstatic, impelling them to go beyond the mere acceptance of reality to affirm life as it is. ("I love life unconditionally!" — Arthur Rubinstein)

In affirming life, Sevens allow the mystery, and the precariousness of human existence to make an impression on them. But rather than feel anxious over the inherent fragility of existence, very healthy Sevens celebrate life for what it is. Possibly for the first time, they are able to perceive something beyond the outer surface of life to the possibility of a metaphysical reality they have never glimpsed before. Affirming reality in the depths of their souls is a special achievement for Sevens, sweeping them up into something beyond mere psychological happiness into an ecstasy that goes beyond words and feelings. They sense that there is something holy about life which is to be revered and respected. Filled with wonder, lost in admiration, they fall on their knees to give thanks and praise.

They are tremendously grateful for everything, starting with the inexplicable fact of existence itself. Life is so wonderful, awe-inspiring, and astonishing that very healthy Sevens can find something good in everything, even in those things which they never thought would make them happy. The incredible richness of existence has a profound effect on them, transforming Sevens from within. Their inner life — the spiritual life — becomes a reality to them. Thus, even the dark side of life, and the knowledge that it will end in death, is no longer so terrifying because this, too, is part of the existence they now embrace. Paradoxically, just when Sevens are able to let go of it, life means more to them than ever.

Because they understand that everything is a gift, not something which exists for their selfish gratification, they learn to appreciate things as they are in themselves rather than as objects to be consumed. Thus, very healthy Sevens acquire faith in the essential goodness of life. ("Consider the lilies of the field . . . they toil not, neither do they spin.") And they discover that, when all is said and done, no matter what they have, it is enough to make them profoundly happy if they use it rightly. They do not have to push to acquire possessions since each moment, if it is comprehended, holds the possibility of satisfying their deepest needs. They will not be unhappy if they focus upon what is truly best in life — not apparent goods, but real goods, things of value which endure.

When very healthy Sevens are in this state of ecstatic affirmation, they are continually surprised by reality, since there are dimensions to it which they have never experienced before, a wonderful irony for those who think they have experienced everything. Their ecstasy, the greatest high they have ever had, can be experienced over and over because reality cannot be exhausted. There will always be enough for them. They cannot be deprived.

THE HAPPY ENTHUSIAST

Even healthy Sevens do not always live at this high degree of psychological balance. Rather than assimilate experience, they respond to it immediately. Their consciousness becomes extroverted, or turned outward, so that every stimulus brings an immediate response, preparing them to be restimulated.

Healthy Sevens are open to experience in a way unparalleled by any other personality type. The sensory world excites them, and they want their excitement to continue for as long, and in as many pleasurable ways, as possible. Their psyches are charged by the tangible world, immediately closing access to their unconscious experiences because they are instantly aware of, and immediately respond to, reality.

The "inner world" of even healthy Sevens is difficult to describe because it is made up of impressions of things from the real world. Their inner life is a catalogue of their experiences. In fact, Sevens do not have an inner world so much as they possess an exterior landscape, a network of activities and interests by which they create yet more sources of stimulation for themselves, which in turn create an aura of energy and excitement around them, as if to say, "I sense, therefore I am alive."

Healthy Sevens see themselves as happy and enthusiastic. They like being happy and make psychological happiness, the feeling of euphoria, the goal of their lives. They are delightful company because they are almost always in high spirits. Their vitality, vivacity, and joie de vivre are infectious, making people feel stimulated by being in their company. They are genuinely fun to be with since they are so upbeat and exuberant. Other people simply cannot help but be caught up in their high spirits. ("Energy is eternal delight." — William Blake)

Given sufficient intelligence, Sevens have wonderful linguistic skills: they are adept at languages, witty and quick with repartee, and gifted with the ability to apprehend form and structure quickly, from the language of music to that of the eye — color, shape, and design. Sevens have excellent memories, since everything registers on their minds like light on film: one brief exposure, and they have it. Instantly and effortlessly, they remember stories, anecdotes, musical scores, lines from movies, and history.

Although healthy Sevens have strong likes and dislikes, they are extremely positive about everything. They "think young" and have a remarkable youthfulness about them, even when they have grown older. They are also extremely resilient, able to rebound from unavoidable setbacks and disappointments like a phoenix rising from the ashes. Sevens never let things get them down for long; they seem to have a way of making the most of whatever situation they are in. ("If life gives you lemons, make lemonade.")

In short, Sevens seem to be blessed with an enormous physical vitality, with the capacity to be recharged by everything that happens to them. Their every contact with the world invigorates them for more; every experience seems to enlarge their capacity for more experience.

THE ACCOMPLISHED GENERALIST

Beyond their great vitality and enormous enthusiasm, healthy Sevens contribute something valuable to others because they are extraordinarily practical and productive people, achievers who do well at whatever they focus on. They are generalists, multitalented, enjoying a dazzling array of skills. They are so good at what they do that Sevens become bridge builders from one area of experience to another. They know a tremendous amount about a wide variety of subjects, particularly practical ones, cross-fertilizing their many areas of interest.

Healthy Sevens are enviably at home in everything: they know several languages, are able to play a number of musical instruments, are exceptionally competent in their professions, can cook well, ski, and know their way around art, music, the theater, and what have you. Quite literally, the whole world seems to be at their disposal.

As a group, healthy Sevens are probably the most talented of the personality types. If they are exceptionally intelligent, they may have been precocious children. But whether or not they are outstandingly gifted, Sevens are usually much more accomplished than their years or experience would lead others to expect. A large part of this is a consequence of the extroversion of their psyches: virtually all their attention and energy is focused outward into the world. Sevens are not distracted by introspective ruminations which might cause them to withdraw from practical action. On the contrary, they are eager to get on with new projects. In fact, one of their hallmarks is that they are not afraid to try something new. Their delight with the world always leads them back to the world. The result is that they constantly acquire new interests and new skills.

The more healthy Sevens accomplish, the more they are able to accomplish — skills beget more skills. Exercising a skill leads them into new areas, and their abilities mount exponentially as Sevens do more and more with them. For example, a Seven may learn to play the piano, and a singer might ask him to accompany her. The Seven might then become interested in vocal coaching, and an opportunity might arise to direct a local opera company or conduct an orchestra — and a career might be launched. Another Seven might enjoy telling stories to his or her brothers and sisters, and decide to write some of them down for publication. Before long the short stories grow into a book, then to novels or movie scripts, which may lead to screen writing or becoming an actor. One thing always leads to another, and as long as Sevens are involved with what they are doing, then not only do they delight themselves, but what they produce is a source of delight and enjoyment for others as well.

One of the enduring sources of their pleasure involves introducing their enthusiasms to others. Whether the object of their enthusiasm is a painting, a cookie, a piece of music, or an idea, healthy Sevens enjoy sharing their excitement. Healthy Sevens want others to have a good time and to appreciate what they appreciate. This delightful trait rightly endears them to many people.

Analyzing the Average Seven

THE EXPERIENCED SOPHISTICATE

Since their experiences are so gratifying to them, Sevens begin to fear that if they focus on only one or two things they will miss out on others, so they begin to want more of those things which have made them happy. This is not an unreasonable desire, but in colloquial terms, "their eyes get bigger than their stomachs," and all their appetites increase. The result is that average Sevens literally become more experienced, trying everything at least once so they can see and do it all, and therefore not experience the anxiety which results from depriving themselves of anything.

The difference between healthy Sevens and average Sevens is that average Sevens are less productive and more materialistic, less genuinely accomplished and more acquisitive. They cast their net wider to have more and different sensations. Their desires increase for ever new and better things, from owning a fur coat to going to expensive restaurants to having fine jewels and clothes. In short, average Sevens want more possessions and more experiences because they think that more of everything will make them happier.

If they have sufficient funds, at this stage average Sevens may become worldly sophisticates and connoisseurs, people who have "class" and know how to live a life of glamour and elegance. Those

Sevens who have less money may acquire less, but they are not necessarily any less acquisitive.

> On the lower levels, this type is the lover of tangible reality, with little inclination for reflection. . . . To feel the object, to have sensations and if possible enjoy them — that is his constant aim. He is by no means unlovable; on the contrary, his lively capacity for enjoyment makes him very good company; he is usually a jolly fellow, and sometimes a refined aesthete. In the former case the great problems of life hang on a good or indifferent dinner; in the latter, it's all a question of good taste. Once an object has given him a sensation, nothing more remains to be said or done about it. It cannot be anything except concrete and real; conjectures that go beyond the concrete are admitted only on condition that they enhance sensation. The intensification does not necessarily have to be pleasurable, for this type need not be a common voluptuary; he is merely desirous of the strongest sensations, and these, by his very nature, he can receive only from outside. What comes from inside seems to him morbid and suspect. . . . If normal, he is conspicuously well adjusted to reality. That is his ideal, and it even makes him considerate of others. As he has no ideals connected with ideas, he has no reason to act in any way contrary to the reality of things as they are. (C. G. Jung, *Psychological Types*, 364.)

As Jung notes, average people of this type are by no means unlovable; they are bon vivants, unashamedly in search of the good life. Sophisticated banter, lightheartedness, and gaiety are the order of the day. Sevens are typically excellent hosts; they love to throw cocktail and dinner parties, entertaining their guests in as fine a style as they can afford. They know fine food and how to cook well — or which caterer is best. They are always fashionable, and usually stylish. Average Sevens know the best and take pleasure in creating a rich, luxurious atmosphere for themselves, their families, and friends. Their dream is to have so much money that they do not have to worry about having money.

However, the style and level of opulence can vary greatly among average Sevens, depending upon how refined their pleasures are, the amount of money at their disposal, their socioeconomic group, education, and intelligence. Some Sevens may be debonair and chic, socialite trend setters at the newest restaurants or at opera and theater openings. On the other hand, if their finances do not permit it, some average Sevens may have to settle for something less lavish, although they still acquire whatever possessions and experiences they can afford. They may go to movies instead of the theater, or to Europe only once a year instead of three or four times, as they would like. Instead of nightclubs, they may go to ballgames and shopping malls. Instead of diamonds, rhinestones. The important thing to average Sevens is the constant acquisition of new, enjoyable experiences. ("I want it all!")

The danger for all average Sevens is, however, that as their appetites grow, they become less discriminating about their experiences, and become mere consumers rather than connoisseurs. Their appetites always increase faster than they can be fulfilled.

THE HYPERACTIVE EXTROVERT

The more they do, the more average Sevens become indiscriminate about the variety and quality of the experiences they allow themselves. They fear the slightest moment in which nothing is going on because anxiety may have a chance to register in their minds. They shift from sophistication to uninhibitedly throwing themselves into constant activity to maintain their stimulation, and therefore their sense of self. They are in perpetual motion, flinging all their energy outward in a centrifugal flight from themselves as they search for ever new experiences. Their credo becomes "I do, therefore I am."

Because they do not say no to anything, average Sevens cram as many experiences into a day as twenty-four hours will allow. They want constant variety and are always looking for something new and different to do to amuse themselves. The faster the pace, the better. They do not have the least interest in thinking about their behavior or in pausing for a moment's reflection amid the swirl of their activities. They literally do everything fast — eat fast, talk fast, think fast — so they can get on with the next event. Average Sevens get so used to life at 120 mph that cutting back to merely 100 would be boring.

The pleasure principle is their guiding principle. Everything should be fun! If it is not, they immediately lose interest and move on to something else. Sevens are gregarious, loud, and flamboyant, public personalities who like nothing more than to be in a party of other "fun people." To hear them tell it, everything they do is "wonderful!" "fabulous!" or "sensational!" — three of their favorite all-purpose adjectives. ("The play was sensational and the acting was fabulous and the staging was absolutely wonderful; then we went to a fabulous restaurant and had a sensationally fabulously wonderful time!")

There is an unmistakable oral quality to Sevens, and many of their favorite activities center around the mouth. Talking, eating, drinking, smoking, laughing, wisecracking, gossiping are typical — and all usually undertaken at the same time, if at all possible. They are, for example, the most talkative of the personality types, saying anything that pops into their heads. Their lack of inhibition makes Sevens very funny, and since they have usually done so many different things, they have a raft of stories which they tell in colorful language and with great verve. Sassy and irreverent, they take nothing seriously and turn everything into a joke as a way of dealing with their anxieties and problems.

There is something of the performer and comedian in average Sevens. Many professional comedians are Sevens; the source of much of their comedy is the insecurity and anxiety which underlies the humor of this personality type. Their humor, like their lives, depends on staying uninhibited and censoring themselves as little as possible. There is nothing subtle about average Sevens: they let others know precisely what is on their minds, even at the risk of hurting other people's feelings. While they may offend some, others find their brashness and outrageousness refreshing.

As funny and gregarious as they are, average Sevens are not usually the best conversationalists because they do not listen to anyone. They want to be the center of attention, to have others listen to them, laugh at their jokes, and be interested in what they are interested in. But they do not reciprocate with genuine interest. ("Oh, that's nice. Now, let me tell you what *I* did today.") They also jump around from one topic to another as new thoughts cross their minds, interrupting others to keep the banter moving along. Even getting into heated arguments is a way of creating excitement, of keeping up the level of stimulation, and of having fun.

The problem with their hyperactivity is that it encourages superficiality and triviality, since average Sevens do too many different things to do anything well. Ironically, for all they do, average Sevens are not perceptive about their experiences because they do not think about anything very much. They are either doing something else (reading the program during a play) or they are off to the next event, too busy to reflect on what they have just done. At most, they give something a one-line review, and that's the end of it. ("The food was all right, but I've had better.")

As gifted and intelligent as they often are, average Sevens throw away many opportunities to do something worthwhile. Instead, they stay on the surface and dabble around. Although they do not like to admit it, they are merely frivolous and glib. The great capacity for accomplishment we saw in healthy Sevens has deteriorated into merely being facile. They are no longer connoisseurs but dilettantes. (They may still sing, but not well, since they do not practice; they learn a few phrases of French, then move on to Russian; they take up needlepoint, then painting, then photography, then the piano. But they never become accomplished at anything because they do not stay with it long enough.) Once an activity requires concentration or effort, average Sevens get bored and move on to something new. They rationalize their superficiality by thinking of themselves as jacks of all trades, but, as the saying aptly goes, they are really masters of none.

People are significant in their lives because average Sevens cannot stand being alone. However, friends and people in general are essentially incidental to Sevens: they continue relationships that contribute to their enjoyment and drop without regret those which do not. Their marriages may last only a year or two, less serious relationships a considerably shorter time. Once the newness wears off, Sevens want to move on to something else.

Their professional work also suffers because doing a good job requires concentration, and average Sevens do not give their time or attention to anything routine. Their minds are elsewhere, on more pleasurable activities. Or they are off on long lunch breaks, shopping, or on vacation because they are exhausted from their whirlwind schedule. This is a turning point in their development because hyperactivity is not so much productive as it is merely busy and restless. They cannot sit still; they must have something to do every minute, even on vacation. (Being in a cabin by the seashore would drive them crazy, unless the cabin was in downtown Rio.) They are easily distracted. Indeed, they build in distractions for themselves to avoid becoming bored. They cannot stand silence — the stereo and television are both on while they talk on the telephone.

Personal assimilation is missing in average Sevens. What makes people interesting is the subjective element, how their experiences affect them. What is interesting, for example, is not how many movies someone attends in a week, but what the movies mean to the person. But since they consume experiences only to keep their level of stimulation high, average Sevens appreciate very little of what they do. And because they do not assimilate their experiences, Sevens ironically become less interesting — less developed and more infantile — as human beings. Interpersonal conflicts often result because their company is less satisfying to others. Relentless activity gets tiresome.

THE EXCESSIVE MATERIALIST

At this stage, they become anxious about being frustrated in any way, so they demand more of everything, especially more of whatever has once distracted or pleased them. (No longer content with a Cadillac, they must have a Rolls and a Jaguar; one fur coat is not sufficient, they must have two or three.) They now become greedy and pushy, insisting that others cater to them so that all their appetites are satisfied immediately. ("I want *more* — and I want it *now!*") They have no tolerance for physical or emotional discomfort, or for any kind of inconvenience. They demand instant gratification of all their desires.

Having a lot of money is a very important value to average Sevens at this Level so that they can get whatever they want when they want it. They typically spend all their money on themselves, usually running up large debts in the process. They cannot say no to anything, and they see no reason to delay gratifying themselves when, with credit cards, they can have anything they want. Sevens who do not have a lot of money make acquiring it their top priority, either by marrying money, or making enough to support themselves in the style to which they have become accustomed. Marrying for love may be a fantasy ideal for them, but materialistic Sevens do not let love, or the absence of it, stand in the way of getting what they want.

Their lifestyle is frankly materialistic, one of conspicuous consumption and the ostentatious display of wealth. By this stage, average Sevens are voracious consumers. ("I see what I want and I go after it until I get it.") Greed is the capital sin of the Seven, and nowhere is it more apparent than in materialism so excessive as to be obscene. They go too far with everything, pushing everything beyond actual need and good taste into the realm of wretched excess. ("If one thing is good, two are better.") Ironically, the sophisticated connoisseur becomes garish and vulgar as he or she deteriorates into the crasser forms of materialism.

Excess touches every area of their lives, including the measures Sevens take to protect their health and youthfulness, which are very important to them. ("You can never be too rich or too thin." — the Duchess of Windsor) They tan themselves until their skin looks like leather and they need cosmetic surgery. They eat and drink so much that they have to go to a fat farm or get a tummy tuck or dry out at a sanitarium. Female Sevens tend to overdress and wear so much makeup and jewelry that they look cheap and brassy even though they may have spent a fortune on their wardrobes. Male Sevens usually look nouveau-riche flashy, sporting loud colors and patterns — all very expensive, but reflecting doubtful taste.

Of course, any of the personality types can be excessive once in a while, but excessiveness is a hallmark of Sevens at this stage because they consciously put no limits on themselves, even when their hedonism would be well served by a degree of moderation. Just the reverse: they are purposely immoderate and inordinate. ("Nothing succeeds like excess.") Profligate and wasteful, they consume and then cast aside once they have gotten what they want. Their attitude is "I have mine, so what do I care about anyone else?"

Despite all they have, they are jealous of those who seem to have more than they do. They are also completely self-centered and totally insensitive about the welfare of others, except as it bears on their own convenience or comfort. Sevens at this stage do not share what they have with anyone else, and they do not want others to depend on them. They feel that others should take care of themselves just as they do. Beneath whatever veneer of sophisticated manners may remain, they are as hard as nails.

It goes without saying that putting their own gratification before everything else makes them poor parents, because they are too self-centered to really care about the needs of their children. Male Sevens are certainly not caring, and female Sevens are far from the mothering type. Rather than allow children to interfere with their lifestyle, they may choose to have an abortion or to put a child up for adoption. Having a family ties them down and makes demands on them, circumstances they want to avoid.

The problem Sevens unwittingly create for themselves is that they become so used to immoderation that nothing *can* satisfy them unless it is done at an excessive dosage. They need more and more of every kind of stimulation for anything to have an impact on them. To get the kind of high they want but are unable to attain naturally, they may begin to be sexually promiscuous or use drugs (especially cocaine and alcohol), or spend great sums of money for new, more expensive toys. But here again, they create problems for themselves because they are addictive. Sevens easily become dependent upon a source of stimulation, no matter what it is —television, going out, sex, or drugs. Once they get used to something, they are hooked — and suddenly cannot do without it.

The pity is that average Sevens at this stage completely lack a sense of real happiness. They have all that money can buy, yet they are not enlarged by their experiences. In fact, just the reverse: they are emotionally hardened and increasingly unsatisfied. Unfortunately for them, they are also insatiable. Habitual excess has made them literally unsatisfiable.

Analyzing the Unhealthy Seven

THE IMPULSIVE ESCAPIST

Since they do not reflect on their experiences, Sevens are usually at a loss to figure out why they are unhappy and dissatisfied, particularly since they almost always possess so many of the good things of life. But they are only aware that they are unhappy, so they begin to strike out at whoever or whatever seems to have denied them what they want.

Unhealthy Sevens continue to stay in motion — actually, in flight — like a surfer riding the crest of a wave before it breaks. They become utterly dissipated escapists. The uninhibited hyperactivity we saw in average Sevens has deteriorated into completely indiscriminate behavior, the feeling that anything goes if it promises to make them happy or to relieve their tensions or anxiety. They may throw themselves into sexual escapades and drinking or drug binges until they are utterly debauched. They may try increasingly depraved sexual practices because unhealthy Sevens are always looking for new thrills and a new avenue of escape from themselves. They become so dissipated that they cannot, and do not want to, center themselves or make real contact with anything.

We have just seen that Sevens are addictive personalities because they become dependent on whatever has given them pleasure or has eased anxiety. The potential for addiction to various forms of "uppers" (so that they can enjoy themselves) and "downers" (so that they can relax and lose consciousness without feeling anxious) is very great now. At this point, Sevens will almost certainly have abused every kind of stimulant and tranquilizer they can get their hands on in their pursuit of happiness, gradually becoming unhappier every step of the way.

If they are frustrated for the slightest moment, they become extremely angry, saying and doing things which are insulting, coarse, and ill-considered. They are like spoiled children, becoming rude and offensive if others do not give them what they want, impulsively saying whatever comes to mind, no matter how untrue or hurtful. Others usually find their behavior obnoxious and detestable, not that they can do very much about it. Unhealthy Sevens do not give a damn whether they hurt anyone's feelings or ruin an occasion. If something is not to their liking, they throw tantrums, start screaming, or otherwise create a scene to vent their rage.

Having no capacity to inhibit their impulses, they act out, doing whatever they are motivated to do at the moment. If they are angry, they will grab something and throw it across the room; if they are sad, they will burst into tears. If they feel like insulting someone, they will do so without hesitation or embarrassment. Unhealthy Sevens hold nothing back because their only way of dealing with anxiety, aggression, or any other disturbing feeling is to give in to it, discharging it right away.

Of course, acting like this not only often gets them their way (others are embarrassed into silence or shocked into acquiescence) but it provides another form of instant gratification by discharging tensions. Nevertheless, by acting out their feelings unhealthy Sevens reinforce impulsiveness, making things worse for themselves in the long run. Furthermore, impulsiveness reveals how infantile and emotionally immature they are. As a result, few people can stand being around them for long, which only frustrates and infuriates unhealthy Sevens all the more.

THE MANIC COMPULSIVE

Unhealthy Sevens deteriorate from impulsiveness to mania, into a total flight from themselves. They are still able to function, however, because they do not yet experience anxiety directly. Nevertheless, neurotic Sevens wreak havoc in the environment and their relationships because they are completely out of control and extremely unstable in both their behavior and their moods. They are as erratic as the path of a tornado, and just as unpredictable.

The hyperactivity we saw in average Sevens has deteriorated into a neurotic mania where moods, ideas, and actions shift rapidly. Their mood may swing from belligerent hostility to tearful remorse to a feeling of elation, all in the space of a few minutes. Naturally, others find this sort of thing very difficult to cope with, and if they try to reason with neurotic Sevens or put limits on their "high spirits," Sevens usually react in any number of unpredictable and dangerous ways.

Although their mood is usually high, Sevens are actually delusionally elated, having a characteristically unnatural, compulsive quality to their moods. They feel higher than high, on top of the world, giddy with excitement. They talk loudly and rapidly, as if on amphetamines. They feel that they can do anything, and so may squander great sums of money on grandiose plans they cannot actually carry out. Or, because they do not stop to consider the consequences, they may use dangerous doses of drugs and alcohol to maintain their feelings of elation.

It is also typical for manic Sevens to throw themselves compulsively into all kinds of different activities so that they can maintain their defenses against becoming depressed. These compulsive activities can take many different forms — from compulsive shopping or gambling, to nonstop, compulsive alcohol or drug binges, to compulsive eating, to compulsive sexual activities. Even formal "manias," such as kleptomania (the neurotic impulse to steal), may be part of the picture, depending on which objects their impulses have become focused on.

If neurotic Sevens do not realize that they have become delusional, it is because they do not understand the degree to which they are out of control. From their point of view, their only defense against anxiety is to act it out before it has a chance to register in their minds. There is a certain logic to this, since, through their manic activities, neurotic Sevens are able to create new (although delusional) sources of experience against which they can discharge their anxiety. Thus, completing their plans is not really the point: having avenues of escape is.

However, what neurotic Sevens cannot appreciate is that they are now in a very dangerous situation. Their minds are like beads of water skittering on a hot iron — slowing down would be the end of them. If they were to lose the ability to stay in constant anxiety-dissipating motion, they would become seriously depressed, precisely what their manic activity is staving off, and why this is called the manic-depressive defense. Moreover, the compulsiveness of their activities inevitably begins to get them into trouble of one sort or another. Other people (and reality itself) must necessarily frustrate them, eliminating the routes they can take to escape from themselves.

THE PANIC-STRICKEN "HYSTERIC"

Manic Sevens eventually reach a point where they have "consumed" everything in their environment, leaving them nothing upon which to ground themselves. The anxiety they have been able to repress by staying in motion finally breaks into consciousness. But now there is nowhere to go, nothing to hold on to. The result is that they become hysterically afraid, as if they were being pursued by a raging beast. They are "hysterical" in the popular sense of the term — panicked, trembling, unable to act or do anything to help themselves, so great is their terror.

Those hardened, worldly people who seemed entirely capable of taking care of themselves are suddenly devastated by a flood of anxiety from which they can no longer escape. Their defenses crumble instantly and completely, leaving neurotic Sevens prey to an overwhelming amount of anxiety. Of course, any amount of anxiety is extremely threatening to even average Sevens since it comes from their unconscious, territory unknown to them. But this is all the more true of neurotic Sevens, and they suddenly feel as if they were being swallowed up. The tangible world which once seemed so solid is not solid enough to save them from the unnameable dread engulfing them as their unconscious breaks into consciousness.

In times of panic such as these, neurotic Sevens experience in their waking hours the kind of terror normal people experience momentarily in nightmares, from which they fortunately awaken. Normal people recontact reality by waking up and are thus able to re-repress their terror. But this is not possible for neurotic Sevens at this stage. They are already fully awake, and there is nowhere for them to hide. They feel claustrophobically paralyzed with fear, terrified of annihilation, of going mad, and of being trapped in endless torment with no way out.

One of the most terrifying aspects of their anxiety is that the source of their terror is still unnameable — and therefore is extremely difficult to deal with, much less resolve. The reason is that Sevens have habitually given themselves to an externalized life, to one of ever increasing experiences and stimulations, and they have, as a result, become totally unequipped to get in touch with themselves. As they deteriorated down the Continuum, they were in a sense "buying time," hoping that there would be no negative consequences for the superficial way they were living. Now they realize that they were wrong.

The Dynamics of the Seven

THE DIRECTION OF DISINTEGRATION: THE SEVEN GOES TO ONE

As we have seen, neurotic Sevens are in a panic, recklessly out of control. When they go to One, they throw all their energy into some direction or plan by which they hope to regain a sense of control. Self-control — a way of centering themselves and of finding emotional stability — is what they most need, and going to One seems to offer it. All the energy they formerly invested in the environment in the pursuit of happiness implodes into a core of hatred both for reality and for those who have frustrated them.

Deteriorated Sevens suddenly streamline their existence, intensifying their interest in a person or thing into an obsession. We saw earlier that mania was a way to create new attachments to the environment as an unconscious means of dealing with anxiety. Now, obsessions serve the same purpose. The manic defense becomes an obsessive defense by which neurotic Sevens hope to regain control over themselves and re-repress their anxiety. Going to One supplies them with a rationale by which they can sadistically punish anyone who does not give them what they want. Punitive impulses and the vilest condemnations of others are all part of the picture.

However, going to One does not work because the rallying point around which deteriorated Sevens hope to find some kind of salvation for themselves is entirely outside themselves, ironically acting as a kind of psychological lightning rod for their destructive impulses. Rather than help Sevens suppress their destructive impulses or deal with them constructively, the person who has become the expected means of salvation becomes instead the focus of the hatred which Sevens have for those who have frustrated their desires in the past.

Deteriorated Sevens are dangerous not only because they are impulsive and violent, but because their thinking is disturbed. Now, in a fit of hysterical passion or a moment of temporary insanity, they may well kill or severely injure the very persons they turn to. Even if they are not homicidal, deteriorated Sevens may become violently abusive to their children or spouses. If they succeed in killing or injuring others, their manic defense may finally give way to severe depression, with suicide the ultimate result.

THE DIRECTION OF INTEGRATION: THE SEVEN GOES TO FIVE

Because they have already attained psychological balance, integrating Sevens no longer fear that they will be deprived of happiness. When healthy Sevens go to Five, they become involved with things in depth. By internalizing their experiences, integrating Sevens create the anchors they need to find stability and security in their lives.

The gratitude for life they feel when they are very healthy leads integrating Sevens to want to know more about what has made them so extraordinarily happy. It is no longer enough just to experience the world, they want to know more about it. The focus of their attention has shifted away from themselves (their experiences and their immediate happiness) to the world around them. Integrating Sevens become more respectful of the integrity of everything, understanding the world as existing for purposes other than their personal gratification. They are no longer the consumers of the world, but its contemplators. Their sense of gratitude blossoms into a feeling of wonder and curiosity about creation.

Integrating Sevens have by now progressed far from their tendency to be dissipated escapists. Sevens at Five concentrate on their experiences and are rewarded for their efforts, gaining vastly in the satisfactions they receive. New depths of experience become available to them as they center themselves. They become more expert, more profoundly penetrating reality, and allowing reality to penetrate them. Integrating Sevens bring the full force of their considerable skills and talents to bear on their experiences. They do not lose their healthy enthusiasm or productivity when they go to Five. On the contrary, integrating Sevens may well become even more productive by contributing something original to the world.

The Major Subtypes of the Seven

THE SEVEN WITH A SIX-WING

The traits of the Seven and those of a Six-wing are in a certain amount of tension with each other: Sixes are oriented toward people, while Sevens are oriented toward things and experiences, quite capable of fulfilling their own needs themselves. In both types, however, there are dependencies; Sixes depend on finding approval and security from others, while Sevens depend on the environment to make them happy. People of this subtype will attempt to find satisfaction for themselves, while looking to other people as additional sources of stimulation and happiness. Noteworthy examples of this subtype include John F. Kennedy, Arthur Rubinstein, Leonard Bernstein, Mae West, Elizabeth Taylor, Zsa Zsa Gabor, Bette Midler, Liza Minnelli, Robin Williams, Peter Ustinov, Carol Burnett, Shelley Winters, Liberace, Richard Simmons, Mickey Rooney, Bob Hope, Sid Caesar, Mel Brooks, Zero Mostel, John Belushi, and Miss Piggy.

Healthy people of this subtype are lovable and endearing. They can be extremely good company because lighthearted playfulness, silliness, and wit characterize their sense of humor. While they are essentially aggressive, they also want others to like and accept them. If they have money, they tend to be generous with others, particularly in their socializing, party giving, and traveling. People of this subtype have a soft, sweet side which can be very appealing. They are a kaleidoscope of contrasting traits — ingratiating and sassy, vulnerable and resilient, spontaneous and dependable, adult and childlike.

Average people of this subtype are defensive and impulsive. They want approval and are afraid of being anxious or alone. They want to be loved and they fall in love easily. But they also fall out of love easily as soon as the romance has worn off. Being in love is a strong sensation, which average people of this subtype enjoy having. They can still be quite funny, but an underlying note of anxiety is closer to the surface. They are gregarious but insecure about what people think of them; impulsive but anxious about their decisions; materialistic yet anxious about money. As their anxieties increase, people of this subtype tend to become increasingly insensitive about others, without being aware of it. They also become self-centered, demanding that others help them through bouts of anxiety. Thus, for better or worse, while the Six-wing softens the Seven's aggressive nature, it also reinforces its anxiety.

Unhealthy people of this subtype tend to be insecure. They want to have the approval and affection of others and will likely experience acute problems with inferiority and anxiety, traits which are problems for each of the component subtypes. They will turn to other people, tearfully but obnoxiously demanding that others solve their problems for them. If this does not work, people of this subtype become hysterical and helpless, alternately thrashing around and lashing out, driving away others and seeking to bring them back to their sides. This subtype is also highly prone to self-destructive behaviors and dramatic, masochistic episodes, such as suicide attempts.

THE SEVEN WITH AN EIGHT-WING

The traits of the Seven and those of the Eight-wing produce a personality combination which is very aggressive, since each component type is aggressive. Persons of this subtype are aggressive in two ways: in the demands they make on the environment and in the strength of their egos to enforce those demands. No one frustrates people of this subtype without hearing about it. Noteworthy examples of this subtype include Joan Collins, Barbra Streisand, Joan Rivers, the Duchess of Windsor, Marlene Dietrich, Phyllis Diller, Helen Gurley Brown, George Plimpton, Cary Grant, Noël Coward, Cole Porter, David Niven, Lauren Bacall, Judith Krantz, Jacqueline Susann, and Martha in *Who's Afraid of Virginia Woolf?*

Healthy people of this subtype are exuberant and enthusiastic, since they are fundamentally Sevens. The Eight-wing adds elements of self-confidence, will power, and self-assertion to help them overcome obstacles and endure whatever hardships might be in their paths. This subtype has a capacity for leadership. Persons of this subtype who are leaders are known for their quick minds and the brilliance of their personal style. They are typically extremely accomplished, since the Eight-wing's self-confidence enables Sevens to engage in the widest variety of activities, and their strong egos allow them to go after what they want until they succeed at what they have begun.

Average people of this subtype are more practical, worldly, and cosmopolitan than Sevens with a Six-wing. They make their desires known, and pursue them with less regard for the needs, desires, or feelings of others, and sometimes without regard for law or morality. The aggressive note added by the Eight-wing makes people of this subtype more forceful and egocentric in everything they do. They are interested in having a lot of money, and because they are willful, they do what they must to obtain it. They do not try to avoid conflicts; indeed, the reverse is usually the case: they are stimulated by confrontations because of the excitement which conflicts produce. In general, this is a harder, more willful, and more selfish subtype. These people care principally about themselves, and are much more materialistic and hedonistic than Sevens with a Six-wing.

Unhealthy people of this subtype mix the manic traits of the Seven with the antisocial, violent traits of the Eight. They can be completely ruthless, particularly if someone has what they want, whether it is a person or a thing. Because unhealthy Sevens fly out of control and unhealthy Eights overestimate their power, unhealthy people of this subtype are extremely reckless and dangerous. They may become physically destructive when they act out, with possibly devastating effects for others.

Some Final Thoughts

Looking back at their deterioration, we can see that unhealthy Sevens have brought about the very thing they most fear. They are deprived of the happiness they seek, not because the world is bent on frustrating them, but because they have not trusted life enough. They have consumed their experiences, tasting them superficially as if everything existed merely for their pleasure. Living for their own immediate gratification has not brought about the happiness they have been seeking, but its reverse.

It is also worth noting that while Sevens fear being deprived, it is exceedingly rare to find Sevens who actually are deprived, at least for long. Because they fear deprivation, they do everything they can never to be the victim of it. Because they are aggressive, they usually succeed in getting what they want. But also precisely because they are aggressive, they tend to go overboard, ruining themselves through excess and destroying the possibility of achieving happiness.

If Sevens do not "experience their experiences," whatever they do will be worthless and wasteful. The most exquisite possessions and the most potent experiences will mean nothing if Sevens do not assimilate them. In the end, if Sevens fail to overcome their fear of being deprived, they will continue to consume, yet remain dissatisfied. There is no way to convince them of this truth because some of the most valuable experiences in life can be realized only after people are psychologically and spiritually prepared for them. Unless Sevens internalize their experiences in the depths of their souls, they will forever bar themselves from the most sublime experiences life has to offer. They unwittingly trade true gold for lead.

Chapter 10

Type Eight: The Leader

The Eight in Profile

Healthy: Becomes magnanimous, self-restrained, courageous, possibly heroic, and historically great. Self-assertive, self-confident, and strong. The natural leader, able to inspire others. Decisive, authoritative, and commanding. Championing people, protective, and honorable.

Average: Enterprising, the "rugged individualist," and wheeler-dealer, often an entrepreneur. Forceful, aggressive, expansive — the power broker and empire builder, dominating the environment. Gets willful, combative, intimidating others to get his or her way: confrontational, belligerent, creating adversarial relationships.

Unhealthy: Can be relentlessly aggressive and ruthless: dictatorial, a tyrant and bully. Develops grandiose delusional ideas about himself or herself: megalomania, feels invulnerable. May brutally destroy everything which does not conform to his will. Vengeful, violent, barbaric, murderous.

Key Motivations: Wants to be self-reliant, to act in his own self-interest, to have an impact on the environment, to prevail over others.

Examples: Martin Luther King, Franklin D. Roosevelt, Mikhail Gorbachev, Lyndon Johnson, Lee Iacocca, Golda Meir, Indira Gandhi, Frank Sinatra, Pablo Picasso, John DeLorean, Napoleon, Idi Amin, the Reverend Jim Jones, and Don Vito Corleone.

An Overview of the Eight

Everyday language comments regularly on the reasons for which power is being pursued. If it is narrowly confined to the interest of an individual or group, one says it is being sought for selfish ends; if it reflects the interest or perception of a much larger number of people, those involved are thought inspired leaders or statesmen. . . .

Much less appreciated is the extent to which the purpose of power is the exercise of power itself. In all societies, from the most primitive to the ostensibly most civilized, the exercise of power is profoundly enjoyed. Elaborate rituals of obeisance — admiring multitudes, applauded speeches, precedence at dinners and banquets, a place in the motorcade, access to the corporate jet, the military salute — celebrate the possession of power. These rituals are greatly rewarding; so are the pleas and intercessions of those who seek to influence others in the exercise of power; and so, of course, are the acts of exercise — the instructions to subordinates, the military commands, the conveying of court decisions, the statement at the end of the meeting when the person in charge says, "Well, this is what we'll do." A sense of self-actuated worth derives from both the context and the exercise of power. On no other aspect of human existence is vanity so much at risk; in William Hazlitt's words, "The love of power is the love of ourselves." It follows that power is pursued not only for the service it renders to personal interests, values, or social perceptions but also for its own sake, for the emotional and material reward inherent in its possession and exercise. (John Kenneth Galbraith, *The Anatomy of Power,* 9–10.)

It is difficult to describe power without roaming into ambiguous matters — into a consideration of leadership, authority, will, courage, self-reliance, and destructiveness. What is the difference between willfulness and self-assertion, for example? "Will" can be thought of as good or bad, although more by its use than by what it is. It is difficult to say what gives a person authority or makes someone a particularly able leader. Is it proper to call the use of power with which we agree healthy, while condemning its use by those with whom we disagree? We cannot possibly begin to do justice to the complexities of power here, although they will, of course, be touched on because this chapter concerns itself with the personality type which most exemplifies power.

In the personality type Eight, we see courage, will, self-reliance, leadership, authority, self-assertion — and the dark side of power — the ability to destroy what power has created.

IN THE RELATING TRIAD

Eights are one of the three types in the Relating Triad. All three personality types of this Triad attempt to adjust the environment to themselves in different ways — Eights by dominating it, Nines by finding union with it, and Ones by striving to perfect it. Eights tend to overrelate to everything in the environment so that they can dominate it and prevail.

Of all the types of the Enneagram, Eights are the most openly aggressive personality. They are take-charge people who want to impose their wills on the environment, including, of course, other people. No one can ignore Eights — others do so only at their peril. Because they are so strong-willed and forceful, Eights are among the easiest types to identify, although for the same reason they are the most difficult to deal with because getting their way is so important to them. If they are healthy, they use their immense self-confidence and will to remake the environment in some constructive way. But if they are unhealthy, whatever power Eights have deteriorates into the desire to prevail over others, no matter what the cost, even if it means destroying anyone who stands in their way.

The source of their problem with relating is that Eights sense themselves as stronger than anyone else. Because they assert themselves so readily, and usually with such favorable results for themselves, they develop a sturdy feeling of confidence in their own powers. Eights have more steely determination and singlemindedness than any other personality type. What Eights do not recognize, however, is that their capacity to assert themselves can become immensely destructive if they allow their willfulness to get out of hand. They do not realize that by asserting themselves at every opportunity, they dominate others so thoroughly that they eventually treat others inhumanly — and become inhuman themselves.

Eights correspond to the extroverted intuitive type in the Jungian typology.

> The [extroverted] intuitive . . . has a keen nose for anything new and in the making. Because he is always seeking out new possibilities, stable conditions suffocate him. . . . Neither reason nor feeling can restrain him or frighten him away from a new possibility, even though it goes against all his previous convictions. . . . Consideration for the welfare of others is weak. Their psychic well-being counts as little with him as does his own. He has equally little regard for their convictions and way of life, and on this account he is often put down as an immoral and unscrupulous adventurer. Since his intuition is concerned with externals and with ferreting out their possibilities, he readily turns to professions in which he can exploit these capacities to the full. Many business tycoons, entrepreneurs, speculators, stockbrokers, politicians, etc., belong to this type. . . .
>
> It goes without saying that such a type is uncommonly important both economically and culturally. If his intentions are good, i.e., if his attitude is not too egocentric, he can render exceptional service as the initiator or promoter of new enterprises. He is the natural champion of all minorities with a future. Because he is able, when oriented more to people than to things, to make an intuitive diagnosis of their abilities and potentialities, he can also "make" men. His capacity to inspire courage or to kindle enthusiasm for anything new is unrivalled, although he may already have dropped it by the morrow. The stronger his intuition, the more his ego becomes fused with all the possibilities he envisions. He brings his vision to life, he presents it convincingly and with dramatic fire, he embodies it, so to speak. But this is not play-acting, it is a kind of fate. (C. G. Jung, *Psychological Types*, 368–369.)

Eights are confident that they can assert themselves until they achieve their goals and, as Jung notes, if they are not too egocentric, their personal goals will be extremely beneficial to others. They may build skyscrapers, cities, or nations which, while personal expressions, are also necessary for the well-being of others. Eights are the natural leaders among the personality types and may even achieve some measure of historical greatness if their goals extend far enough beyond themselves to the common welfare. Their enormous self-confidence inspires others so that everyone's energies can be harnessed in a worthwhile undertaking.

Unfortunately, as Jung implies, Eights tend to become egocentric. They get carried away by the momentum of their egos and the projects they have set in motion. Even average Eights begin to pit themselves against others in a struggle for power and dominance, as if the welfare of others automatically means that their own welfare must suffer. Average Eights feel that there can be only one person on top, and they intend to be that person. They feel that the world must adjust itself to them and that others must fall in line to help them accomplish their goals.

Given this disposition, it is not surprising that if they become unhealthy, Eights can be extremely dangerous. They become ruthlessly aggressive in the pursuit of their goals, even if it means, as it ultimately does, that the rights and needs of others will be sacrificed so that they alone can prevail. Thus, the two ends of the spectrum of their traits are starkly contrasting: when healthy, no other personality type has as great a capacity for exerting a constructive influence in the lives of so many people. But the reverse is that no other personality type can so completely misuse power or become so totally destructive as unhealthy Eights.

PROBLEMS WITH AGGRESSION AND REPRESSION

The three personality types of the Relating Triad have common problems with aggression and with the lack of self-development as a result of repression. Each of these types has aggressive impulses which are either totally repressed (the Nine), or sublimated into idealistic work (the One), or forcefully expressed (the Eight). Also, each of these three types represses some aspect of the self, resulting in a characteristic effect on their personalities: in general, none of these three types thinks there is anything wrong with them. They think that all significant problems lie outside themselves in the environment, which they attempt either to dominate (Eights), find union with (Nines), or improve (Ones). Moreover, repression protects these types from feeling anxiety about the consequences of their actions, so that they are able to go about their lives relatively unencumbered by emotional conflicts or self-doubt. In the short term, such a disposition is pleasant for these types, but it can make life very difficult for others.

Repression produces a fundamental imbalance in the Eight's psyche. It is as if something is missing in them. They develop one-dimensionally; in Freudian language, their egos and ids dominate their psyches at the expense of their superegos and, hence, of their consciences. In short, what is missing in Eights (because of the overdevelopment of their egos) is the ability to identify with others, to see that others also have legitimate needs and rights. Unless they are very healthy, Eights never develop a capacity for empathy: they do not care whether they are right or wrong as long as they get their way. They feel that their own needs and desires are the only ones which count — that they alone have any rights. They look on everyone and everything in the environment merely as chattel to be used for their own ends — to obtain what is in their self-interest, to extend their power, and to ensure their survival.

Because of the forcefulness of their ids, what is also missing in average to unhealthy Eights is the ability to put limits on themselves. They are assertive, enterprising, aggressive, lustful, and confrontational, constantly pushing outward, testing themselves, and stretching their limits. Dominating everyone is essential because average to unhealthy Eights fear that if they do not prevail, they will be forced to submit to someone else, and they fear submitting to anyone lest they be treated as badly as they tend to treat others. (As with many other developments, there is a self-fulfilling prophecy operative here: Eights would not have to fear others if they did not tend to treat others so ruthlessly.)

CHILDHOOD ORIGINS

For a number of possible reasons, Eights, as children, became ambivalent to their mothers or a mother figure. They wanted to be loved and cared for by their mothers, but they learned that their mothers would not respond to their needs unless they asserted themselves aggressively. Their ability to dominate their mothers caused Eights to realize that they, mere children, were stronger than an adult. Very early on, they learned that they possessed the capacity to get their way when they wanted something, that "the squeaky wheel gets the oil." Before long, Eights learned to be comfortable dominating others without guilt or fear of retribution.

Eights also learned to protect themselves from fear and guilt by defying these feelings in the same way that they learned to defy their mothers. They learned to refuse to be soft or to seek forgiveness from anyone. Learning to defy fear and guilt prepared them for greater acts of defiance later in life so that these feelings can remain repressed.

Since each of the personality types tends to think that others are more or less like itself, average Eights think that everyone else is as capable of defending their self-interest as aggressively as they are. Eights think that others enjoy the rough and tumble of confrontation and conflict as much as they do. But, of course, different personality types are not alike, and everyone is not as capable as Eights of working their wills in the environment. Eights do not take into consideration the feelings of others, or their physical, economic, or emotional handicaps.

Instead, average Eights see all of life solely in terms of power and its exercise: rather than help those who are less strong than they, they take advantage of whatever weakness they perceive in others. Their aggressive stance toward the environment — particularly toward people — will almost certainly have negative consequences for others. And their aggressions will eventually be disastrous even for themselves, since the more illegal, immoral, and barbarous their actions become, the more their own survival will be threatened.

Analyzing the Healthy Eight

THE MAGNANIMOUS HERO

At their best, healthy Eights restrain their tendency toward self-assertion. They master themselves and their passions, proving the depth of their genuine strength by not acting when they could act forcefully against others if they chose to do so. Paradoxically, Eights never seem as strong as when they act with self-restraint. They become forbearing, attaining the quality of magnanimous dominion rather than domination.

Self-restraint manifests great courage, and the depth of their courage is tested because what they do, or do not do, may well put their own lives in jeopardy. Very healthy Eights possess not only physical courage, but moral courage, putting themselves on the line for what they believe in. Thus, they may be thought of as heroes whom others look up to and deeply respect.

Eights have the psychological potential that enables them to do the greatest good for the greatest number of people. Very healthy Eights are invariably charismatic, emanating an aura of absolute self-mastery which inspires others to gather around them for guidance, safety, and protection. Their largeness of spirit uplifts and ennobles everyone. Very healthy Eights are in the best possible position to achieve something truly great because they have gotten past their egos to actualize an objective value, such as achieving peace, building schools, or helping others in important concrete ways.

The essence of their greatness lies in their ability to find ways of alleviating the burdens of others, making life better for everyone. Very healthy Eights take it on themselves to solve problems by using whatever personal resources they possess for the common welfare. They are therefore inevitably seen as benefactors — to their immediate circles, to their countries, or to the world. People are enormously grateful to them for creating the opportunities in which they can improve their lives in peace and prosperity. As a result, people are extremely loyal to healthy Eights, responding to them with almost worshipful devotion.

Eights may be judged great even if they do not personally succeed in their quest. They may see little of their vision become reality while still having an enormous effect on the world because the example of their heroism and their vision inspires millions to carry on their work, accomplishing great things in their name. And if Eights of this caliber should die before they complete their life's work, their death leaves others feeling desolate. People feel that their protectors have been taken away and that without them they are without a defender before the uncertainties of fate. No other personality type has this kind of elemental, passionate effect on others, who are proud to be called their followers.

Thus, heroic Eights achieve immortality by earning a permanent place in the hearts and minds of their fellow human beings. They make a very particular kind of mark on the world — a mark possible only to those who are loved and revered.

THE SELF-CONFIDENT PERSON

Healthy Eights do not always remain this healthy. If they succumb to their fear of submitting to anyone else, they desire to become self-reliant. They want to make their own way in life so they assert themselves against the environment, creating and reinforcing their will power. They never question their ability to effect their wills, giving healthy Eights enormous self-confidence.

Their sense of self as a strong individual comes from experiencing the full weight of their wills bearing on the world outside. Eights feel they are solid and communicate their inner strength to others by their self-confidence. They know that they are able to overcome obstacles and come back stronger. They know that they have the ability to stand up for their own rights and needs and the will power to resist whatever pressure may be put on them.

The more they assert themselves, the more healthy Eights believe in themselves and their ability to overcome difficulties. They have the knack of turning apparent setbacks into new opportunities, thriving on and learning by adversity. Rather than ask why something cannot be done, healthy Eights feel confident that they can do whatever they set their minds to. Unlike some of the other personality types, healthy Eights do not suffer from self-doubt, anxiety, or insecurity, nor are they given to introspection or concern about their identities.

Throughout the entire spectrum of traits, we will see their self-confidence, enormous will power, and ability to assert themselves. There is nothing subtle or indirect about Eights: since their sense of self is reinforced the more they overcome resistance in the environment, they have every incentive to assert themselves at every possible opportunity.

Their self-confidence and self-reliance also make healthy Eights very resourceful. Self-motivated, they take the initiative when things must be done. In a word, they are confident that they can make their way in the world. This is an extraordinarily effective psychological foundation to build upon — the perception of themselves as strong, confident, capable, secure, having will and ego, and the ability to affect the environment. The Eight is the only personality type which has such inner solidity. And as long as Eights are healthy, it is a very desirable disposition to have.

THE CONSTRUCTIVE LEADER

Healthy Eights test themselves by acting to prove their strength, although primarily to themselves. They become constructive, authoritative leaders, rising to new challenges, using their strength to achieve worthwhile goals.

While the qualities which make up leadership are complex and difficult to define in the abstract, the Eight is the personality type to whom people naturally turn to find these qualities embodied. Healthy Eights exhibit a masterliness and authority, decisiveness, and sense of honor. They are believed in, trusted, and looked up to — people who can be called on to solve problems or use their strength to do battle on behalf of others. People rightly see healthy Eights as personifications of the father figure and as protectors and providers who take care of others' needs.

When Eights are on the scene, they are in charge. When Eights are healthy, others do not mind their being in charge because they are clearly honorable and have everyone's best interests at heart. While Eights are resolute and decisive, their decisions are also fair. Moreover, they are very effective leaders because they are extremely persuasive. As we have seen, their enormous self-confidence and belief in the importance of what they do enable them to motivate others, who willingly submit to their leadership. ("Leadership is the ability to get men to do what they don't want to do, and like it." — Harry Truman) Healthy Eights exude the aura of natural leaders, taking a justifiable pride in themselves and their genuine accomplishments. Healthy Eights at this Level are not without ego, but their egos are in the service of something outside themselves, influencing others to obtain goals which will be valuable for everyone.

By looking at the characteristics of good leadership, in effect, we see the traits of healthy Eights. Good leaders give people a clear and worthwhile sense of direction as well as the means to attain common goals. Good leaders create and maintain a stable social order on whatever scale of influence they have, from a family to a corporation to a nation. They inspire others to want to work for something larger than themselves, such as winning a war, launching a space station, or building a city. They know how to create a community, or a people, and, in rare circumstances, they become the symbol and embodiment of the aspirations of that community. They help build self-esteem, courage, and self-confidence in others by inspiring them to accomplish more than they thought they could. And while good leaders enjoy preeminence, they are willing to take ultimate responsibility for the actions of their followers and to suffer the consequences of failure. As long as they are good leaders, as judged by their effects on others, Eights are worthy of loyalty, honor, and obedience.

Analyzing the Average Eight

THE ENTERPRISING ADVENTURER

The difference between healthy Eights and average Eights is that the self-interest of healthy Eights coincides with the interests of others, whereas that of average Eights does not. The aggressive aspect of self-assertion emerges in the desire of average Eights to act on their own self-interest.

While they may still play the role of some sort of leader, the increase of their self-interest spoils the positive quality of their leadership. Average Eights are really not worthy of the name leader. They are adventurers and entrepreneurs, interested in their own affairs, particularly their financial interests, and in achieving their own ends.

They see themselves as self-sufficient "rugged individualists," who believe in the free enterprise system which allows them to pursue their own interests and others to do the same. Average Eights are not cooperative, not good team players, and not much concerned with the welfare of others unless others contribute to the success of their efforts. As entrepreneurs, average Eights are particularly plentiful in the business and political worlds as the movers and shakers of society. They are probably best epitomized by the Horatio Alger self-made man who rises from humble origins to make a fortune for himself.

Eights at this stage are typically businessmen, real estate mag-
nates, industrialists, financiers, or tycoons of some sort. Making
money is the means by which they become self-sufficient so that
they will not have to depend on or submit to anyone else. The profit
motive is their own motive. Money also allows average Eights to
get involved in whatever projects they want to, without regard to
the loyalty or devotion of others. With sufficient funds, they can
buy what, and whom, they need. ("I believe in Rhett Butler. He's
the only 'cause' I know." — from the 1939 movie *Gone With the
Wind*) They are often extremely persuasive salesmen, and the more
unscrupulous individuals of this type are outright con men.

Even if they do not start out in life with a lot of money, average
Eights are so enterprising and have so much drive that it is not
unusual for them to get rich rather quickly. They are effective ne-
gotiators and deal makers because they go after what they want
until they get it. They can withstand pressure and say no to others.
They can also compromise when it is in their interest to do so. They
are *Homo economicus*, always ready to buy, sell, trade, and make a
buck. Their line of work does not matter much to them as long as
they are turning a profit. They could be manufacturing shoes or
computers, mining gold, or selling pizza. The important thing is not
what they do but the bottom line, making money.

Average Eights are competitive with others, although strictly
speaking, Eights are more properly "enterprising," a form of self-
assertion. They assert themselves in the environment, and they
would prefer it if others would capitulate to them immediately. If
others cede the lion's share to them right away, Eights get what
they want, and they do not have to waste time and energy engaging
in competition.

Risk taking is a necessary aspect of the quest for success in any
venture, and average Eights take risks so they can reap the financial
and psychic rewards. They love danger and excitement, not only in
the business world, but in all their activities. They enjoy the high
feeling they have when they prevail in challenging situations. Average Eights want to do the impossible, to succeed where others
have failed, to do what cannot be done. They may fly airplanes, sail,
scuba dive, or race cars for the thrill of putting themselves in danger
and triumphing over the risks.

Average Eights usually succeed both at business and in their other goals because they work constantly. They enjoy working because work offers an arena in which to assert themselves, and hence to maintain the sense of self. Making deals and taking risks is not only a way to make money, it is a way of literally making more of themselves.

THE DOMINATING POWER BROKER

Every successful action gives Eights another reason to believe in themselves, strengthening their self-confidence and their egos. Average Eights are like healthy animals which eat more than other animals — allowing them to grow bigger and eat more and grow bigger still, expanding into the environment, dominating it by taking over more territory and extending themselves even further. Eights want to have a personal impact on the environment; they want to see themselves — their wills and egos — extended in it. The healthy leader has deteriorated into the dominating boss.

Average Eights at this stage have an innate sense of the use of power, and they do not hesitate to wield it. They are "power brokers," exercising power in whatever form is at their disposal. They understand that power is not a thing, but the ability to get things done, the ability to shape events and make the environment conform to their vision. Power is not something which can be enjoyed in the abstract: it must be continually used if it is to be maintained.

Their style of power is expansive. Average Eights move forcefully to fill a void wherever they perceive one, taking over situations because they want to continue expanding. Average Eights see the world the way chess masters see the board: everything is merely a pawn to be used to further their ends. They may take advantage of a weakness in someone, or simply advance their own interests if someone hesitates to move first. They do not want to be limited or tied down in any way since expanding their sphere of influence increases their sense of self, particularly the sense of their own greatness. Average Eights would feel anxious if they were not expanding and impressing themselves on the environment, so they constantly look for ways to do so.

A typical expression of their expansiveness is their "edifice" complex. The epic scale appeals to them, both literally and figuratively. They enjoy building, whether a house or a financial empire, as long as it reflects themselves. In their private lives, average Eights would like to be monarchs ruling a large and powerful family dynasty which perpetuates their influence for generations. The wider their influence, the more they can have an impact upon the environment and ensure themselves of immortality, a goal which, in various forms, average Eights begin to seek.

Indeed, average Eights are expansive in every area of their lives, including their sexual lives. Male Eights see themselves as extremely macho, a man's man, although others may regard them as merely boastful and arrogant. In psychoanalytic terms, they are phallic exhibitionists ("I am the biggest and the greatest!"), wanting to prove their superiority by what and whom they control and dominate. At home, they are the undisputed lords and masters of their castles, making everyone aware that others are present to serve their needs, not the other way around. Male Eights dominate women, seeing them ambivalently, just as they did their mothers, typically creating master-slave relationships with them. Since aggression and sexuality are interrelated in their psyches, average Eights often have stormy relationships with the opposite sex; they are frequently womanizers, treating their women either as whores or Madonnas, but in either case as possessions who exist solely for their pleasure and to gratify their egos.

Female Eights also dominate their spouses, since they are just as aggressive as male Eights. However, female Eights have more difficulty expressing themselves aggressively because the culture discourages them from doing so. Therefore, they may limit the expression of their aggressive impulses to the domestic front, where they dominate their husbands, are sexually aggressive, control the finances, demand sexual and psychological gratification in master-slave relationships of their own, and so forth. As aggressive behavior in women becomes more acceptable, we will see more of it, particularly in the business world, as female Eights feel free to express themselves as they are.

Through their enterprise, which we saw at the previous stage, average Eights have already built a "power base" whose effectiveness is in proportion to the amount of control it allows them to exert over others. Their power is most effective when average Eights make it their business to have what others need. They attempt to control such necessities of life as food, shelter, and security so that

people must do what they want. Of course, one of the primary needs
of people is money, so having a lot of it becomes an even higher
priority to average Eights because they regard money as power.
Money becomes the yardstick by which they measure themselves
and their success in life. Above all, since it is in their control,
money is the only thing they can depend on to feel self-sufficient. It
is the source of their security. The love of spouse, the devotion of
children, the loyalty of friends and associates are all undependable.
Only money seems certain, the one sure means by which they can
get their way.

It is a great temptation for average Eights who are powerful to
begin to believe in their own "larger-than-life" image of themselves.
They begin to think of themselves as big shots, swaggering around
like Mafia dons or four-star generals. The more they dominate everyone and everything, the more likely it is that conflicts with
others will arise because Eights want to retain all power for themselves. They do not delegate authority; they do not allow anyone to
threaten their preeminence, and they trust no one. They want total
obedience. As much as they enjoy exercising their wills, average
Eights ironically do not allow anyone else to do so.

Unfortunately, once the process of ego inflation has begun, it is
difficult to check since it is fed so mightily. Average Eights are
literally egocentric: their egos are the center of their lives. They
indulge in the care and feeding of their egos with all the attention
that a gardener gives his most prized flowers. Given such careful
cultivation, their egos bloom to grotesque proportions, choking off
the rest of their psyches and blocking any possibility of identification with anyone else.

At this point average Eights begin to play God, relating to the
environment as beings who are greater than anyone or anything
else. Without regard to their personal qualities (such as being just or
honorable, or even right), average Eights want others to obey and
respect them unquestioningly. Their power understandably goes to
their heads: it is intoxicating to affect the environment, to have
their will done, to see themselves extended in flesh or stone.

The greater their dreams for glory, however, the more average
Eights need the cooperation of others to achieve them. Average
Eights therefore typically offer subordinates patronage in some form,
usually money or protection. Ironically, Eights unwittingly become

dependent on others to carry out their orders precisely when they are loath to share power or glory with anyone else. This stage is a turning point in their deterioration because the use of power to dominate others begins to dehumanize everyone, making aggression and destructiveness all the more likely.

THE CONFRONTATIONAL ADVERSARY

Ego inflation, once set in motion, is difficult to stop. Average Eights now push forward even more, in confrontations against others, seeking to emerge as the victor, the superior person of stronger will.

At this stage, average Eights turn everything into an adversarial relationship, attempting to make others back down rather than do so themselves. They see themselves as fighters, purposely creating conflicts even out of those things which have very little objective importance to them. What is always important to them, however, is their ego: Eights do not back down because pride is at stake.

Everyone, from business associates to the greengrocer, becomes an opponent. Eights enjoy putting pressure on people, no longer merely dominating them, but threatening and intimidating them until they get what they want. Eights at this Level are belligerent, strong-arming people if that will get them their way. They are bullies who make no apologies, ordering people around, exploding in a rage if their orders are not carried out immediately. They relish menacing people into submission, making others cower before them. ("What I say goes!")

Confrontational Eights are proud of their combativeness. Their egos are so involved with getting what they want that they cannot compromise with anyone. No other personality type is as willful. Prevailing in every contest of wills becomes all-important because it is by doing so that Eights continue to inflate the sense of self.

It is also a source of pride to get others to concede to them what they want without having to fire a shot, as it were. Eights usually prevail because they are able to bring more pressure on their opponents than their opponents bring on them. They can shout longer and louder and threaten others more convincingly, never letting up until others give in. This is why no personality type is better at waging psychological warfare than average Eights. No type is better at bluffing others to make concessions without having to resort to violence. There is, however, always the implicit threat of violence if their commands are not carried out. People fear that they will be punished swiftly if they do not knuckle under to what Eights want. Others rightly sense that they have the will and the audacity to back up their threats.

Eights believe in being tough with everyone around them. They hate softness in themselves and even more so in others. Not only do business associates and rivals come in for forceful treatment, so do spouses and children. They use fear to motivate people, employing the carrot and the stick, promising rewards for obedience while threatening reprisals to those who disobey. When they say jump, they expect immediate compliance: the message they give others is "Take it or leave it!" They brook no disobedience or disloyalty and forbid all questioning of their commands. Their word is law.

There is, however, an irony here: average Eights usually intimidate only those they are sure they can beat. Before they act, they find some weakness in their opponent, and strike at the most vulnerable point. Only if their backs are to the wall do Eights confront someone whose strength is equal to or greater than their own. This is not to say that they are all bluster and no substance. Far from it. But belligerent Eights would rather get their way by bluffing than by risking defeat. If they should ever lose, it would be catastrophic. Not only would they lose whatever is at stake, but their sense of self, their pride, would be crushed.

A further irony is that by bullying others so much, Eights make enemies of the very people on whom they depend to carry out their orders, creating a vast pool of resentment against themselves. As they intimidate everyone around them, Eights cannot help but wonder what others might do if they could act freely. Having pushed people around, Eights must either brace themselves to be pushed back or maintain the level of intimidation. They can never relax once they have taken an adversarial stance toward others.

It is frightening not to know how far Eights will go with intimidation. Confrontational Eights are not psychopaths; they recognize limits on their behavior, the limits of their self-interest. They will push others until they see that their self-interest is no longer being served, then push no longer. But each situation is different, and the degree to which Eights intimidate others depends on their perception of their opponents. If they think their opponents are weak,

Eights will go much further than if they think they are strong. But, of course, they may misjudge. Violence may erupt.

Analyzing the Unhealthy Eight

THE RUTHLESS TYRANT

If Eights have provoked others seriously enough, it is likely that others will have banded together against them. Prevailing in what has become a life-or-death situation — perhaps literally and certainly figuratively — is all that matters.

The difference between average Eights and unhealthy Eights is that average Eights need other people and are willing to give them something in return for obedience and cooperation. On the other hand, unhealthy Eights are completely ruthless, despotic, and tyrannical: they oppress people, taking away their rights, their freedom, and their dignity.

At this stage, they have deteriorated into a might makes right philosophy. The law of the jungle and the doctrine of survival of the fittest give unhealthy Eights a rationale for using force when it suits their ends. They are now a law unto themselves, cynically living in the world of realpolitik where what matters is having the might to prevail, regardless of right or wrong. Expedience is all.

It is impossible to be intimate with and dangerous to trust unhealthy Eights, since they take every sign of friendliness or cooperation as a sign of weakness and therefore as an invitation to take advantage of others. Treacherous and immoral, unhealthy Eights have absolutely no compunction about lying, cheating, stealing, or reneging on their promises. They will resort to any illegality or ruse to get what they want. (They are the most frequent perpetrators of the Big Lie, a blatant and outrageous lie repeated so endlessly and vehemently that it begins to be accepted as the truth.)

What is especially dangerous at this stage is their willingness, even eagerness, to use violence with very little provocation. The smallest hint of aggression from others will bring an avalanche of retaliation from unhealthy Eights. While some of the other personality types also resort to violence, they usually do so if there are no alternatives for defending themselves. And when the other personality types use violence, they generally feel guilty and fear retribution from others.

This is not so of unhealthy Eights, who think nothing of using violence, doing so without guilt. Eights are *capable* of feeling guilty for their actions, but they defy guilt feelings so that they will not have to modify their behavior. They intentionally make themselves pitiless.

> Power as a means of combating guilt feelings is easily comprehensible; the more power a person has, the less he needs to justify his acts. An increase in self-esteem means a decrease in guilt feelings. In the same way that "identification with the aggressor" is of great help in fighting anxiety, guilt feelings, too, may be refuted by "identification with the persecutor" by stressing the point: "I alone decide what is good and what is evil." However, this process may fail because the superego actually is a part of one's own personality. Thus the struggle against guilt feelings through power may start a vicious circle, necessitating the acquisition of more and more power and even the commitment of more and more crimes out of guilt feelings in order to assert power. These crimes may then be committed in an attempt to prove to oneself that one may commit them without being punished, that is, in an attempt to repress guilt feelings. (Otto Fenichel, *The Psychoanalytic Theory of Neurosis*, 500.)

To put this less technically, defying guilt and such other emotions as empathy for others and fear of retribution allows unhealthy Eights to act ever more ruthlessly. By escalating the abuse of power, they become so immoral that they must do ever more immoral things to avoid feeling guilty. Very simply: the more terrible they are, the more terrible things they must do so they will not feel guilty about doing them.

Unhealthy Eights inflict some of their worst abuses on those closest to them: they demean others, subjecting them to verbal, and possibly physical, abuse. Rape, child molestation, and wife beating are common expressions of aggression, especially damaging to those who are unable to defend themselves. Unhealthy Eights play for very high stakes — for the control of families, fortunes, businesses, or nations — literally for matters of life and death.

Moreover, once unhealthy Eights have begun to defy the law, morality, and common decency, there is almost no way they can stop. Indeed, they do not want to stop because they are in too deeply. If they did stop, they would be terrified of retaliation from those they have wronged. Having begun to violate others, they are desperate to hold on to their power at all costs. To do otherwise would jeopardize not just their way of life, but their very lives.

THE OMNIPOTENT MEGALOMANIAC

If they continue to get away with doing whatever they want, neurotic Eights develop delusional ideas about themselves and the extent of their power. They become megalomaniacs, feeling omnipotent and invulnerable — God-like in the scope of their absolute power.

By relentlessly exercising their power, Eights gradually persuade themselves that human limitations do not apply to them. Not having previously submitted to any limits on themselves, neurotic Eights become convinced that Fate has given them privileges which other people do not have. They think of themselves as supermen who are beyond morality and who can do whatever they please. Having always gotten their way, neurotic Eights find it difficult to believe that they are not invincible. Given that no one has stopped them before, there is no reason for them to think that they will be stopped now.

Having no capacity for self-restraint, neurotic Eights play God in ever more outrageous ways for a momentary confirmation of their absolute power. An obscene fascination with death manifests itself at this stage. The fear of death, a reflection of their more basic fear of submitting to anyone, impels unhealthy Eights to defy death by killing others, if it is within their power to do so. They may put others to death not so much for sadistic pleasure, but as a magical way of warding off their own death, thinking that they will be invincible if they can kill without being killed.

> Amin claims to believe he is God's instrument. But you feel, as you watch him, that he doesn't believe in anything except his own survival. He will use anything — showoff, clowning, flattery, seductive promises, threats, the Big Lie, murder — to remain in control. Yet he sweats like a cornered beast while proclaiming his invincibility. The threat of death hangs thick around him. No one is an individual to Amin. All are potential victims. (Silvia

Feldman, *Psychology Today*, review of Barbet Schroeder's movie
General Idi Amin Dada.)

Neurotic Eights are out of touch with reality, especially the reality of their power. Their egos have completely taken over, like a
cancer destroying them from within. Furthermore, their egos have
become so inflated that the self has no grounding in reality. The
judgment needed to make shrewd decisions to guarantee their own
survival is undermined. The irony is that the more delusional they
are about their invincibility, the more overextended and reckless
they become — sowing the seeds of their own ultimate destruction.

Delusional Eights are thus in a conflict: they must isolate themselves from an increasingly hostile environment while they convince themselves, and those in their entourage, if there are any left,
that they are the absolute masters of their world. They may try to
reconcile this conflict by using whatever power they still retain to
degrade others psychologically or physically and to increase the
level of violence. But since they are reckless, they are doomed to
fail, especially once they become killers. They must and will eventually be stopped.

THE VIOLENT DESTROYER

Even megalomaniacal Eights realize that they cannot hold out forever against the forces amassed against them. They will therefore
attempt to destroy before they are destroyed. Neurotic Eights are
the most widely destructive and antisocial of all the personality
types, just as, if they were once healthy, they were the most constructive of the types.

Since survival is the only thing which matters to them now, they
will sacrifice anyone and anything to survive: wife, children, friends,
business associates, and everything they have built or achieved.
The dark side of power is its willingness to destroy, and if the world
does not conform to their wills, neurotic Eights will destroy it so
that nothing is left. They become barbarically destructive on as
great a scale as is within their power.

It is as if they were on a death trip. Their willingness to sacrifice
everything for their own survival is absurd and obscene, especially

since Eights, like everyone else, will eventually lose their lives anyway. The deaths of others will not assure them of their survival. Just the reverse: by the horror of what they do, destructive Eights bring destruction on themselves. They also lose their bid for greatness and immortality, becoming accursed and, at best, infamous.

It is ironic that what ends in destruction began as a desire for self-preservation. Thus, creation and destruction are the opposite ends of the spectrum of the Eight's personality. The desire to create and the desire to destroy originate from the same impulse; but when the impulse for life becomes defined as saving one's own life at any cost, it becomes corrupt and turns destructive.

Neurotic Eights are able to destroy because they have never identified with anyone else. Their egocentricity allows them to see only themselves in the world, and if the world does not reflect them, they eventually hate the world so much that they want to destroy it. Yet what kind of world would it be if it actually did reflect them? As the philosopher Hillel said, "If you are not for yourself, who will be? But if you are for yourself alone, what are you?"

The Dynamics of the Eight

THE DIRECTION OF DISINTEGRATION: THE EIGHT GOES TO FIVE

Unhealthy Eights have abused their power so completely that they have made enemies of everyone. The main enticement for Eights to go to Five is that they see such a development as a tactical retrenchment from belligerent action into the safety of thought. They think that they will be able to maintain their power by being shrewder and more premeditated. Instead of acting recklessly, they will attempt to act with more foresight; by being more secretive, they will be able to strike without warning; by being more wily, they will be able to hide from their enemies until they are ready to destroy them utterly. In short, the temptation for neurotic Eights to go to Five lies in the union of absolute power and perfect safety, an unbeatable combination.

This, however, is not what actually happens. When neurotic Eights go to Five, they become extremely paranoid about their continued survival. By going to Five and isolating themselves from others, they can no longer act effectively either in defending or asserting themselves. What power they still possess swiftly crumbles, giving deteriorated Eights real reasons for at least some of their paranoid fears.

As their paranoia increases, so does their isolation, and their isolation feeds their paranoia, a vicious circle. For the first time in their lives, Eights become extremely anxious because their defense mechanisms, especially counterphobia and denial, no longer protect them. They are terrified of being punished for their many crimes, some of which may have been so heinous as to warrant their death. If paranoia continues, they may break more or less completely with reality and lose whatever ability they have to defend themselves. (It is difficult to say whether all deteriorated Eights would become true schizophrenics. Probably not, although if this condition lasts for long, a genuine schizophrenic illness may well result.)

If their enemies have not been able to defeat them before, they certainly will have the opportunity now that Eights have deteriorated into such an extremely vulnerable condition. The irony is that the person who was once so mighty lives in abject terror —terrorized not only by the vengeance of others but by the anxiety which floods their minds. This is no omnipotent god, but an inhuman monster in torment.

THE DIRECTION OF INTEGRATION: THE EIGHT GOES TO TWO

Growth for Eights lies in the direction of opening themselves to others rather than dominating them. When healthy Eights go to Two, they learn to use whatever power they have to nurture others, as individuals. Healthy Eights, as we have seen, are heroic and magnanimous, but principally to groups of people from whom they stand apart. But when healthy Eights integrate to Two, they put aside their lofty position, relating to others as individuals and as equals.

When healthy Eights move to Two, they identify with others rather than against them, realizing that others are not unlike themselves and are therefore worthy of the same rights and privileges. Integrating Eights have empathy and compassion. They are nurturing, generous, helpful, and genuinely concerned for the welfare and aspirations of others. Integrating Eights no longer care about self-interest, but about the needs of others as if they were their own. Thus, their newly emerging capacity for love crowns their other leadership capacities. They learn the power of love rather than being obsessed with the love of power.

They also discover a wonderful truth: that it is in their most profound self-interest to love others. As we have seen, if their power is not used for others, it quickly turns destructive. And even if it is not used brutally, dominating others will never bring Eights what they ultimately most need, to be loved for themselves. On the other hand, by using their power for others, they discover that they are not diminished or in jeopardy. They create something truly new, extending themselves in the world by that most powerful force, love itself.

The greatest and most noble of Eights learn the higher lessons of love at Two, ultimately seeing themselves as the servants of others. Putting themselves in this humble yet exalted position is an extraordinary act of heroism, especially for those whose orientation has been to take pride in self-sufficiency. To open themselves to others, to identify with them, and to take their burdens on themselves — indeed, to sacrifice themselves for the sake of others — are the most courageous and difficult things anyone can do, especially Eights. Rising to this level of heroism will truly make them immortal.

The Major Subtypes of the Eight

THE EIGHT WITH A SEVEN-WING

The traits of the Eight and those of a Seven-wing reinforce each other to produce a very aggressive subtype. Eights with a Seven-wing are the most openly aggressive of all the subtypes because each of the component types is aggressive — Eights in their quest for power and Sevens in their acquisition of experiences and possessions. This is also the least other-related and most egocentric of all the subtypes, making it one of the most difficult for others to get along with easily. Noteworthy examples of this subtype include

Mikhail Gorbachev, Franklin D. Roosevelt, Lyndon Johnson, Indira Gandhi, Ferdinand Marcos, Lee Iacocca, Henry Kissinger, Richard Burton, Barbara Walters, Billy Jean King, Bella Abzug, Norman Mailer, Frank Sinatra, Mike Wallace, Muhammad Ali, Aristotle Onassis, J. Pierpont Morgan, John DeLorean, Al Capone, Joseph Stalin, Mao Tse-tung, Howard Hughes, the Shah of Iran, Muammar Qaddafi, Idi Amin, the Reverend Jim Jones, and Don Vito Corleone.

Healthy people of this subtype are highly extroverted, action-oriented, and extremely energetic. They take the initiative almost all the time — from business deals to romantic engagements —with great gusto and confidence of success. The healthy Eight's charisma combines with the healthy Seven's capacity to enjoy life, producing an extraordinarily outgoing personality whose inner strength and vitality may be so outstanding as to allow Eights with a Seven-wing to have a public, and possibly historical, impact. Their magnanimity will have a practical focus in the concern they show for the material well-being of others.

Average people of this subtype are very interested in power and money, two concerns which reinforce each other. They have a strong business sense, are highly extroverted, and possess an enormous drive which they pour into their work, interests, and adventures. These are robust, earthy, and materialistic people whose feet are firmly planted on the ground. They easily dominate their environments, particularly other people. They are aggressive, pursuing what they want like a hungry animal after its prey. They can also be extremely egocentric, selfish, and rapacious. People of this subtype use money to manipulate others, treating them as possessions or as pawns in their power games. They have no compassion for others and do not feel guilty for their actions. Nevertheless, people of this subtype betray a certain insecurity about money and power, since they never feel that they have enough of either to make them fully independent or secure in life.

Unhealthy persons of this subtype are ruthless and impulsive: they can do and say things which will later be regarded as either a stroke of genius or a fatal mistake. They are offensive and tyrannical, verbally and physically brutish to others, lashing out at anyone who has frustrated them or dared to resist their wills. They have explosively violent tempers and quickly get into a rage. Their manic tendencies reinforce their delusions of omnipotence: they may spend vast sums of money to feed their inflated notions of themselves. They tend to get out of control when they are anxious or feel threatened. Since they are susceptible to anxiety, they defend themselves against it by acting out, impulsively striking first, attempting to destroy before they are destroyed.

THE EIGHT WITH A NINE-WING

The traits of the Eight and those of a Nine-wing are in some degree of conflict with each other. Depending on the Nine-wing's strength, individuals of this subtype are somewhat more oriented to people and less to possessions than the other subtype. They are also less self-assertive, exuding an aura of quiet strength and of power held in reserve in this subtype. In general, this is a less openly aggressive overall personality pattern, although since Eight is the basic type, persons of this subtype can still be quite aggressive, especially when they need to be. Noteworthy examples of this subtype include Martin Luther King, Golda Meir, Charles de Gaulle, Pablo Picasso, John Huston, Johnny Cash, Fidel Castro, Leonid Brezhnev, Darth Vader, Othello, and King Lear.

Healthy persons of this subtype are noticeably more at ease with themselves and with other people, not feeling that they must assert themselves at every moment or in every situation. They are, at times, more open to concerns beyond their immediate self-interest, particularly those involving members of their own family. They are the kinder, more benign patresfamilias, strong willed but mild mannered, who have deeper feelings and more subtle appreciations than Eights with a Seven-wing. Eights with a Nine-wing are able to forge a personal, almost mystical, bond between themselves and others. They may be involved with the arts, nature, and children.

Average people of this subtype begin to show a definite split between the two sides of themselves — the aggressive side (which they show in public and in competitive situations) and the passive, more accommodating side (which they reveal to very few, principally their spouses). Their expansive forcefulness is grounded on some inner fortress of imperturbable strength which others are not allowed to breach. This inner sanctum is undisturbed and at peace, although it is doubtful that people of this subtype visit that inner part of themselves as much as they should. It remains an ideal.

Since Eight is the basic personality type, people of this subtype dominate others, although with a velvet glove over an iron fist. They can be intimidating and belligerent, then accommodating and kind-hearted, especially to those who are close to them.

Since this subtype is almost immune from anxiety, unhealthy Eights with a Nine-wing can be destructive without remorse, combining ruthlessness with indifference. They can get into a strangely dissociated frame of mind, acting in a depersonalized way, as if they were some sort of cosmic force which swatted people aside, crushing them without personal feelings entering the picture. People in this subtype tend, in general, to be less violent and destructive than those in the other subtype. However, if necessary, they may be violent toward others, personally regretting the suffering they cause, but not feeling any empathy or having any real understanding of what they do. They may make up for the lesser degree of violence they wreak on the environment by generally living longer, thus possibly doing more damage in the long run to those who have the misfortune to live with them.

Some Final Thoughts

Looking back on their deterioration, we can see that from the average Levels onward, the self-esteem of Eights came from being increasingly destructive rather than constructive. But is the ability to destroy a reflection of real power? Who is more genuinely powerful, the person who destroys a city or the person who builds one?

We can also see that Eights have brought about the very thing they most fear: having destroyed all they can, they have depleted their resources and become vulnerable to the just retaliation of others who, they rightly fear, may treat them without mercy. They have succeeded in creating a self-fulfilling prophecy: they fear having to submit to others, and now this comes to pass.

How to stop a tyrant without becoming a tyrant oneself is an age-old problem. Must one become ruthless to fight ruthlessness, unjust to fight injustice? How far can one go to protect oneself from predators, from those who destroy without remorse? In searching for an answer, no other personality type makes others consider what they really believe the ultimate values of life to be. Is the ultimate value self-interest? Is getting your way by trampling on others really all that matters?

If there is no God, then Eights are the most expedient and shrewdest of people: self-interest is indeed all that matters. Since we cannot be certain about God, or what form God's justice might take, at least this is certain: no matter how Eights have lived, they cannot escape mortality. Like everyone else, they will have to submit to death and ultimately to the judgment of others about their actions.

The last irony is one of the most poignant: if they have been destructive, they will not have remade the world in their image. They will ultimately be frustrated in one of their deepest desires.

Chapter 11

Type Nine: The Peacemaker

The Nine in Profile

Healthy: Becomes self-possessed, feeling autonomous and fulfilled: has great equanimity and contentment. Deeply receptive and unselfconscious, emotionally stable, and peaceful. Optimistic, reassuring, supportive of others. Patient, good-natured, unpretentious, a genuinely nice person.

Average: Self-effacing, accommodates self to the other too much, accepting conventional roles and expectations. Unreflective, too easygoing, oblivious, and unresponsive. Disengaged, passive, and complacent. Begins to minimize problems to appease others, becoming fatalistic and resigned, as if nothing could be done to change anything.

Unhealthy: Can be too repressed, undeveloped, and ineffectual. Neglectful, does not want to see problems: becomes obstinate, dissociating self from all conflicts. Eventually cannot function: becomes disoriented, depersonalized, and catatonic. Multiple personalities possible.

Key Motivations: Wants union with the other, to preserve things as they are, to avoid conflicts and tension, to ignore whatever would upset him or her, to preserve his peace at any price.

Examples: Ronald Reagan, Corazon Aquino, Walter Cronkite, Rosalynn Carter, Linda Evans, Princess Grace of Monaco, Ingrid Bergman, Perry Como, Walt Disney, Bing Crosby, Edith Bunker, and Mary Hartman.

An Overview of the Nine

The inner landscape of the Nine resembles someone riding a bicycle on a beautiful day, enjoying everything about the flow of the experience. The whole picture, the entire situation, is what is pleasant and identified with rather than any particular part. The inner world of Nines is this experience of effortless oneness: their sense of self comes from being in union with the other. Naturally, they would like to preserve this quality of oneness with the environment as much as possible.

Their receptive orientation to life gives Nines so much deep satisfaction that they see no reason to question it or to want to change anything essential about it. Because Nines develop psychologically this way, we should not fault them if their view of life is open and optimistic. But we may fault Nines when they refuse to see that life, while sweet, also has its difficulties which must be dealt with. Their refusal to fix the tire when it goes flat, so to speak, is symbolic of their problem. They would rather ignore whatever is wrong so that the tranquillity of their ride will not be disturbed.

In this personality type, we will see the personal cost of the philosophy of peace at any price. Refusing to deal with problems does not make them go away. Moreover, the peace Nines purchase is inevitably at the expense of others, and ultimately, at the expense of their ability to relate to reality. With all the good will in the world, Nines still may do terrible harm to others while coasting along, turning a blind eye on what they do not want to deal with.

IN THE RELATING TRIAD

The Nine is the primary personality type in the Relating Triad — the type most out of touch with its ability to relate to the world as an individual. Nines relate to the world by identifying with another. As a result, unless they are very healthy, Nines do not develop an awareness of themselves as individuals or even a well-defined awareness of the world around them.

Because they maintain their sense of self by subordinating themselves to the other, whether a person or an idealized entity, Nines risk never becoming independent, fully functioning human beings with identities of their own. They desire to merge with someone else because having a feeling of union with the other allows Nines to maintain their emotional stability. Thus, their problem with relating is twofold: by identifying with someone else, their sense of self eventually becomes ill defined, so they do not relate to the world as individuals. Second, by identifying with someone else, Nines do not develop their potentials. Preserving their inner peace becomes their all-important motivation.

Only the healthiest Nines achieve an awareness of themselves as distinct persons who can actively choose what they need and want. By contrast, average Nines have a passive orientation to life. What they do not see is that they cannot really contribute to others, or really even love them, if they do not develop themselves as persons. But this does not matter to them since, for average Nines, personal growth, individuality, and self-determination are not values, whereas self-effacement, peace, and accommodation are.

PROBLEMS WITH REPRESSION AND AGGRESSION

Nines, like Eights and Ones, have a problem with the repression of some part of their psyches. All three of these personality types overcompensate in one area for an underdevelopment in another. The problem Nines have with relating is that they have repressed the self so they can be more receptive to the other. Eventually, their sense of self can become so repressed that they are barely functional as individuals, so totally do they live through someone else, or just as bad, so completely do they live in a world of hazy illusions. By repressing themselves, their awareness of themselves, other people, and the world gradually becomes leveled out so that nothing can bother them. They become disengaged — at peace, but unrelated to the world.

While there is certainly nothing wrong with wanting to be at peace, the problem is that average to unhealthy Nines tend to go too far to avoid all effort and conflict. They do not see that it is sometimes necessary to assert themselves, since Nines equate self-assertion with aggression, as if asserting themselves automatically threatens their union with others. The result is that Nines repress their aggressive impulses so thoroughly that they are not aware of having them. However, just because they are not aware of their aggressions does not mean that these feelings do not exist or that these impulses do not affect their behavior.

Nines typically "solve" the problem of having aggressions by ignoring them out of existence. When Nines inadvertently act aggressively, they simply deny that they have done so. To a certain degree, the peace of average to unhealthy Nines is therefore something of an illusion, a form of willful blindness, a kind of self-deception. They do not realize that to maintain their peace, they have dissociated themselves from themselves — and from reality. However, the irony is that their passivity and denials, their inattention to others, and their increasing disengagement from the environment are all negative forms of aggression — passive resistance — an aggressive withholding of themselves from reality. Nines are far more aggressive than they think they are, and the effects of their denied and repressed aggressions can be devastating on themselves and others.

CHILDHOOD ORIGINS

As children, Nines identified positively with both parents or parent substitutes. The impetus to differentiate themselves from their parents was minimal because their emotional needs were so thoroughly satisfied by identification with their parents.

Nines also typically had stable, happy childhoods, at least for the initial years during which the patterns of their personalities were formed. Their childhoods were an idyllic time recalled with fondness, a time they would like to recapture. There may have been a

period in later childhood when poverty, illness, or some other ca-
lamity shattered their early carefree existence, but by that time
their most important personality structures were already firmly in
place.

Because Nines identified positively with both parents, they
learned to maintain their sense of self by identifying deeply with
other people. Later in life, they want union with others and peacefulness, which is a form of union with themselves, just as they
enjoyed an early, extremely satisfying union with their parents.
What Nines most fear is separation from those they have identified
with. This is why average to unhealthy Nines do everything possible to maintain and strengthen the emotional ties between themselves and others, even if it means subordinating themselves to
others too much.

PROBLEMS WITH AWARENESS AND INDIVIDUALITY

Whether or not they want to recognize it, Nines are individuals.
They cannot ignore themselves and allow their potential to go undeveloped without paying a serious price: rather than find union
with others, they will inevitably lose it while living in a dreamy
half-awareness in which their relationships are little more than
idealized illusions.

The personality type Nine corresponds to Jung's introverted sensation type. Jung describes what we would regard as average to
unhealthy Nines, people who maintain their peacefulness and union
with others not as they are, but through an idealization of them.
The other person may feel "devalued," as Jung says, for the following reasons:

> He may be conspicuous for his calmness and passivity, or for his
> rational self-control [especially, for example, if the Nine has a
> One-wing]. This peculiarity, which often leads a superficial judg-
> ment astray, is really due to his unrelatedness to objects. Nor-
> mally the object is not consciously devalued in the least, but
> its stimulus is removed from it and immediately replaced by
> a subjective reaction no longer related to the reality of the
> object. This naturally has the same effect as devaluation. Such
> a type can easily make one question why one should exist at
> all. . . .

Seen from the outside, it looks as though the effect of the object did not penetrate into the subject at all. This impression is correct inasmuch as a subjective content does, in fact, intervene from the unconscious and intercept the effect of the object. The intervention may be so abrupt that the individual appears to be shielding himself directly from all objective influences. . . . If the object is a person, he feels completely devalued, while the subject has an illusory conception of reality, which in pathological cases goes so far that he is no longer able to distinguish between the real object and the subjective perception. . . . Such action has an illusory character unrelated to objective reality and is extremely disconcerting. It instantly reveals the reality-alienating subjectivity of this type. But when the influence of the object does not break through completely, it is met with well-intentioned neutrality, disclosing little sympathy yet constantly striving to soothe and adjust. The too low is raised a little, the too high is lowered, enthusiasm is damped down, extravagance restrained, and anything out of the ordinary reduced to the right formula — all this in order to keep the influence of the object within the necessary bounds. In this way the type becomes a menace to his environment because his total innocuousness is not altogether above suspicion. In that case he easily becomes a victim of the aggressiveness and domineeringness of others. Such men allow themselves to be abused and then take their revenge on the most unsuitable occasions with redoubled obtuseness and stubbornness. (C. G. Jung, *Psychological Types*, 396–397.)

At the lower end of the Continuum, Nines are a "menace to [their] environment" because, like everyone else, they have a characteristic form of selfishness, although it is more difficult to perceive in Nines than in other types because they are so apparently accommodating to others. The particular form their selfishness takes is their willingness to sacrifice a great many values — in a sense, their willingness to sacrifice all of reality — so they can maintain their inner serenity. Being anxious or emotionally stimulated in any way is extraordinarily threatening for average to unhealthy Nines because they are unused to being aware of their feelings. Virtually any kind of emotional reaction disrupts the fullness of their repression, whether the reaction is caused by anxiety, aggression, or something else. The result is that average Nines seek peace at any price, although the price they selfishly but unwittingly pay is that they turn an increasingly blind eye on everyone and everything.

As they cling desperately to peace by "burying their heads in the sand," they eventually become unable to deal with anything. In their haste to get problems behind them, nothing is faced squarely and problems are never solved. They become disoriented, as if they were sleepwalking through life. They exercise poor judgment, sometimes with tragic results. Moreover, the consequences of their inattention and disengagement cannot be ignored forever, at least by others. Unhealthy Nines may be forced to come to grips with what they have done, although they will try to avoid doing so at all costs. They would rather turn their backs completely on reality than face how neglectful they have been.

Healthy Nines, however, can be the most contented and pleasant people imaginable. They are extraordinarily receptive, making people feel accepted as they are. Their peace is so mature that they are able to admit conflict and separation, growth and individuality into their lives. They are their own persons, yet they delight in giving themselves away. But once they begin to seek union with others incorrectly, average Nines become too self-effacing, complacent, and fearful of change. They do not want to deal with reality — either the reality of themselves or of others. And unhealthy Nines totally resist anything which intrudes upon them. They live in a world of unreality, desperately clinging to illusions while their world falls apart.

Analyzing the Healthy Nine

THE SELF-POSSESSED PERSON

At their best, very healthy Nines allow themselves to become independent persons. Having overcome their fear of separation from others, they become self-possessed and autonomous. They feel extraordinarily fulfilled and enjoy a profound contentment and an unshakable equanimity because they are in union with someone from whom they can never be separated: themselves. They achieve the peace they are always seeking because they are truly at one with themselves.

Although extraordinarily peaceful, they are also paradoxically vital and alive, in touch with their thoughts, feelings, and desires. Very healthy Nines are aware of even their aggressive feelings without being alarmed by them. They realize that having aggressions is not the same as acting aggressively or being destructive toward others. Thus, self-possession enables Nines to bring more of themselves to others than they ever could before, and so their relationships become more satisfying as they acquire new depth.

Self-respecting, they have enormous dignity because they are aware of their true worth without the faintest whiff of egocentricity or self-congratulation. They are fully present as individuals. And because they can see themselves as they really are, they are able to see others as they really are. People are no longer idealized, so for the first time, they become truly other to Nines — and for that reason they are loved much more realistically.

Very healthy Nines are firmly in their own center, enormously capable of dealing with problems because of the deep inner unity they have achieved. They feel fulfilled, if not as persons who have completely developed all their potentials, then as persons who are able to bring themselves to bear on the world, the moment, and the other. They actively inhabit their own consciousness, as it were, possessing themselves and taking control of their lives. This is an extremely private, almost spiritual event, difficult to observe directly or describe. But it is a real, decisive event nonetheless. Very healthy Nines are just being born psychologically, as centers of awareness. A new force is entering the world — a new being, an ancient child, an indomitable spirit.

At their best, therefore, very healthy Nines are an example to all the personality types of what it means to be at one with the self and at one with the world. They are an example of the profound unity which is possible for human beings — the unity of the self as well as the unity of the self and the other. They teach us of a self-possession and self-surrender so profound as to have mystical overtones. They are so effortlessly themselves and so completely receptive that very healthy Nines must reflect what human beings were like before the Fall into self-consciousness and alienation. They are a living reminder that, when all is said and done, we are each a gift to the other, just as the other is a gift to us. To be

completely ourselves and yet fully related to the other is a mystery
to be surrendered to in silence.

THE RECEPTIVE PERSON

Unfortunately, even healthy Nines are not always so healthy. Self-
possession is difficult to sustain, and the fear of separating from
those who are important to them always remains in the shadows of
their minds. If they succumb to it, Nines desire to merge with
others to find union with them instead of with themselves.

Nines are able to identify with others, giving themselves to those
who are central in their lives. They are extraordinarily receptive,
capable of identifying with others so completely that, for better or
worse, they are not self-aware, introspective, or self-doubting. Not
only are healthy Nines free to give themselves to others, they positively want to do so. Because of their ability to identify with others, healthy Nines have a great capacity for loving and sustaining
others, both physically and in their imaginations.

Since they are so unselfconsciously accepting, there are few conflicts either in their emotional lives or in their relationships. Nines
see themselves as peaceful, and as long as they are healthy, they
really are at peace with the world. They have a high tolerance for
stress and irritation; they are patient, imperturbable, relaxed, and
tranquil. They do not fly off the handle over the little annoyances of
life. There is also an unmistakable innocence and simplicity about
healthy Nines. When you deal with a healthy Nine, you are dealing
with someone who is guileless, to whom lying or trying to take
advantage of you would never occur. (It is incomprehensible to
them how others can be guilty of this sort of thing.)

Their receptivity allows healthy Nines to be the most trusting of
the personality types. They trust others, they trust themselves, and
they trust life. Because they communicate the feeling of unques-
tioned acceptance of others, Nines serve as emotional anchors for
people; stable and solid, they are always there when others need
them. Modest, gentle, and approachable, they are sanctuaries of
peace to whom others come for solace, rest, and comfort. Uncritical
and unthreatening, they do not have unattainable standards either
for themselves or for anyone else. They are easy to please and make
very few demands on anyone. (Healthy Nines are not, however,

totally uncritical and equally receptive to everyone. Some people repel them, of course, but healthy Nines are more gracious to those they dislike than any other personality type.)

Although healthy Nines feel at ease among people, they also love to commune with nature. Sailing, hiking, camping, gardening, or taking care of animals makes them feel very much at peace. Nature — especially its mystical and mythological side — strikes a receptive chord in them because by identifying with nature, Nines feel at one with something larger than themselves. Moreover, since they are used to identifying with others, personalizing them in their minds, nature, animals, and even abstract ideas have a deep emotional resonance for them. For example, Nines do not think of their country as an abstraction but as a living thing; their pets are people to them; the countryside is populated by mythological creatures; mountains, trees, and rivers are archetypal forces; elves, ghosts, and leprechauns populate their living room or favorite shady spot.

The archetypal imagination we find in healthy Nines also has a deep appeal to other people, since it taps the desire for union with the cosmos which, at some level, everyone desires and needs. Healthy Nines supply the other personality types with a vision of the magic of the world. They have a way of looking at the world through innocent eyes. Their mythological imagination recalls the consciousness of childhood in which everything seemed to glow with enchantment. Healthy Nines never lose the contemplative side of themselves or their sense of wonder.

Finally, since Nines see themselves as part of nature, the physical processes of sex, birth, aging, and death itself seem natural to them, things which should be accepted as part of the way things are. Their acceptance of nature and nature's ways is yet another source of their peacefulness because they are not at odds with existence as many other personality types are. Nines are not defiant of the natural order, but happy to be part of it, yielding themselves to it.

THE SUPPORTIVE PEACEMAKER

Because their peace is threatened by any tension between them and others, healthy Nines want to ensure that peace reigns everywhere in their lives. Achieving and maintaining peace motivates them to become peacemakers, mediating disputes and conflicts between those they are close to. Nines want to reconcile people to each other so that everyone will be at peace, just as they are with themselves.

They are also good mediators because they take the complaints of others seriously. They understand real differences between people, why others are upset and concerned about whatever is on their minds. Healthy Nines also are able to see areas of common ground, and they work toward achieving reconciliation because they feel that there is much more to be gained by cooperation than by divisiveness.

The list of their positive qualities is a long one: healthy Nines have a healing touch and go out of their way to pour oil on troubled waters. They have a soothing effect on others because they are so calm themselves. Others find that they are mysteriously at peace simply for being in their presence. They are also optimistic and reassuring, and whenever they can responsibly do so, they stress the positive because they believe that looking on the bright side of things is preferable to dwelling on the negative. They are able to forgive and forget, to put conflicts completely behind them and get on with their relationships and their responsibilities. They are extremely affable, pleasant people, the kind others spontaneously (and rightly) call "nice," or the "salt of the earth." They are jovial and have sunny dispositions, a natural, unaffected sense of humor, and a warm, easy laugh. They are unpretentious, treating everyone with the same honest directness no matter whether the person is royalty or a cab driver. They are easygoing and as comfortable as an old shoe. It must be the rarest of persons who does not like a healthy Nine.

Healthy Nines are not simply good natured, however. They bring other qualities to society, particularly the support which they give others so that they can thrive. Whoever is significant to Nines — spouses, children, and close friends — will be the beneficiaries of their unstinting love and generosity. And since healthy Nines possess a gut instinct about others (as a result of their identification with them), what they do for people is both appropriate and valuable for their development.

And, when Nines feel something important needs to be said, they can be extremely candid, perhaps saying more than other types would find it politic to say, although Nines do so without desiring to hurt anyone. Their candor can be very valuable since they distinguish themselves by their uncommon common sense, a combination of simplicity and guilelessness so true as to be extraordinary. They have no ulterior motives, no pretensions, no large ego to protect or inflate, no concern for status or prestige, no desire to impress or condemn others. Hence, they speak with the honesty of children and the wisdom of adults.

Last, even though healthy Nines are easygoing, they may become extremely successful in their professions because of their ability to bring out the best in others by creating a nurturing environment. But precisely because they are not competitive and never call attention to themselves, others tend to underestimate them. People take Nines for granted, until they realize how much they have contributed to everyone's welfare.

Analyzing the Average Nine

THE ACCOMMODATING ROLE PLAYER

Outwardly, average Nines seem little different from healthy Nines, although a shift has taken place, not so much in their actions as in their attitudes. The difference between healthy Nines and average Nines is that healthy Nines are in touch with themselves and others, whereas average Nines gradually lose touch with themselves and others by subordinating themselves to roles and social conventions too much, seeing themselves through someone else's eyes.

The problem is that average Nines begin to feel that their role in life is to fulfill others rather than themselves. Fearing to assert themselves, they become self-effacing and accommodating.

Average Nines willingly accommodate themselves to others because their sense of self depends on it. The more the other is idealized, the stronger the emotional bonds and the more at one with themselves Nines feel. They become like a mother who lives for her children or a wife for her husband. Of course, it is appropriate for a mother to accommodate herself to the needs of her children when they are infants and cannot do without her. But it becomes a problem if, as they get older, she continues the same pattern of self-effacement. The essential problem is that average Nines go too far in identifying with the other, losing too much of themselves in the process. Too readily do the wishes of others become their wishes, the thoughts of others their thoughts.

A reciprocal motion occurs: as they accommodate themselves, they idealize the other. If the other is a person, he or she can do no wrong; if it is a value or belief, it is never questioned. Thus, average Nines easily fall into conventional roles, defining themselves as persons whose place in life is to fulfill the functions — husband, wife, breadwinner, parent, citizen — which have been assigned by someone else or by the culture in which they live. Getting married, having children, and holding down a job, among many other things, are expected of them, so they accommodate themselves. Their lifestyle, their religious and political beliefs, their expectations for themselves and their children are all defined by the conventions which they have accepted.

This is why average Nines are so aptly thought of as the archetypal common man. They are the glue of society, which by its very willingness to be molded into whatever niches are needed is valuable to society, although at a cost to the individuals involved. Without a thought about developing themselves, average Nines embrace the conventional values and middle-of-the-road ways of thinking and living of the mass of society. Respectability is therefore very important to them. Nines are not so much interested in keeping up with the Joneses as in being respectable members of society, doing what is proper, and not doing what a respectable person would not do. In this sense, average Nines are also usually conservatives, committed to preserving the traditional values centered around family, religion, and work.

Because they are conservative, average Nines also tend to be past-oriented and old-fashioned. The past is always more comfortable than the present or the future, since the past is a known quantity. It is less threatening because it has already been lived through. Moreover, average Nines can be nostalgic about the past, getting sentimental or idealizing it because doing so creates a source of good feelings for themselves and others.

It is difficult to quibble with many of the particular values of average Nines. The problem is not so much with their values as with their not thinking them through. They simply adopt their way of life wholesale, naively accepting everything at face value.

THE PASSIVELY DISENGAGED PERSON

Because their emotional stability depends on maintaining their inner world of beliefs and idealizations, average Nines at this stage fear change. They want to do nothing which would upset them, and therefore want to maintain the status quo as much as possible. Rather than exert themselves in any deep, essential way, they would rather that everything simply work out on its own, without their intervention or response.

The irony is that average Nines must actually do something to do nothing: they must disengage themselves from anything in the environment which they perceive as a threat to their peace. Their healthy unselfconsciousness has become a certain unreflective disconnectedness, a lack of awareness of much of the world around them. They remain on friendly terms with reality, but not slavishly so. A sluggish complacency, intellectual laziness, and emotional indolence set in. ("Oh, well, we don't have to worry about that.") They become passive: life begins to happen to average Nines.

There is a distinctive vagueness about Nines at this stage because they maintain an uninvolved distance between themselves and their activities, an impassiveness, which does not allow anything to get to them or upset them. They are extremely easygoing, but they do not make real contact with the environment — or with those in it — becoming inappropriately matter-of-fact, even about things which would rightly call for a more personal response. They slip into an indifferent "I can take it or leave it" attitude, which prevents them from getting too excited about or involved in anything. They move from one thing to another, equally content and equally neutral about it. In short, average Nines are mellow and "laid-back" to a fault, the classic phlegmatic temperament personified. Being "on cloud nine" takes on new meaning.

Because they do not allow themselves to feel anything very deeply, their highs are not high and their lows are not low, as Jung noted. Everything is kept on an even keel. Average Nines are not even aware that their feelings are diminished because they have disconnected themselves from their feelings. At this stage, average Nines begin to be so vague and undefined that others cannot help but notice that something is missing in them, as if they were not all there. They are unfocused and spacey, a million miles away, as if grooving on some inner trip or secret thought — or on nothing at all.

Nothing seems particularly important or urgent to average Nines, and they put no particular mental energy into anything unless they absolutely have to. Details do not interest them, they forget things, and they do not concentrate on their work for more than a few minutes before mentally floating off. Their conversation rambles or they change the subject abruptly, revealing their lack of attention to what is being said. Average Nines are life's dreamers, enjoying the contemplation of their inner vision of whomever or whatever they have idealized. But, unfortunately, because their attention is inward on their contemplation, they become inattentive to the real world. If they are intelligent and well-educated, they may enjoy talking about philosophy, theology, the arts or sciences, although even so much of their thinking is frankly little more than vague woolgathering, the purpose of which is to pass the time rather than actively engage themselves with anything requiring intense involvement or effort.

Their healthy simplicity has deteriorated into obliviousness, a permanent absent-mindedness, as if they were constantly daydreaming about nothing in particular, perceiving the world like someone who looks at a clock without seeing the time. Indeed, the way most people have trained themselves to ignore television commercials is how average Nines experience a lot of reality, disconnecting themselves from whatever they do not want to see or hear until inadvertence becomes habitual. They are like sleepwalkers, physically present but not aware of what is going on around them.

Their energy is spent maintaining their peace, ignoring anything which would excite or trouble them. Physical and emotional comfort is an important value, and average Nines do not push themselves too hard intellectually or physically lest they get either too stimulated or too exhausted. They pass the time in undemanding ways, puttering around the house, going on errands, collecting knickknacks, or mindlessly watching television. At this stage, they become accustomed to living in a state of semiawareness, like people who have been on tranquilizers so long that they forget what it is like to be off them.

It is important to understand, however, that psychological passivity is not the same thing as complete inactivity, although it is a precursor to it. Average Nines may be the heads of multimillion dollar corporations, leading vast enterprises while still maintaining an inner disconnectedness from their activities. Nines are able to be uninvolved because one of their defense mechanisms is compartmentalization (isolation), which allows their subjective experiences to be broken into unrelated segments so that they can move from one thing to another without engaging themselves. As a result, reality has little impact on them. They can be relatively busy while remaining emotionally and intellectually detached from their activities.

Because they disconnect from their experiences, average Nines do not make the cause-and-effect connections one would normally expect: cause and effect simply do not seem to go together for them. They do not think of the consequences of their actions or of the fact that their omissions will also have consequences. They do not think through anything, unquestioningly feeling that everything will work out for the best.

Their lack of self-awareness is at the root of what is going on here. Inattention arises because, unless they are healthy, Nines never learn to focus on anything, including themselves. Just the opposite, their entire orientation is to be unselfconscious and receptive to the other, as we have seen. Because they are unable to sense themselves as discrete individuals, they get used to perceiving all of reality vaguely. When practical problems arise, especially with other people, their inability to attend to reality only makes things worse. Average Nines increasingly become part of the problem rather than part of the solution.

They also disconnect from interpersonal conflicts by compartmentalizing their relationships, splitting people into two major groups: those with whom they have identified and everyone else. The second group of people has little meaning to average Nines because they are essentially unreal, little more than an abstraction.

Average Nines can be surprisingly callous and indifferent about this group of people. They may as well not exist.

Nor do average Nines put much energy into their relationships even with those in the first group with whom they have identified. Nines idealize these people, and then shift their attention from the real people to their idealization of them. The result is that others sense a lack of attention to themselves or to their real needs. Ironically, others may also begin to lose interest in average Nines because there is so little energy or relating going on in the relationship. As Nines drift off, others drift away.

THE RESIGNED FATALIST

If doing nothing does not succeed and they must face a problem, average Nines at this stage attempt to minimize its importance. They underestimate the seriousness of the consequences of their passivity and underestimate how difficult it will be for someone else to correct the problems they refuse to deal with. In fact, they underestimate the necessity of doing anything at all.

In a time of crisis, everyone else can see that something must be done, but average Nines take pride in their ability to endure whatever happens: they know that they can get through problems by tuning them out. Thus, rather than exert themselves, they become fatalistic, feeling that nothing can be done to change things, and that in any event, whatever the problem is, it is not so much a problem after all. ("Well, it doesn't really matter anyway.") Their healthy receptivity has deteriorated into resignation, a giving up rather than a mature letting go. This is not optimism but selfishness. ("I don't want to hear it — I just don't want to be upset.")

The problem is that Nines refuse to see the problem. As far as they are concerned, no matter what happens, they are resigned to their fate. They show no interest or understanding about what is at stake either for themselves or for anyone else. If others get angry at them because of their refusal to act, Nines quickly try to appease them. They want peace at any price, and will make whatever concessions are necessary to "get their problems behind them," a typical phrase. Once they have appeased others, they feel the crisis has passed, and they can continue as before. But because Nines do not want to deal with anything upsetting, it is hard to resolve difficulties with them. They forget how problems were settled. The following week the problems still exist: nothing that was supposedly worked out has actually sunk into their heads or made a real, permanent difference.

At this stage, they are so eager to avoid conflicts that they water down conflicting positions, give a false sense of hope by minimizing issues, and tell people prematurely to "calm down — everything will be all right." They want to down-play problems so that everyone can get back to a more peaceful, harmonious existence and so that whatever threatens their tranquillity will go away.

But in doing so they can be penny-wise and pound-foolish. Their judgment becomes extremely poor. If they are forced to deal with a problem which they alone can solve, they will go only as far as they absolutely must and then drop it. They lack staying power; they simply do not see a problem through to the end. If forced to act, their every tendency is to think that they have done enough once they have made a little effort. Thus, they often undo the good they may have begun and disappoint others who may be counting on them.

Furthermore, others realize that they will have to suffer the consequences of the fatalism and unwillingness of Nines to exert themselves. Even so, it is frustrating for others to confront fatalistic Nines. They are still so nice that few people are willing to press them or get them upset. People tend to leave Nines alone because they want to be left in peace.

The nature of their selfishness is now clear: without being aware of it, Nines are able to put their peace above the more serious needs of others, in effect, above reality and the harm they do by ignoring it. Their appeasement of others is a defense against changing anything essential about themselves or the idealization of their important relationships. By minimizing reality, average Nines in effect sacrifice others to continue the illusion of union with them, so that they can maintain their identities and their tranquillity. In this way, they are able to sacrifice their spouses, their children — and themselves — to the god of peace.

There is much aggression in this, but it is so subtle that other people usually do not even notice it. However, others are no longer real to Nines. Their lives have been taken away — not literally, but psychologically. Nines have created a relationship with a fantasy and have turned their backs on reality, particularly the reality of others. There can scarcely be a more pervasive kind of aggression.

Analyzing the Unhealthy Nine

THE NEGLECTFUL PERSON

Unhealthy Nines become adamant about not facing conflicts and problems. They actively resist seeing the problems they have caused or perpetuated so they can protect themselves from guilt and anxiety and maintain their relationship with their illusions. As a result, unhealthy Nines are obstinate and neglectful and absolutely impervious to pressure to change. Problems can even have the most obvious and relatively easy solutions, yet unhealthy Nines do not do anything *and do not want to.*

All their energy goes toward maintaining their defenses against dealing with reality so that nothing will get to them. This defense, known as repression resistance, is extraordinarily frustrating to deal with and makes it almost impossible to get through to unhealthy Nines. It is as if they have bolted shut some inner door, preventing anyone from having access to them. Ironically, those who were once so open and receptive have become impenetrable. They are mad at others for trying to force them to do anything, and hence for arousing their anxiety. But the only way unhealthy Nines can express anger is to resist others and block them out all the more. Passive resistance is as aggressive as unhealthy Nines become, except perhaps for an occasional inadvertent eruption of anger when the repression momentarily fails.

Since they absolutely resist taking any action, they become seriously neglectful, not only of their responsibilities toward others, but even toward themselves. They will not go to a doctor if they are ill, much less recognize the medical or emotional problems of their spouses or children. They refuse to do their work at the office if it upsets them in the least. Not only are they extremely frustrating, but those who depend on them realize very clearly that they are completely unreliable. Getting unhealthy Nines to do anything at all is like running into a stone wall.

Because repressed Nines obstinately resist contact with reality, they become inadequate and undeveloped as persons, virtually helpless about doing anything on their own. Ironically, for people who exert themselves so little, unhealthy Nines have little energy. They are often fatigued because their energy goes into warding off reality rather than dealing with it. They cannot cope with any tension or pressure whatsoever because everything upsets them (or rather, they think it will) or demands more attention and effort than they are able to muster. Others — usually those they have harmed by their neglect — must step in to save them from themselves, correcting the problems unhealthy Nines have refused to face.

Serious interpersonal conflicts are certain to arise at this point, if they have not already done so. When hostilities break out, unhealthy Nines are invariably mystified by the intensity of other people's negative feelings toward them. They do not realize how much their inattention has cost others.

Having to face the fact that through their negligence they have harmed someone with whom they have identified would provoke extreme anxiety and guilt in unhealthy Nines. They would be plunged into despair and possibly driven toward suicide. However, repression spares them from being aware of their failures and inadequacies, although not from all realization. Moments of insight into the finality of their actions — or more properly, the consequences of their neglect — break in on them now and then. They realize that their omissions have had consequences which cannot be undone. It is too late to go back. The horror of this is like a beast pounding at the door of their unconscious. How to keep it out?

THE DISSOCIATING PERSON

Pressure from reality and antagonism from others may get so strong that to protect themselves from having to face the awareness of what they have done, neurotic Nines cut themselves off entirely from everything. They blank out subjectively so that they do not make contact with reality and so that reality does not make contact with them. Their fear of anxiety is so intense that neurotic Nines dissociate themselves from reality, becoming depersonalized. They regress to an infantile state of denial, as if they desired to return to the womb. They block out so much that they withdraw into a

numb, affectless condition, as if in amnesia, completely dissociating from the self.

Neurotic Nines are like automatons: they do not feel or react to
anything. It is as if the self had been removed from the body which
functions on its own. The extent of their denial of reality can be
astounding. They may have lost a limb, but either deny that it
happened or think that the arm or leg will grow back. They may
think that they were not really fired or that a divorce or death did
not really happen. As pathetic as this state is, there is a poetic
appropriateness to their condition, since Nines have been increasingly absent from themselves for some time. By now, however,
their dissociation from themselves has become habitual, a way of
life, or more precisely, a way of not living.

They are in the fog of dissociation, feeling that life is a bad dream,
a sort of make believe from which they must take flight so that
reality will not really happen to them. Of course, in times of severe
loss and trauma, other personality types also react by denying reality until they can begin to deal with what has happened. However, neurotic Nines dissociate because they do not want to deal
with reality ever again.

There is a hysterical element in their flight from reality, although
this is difficult to perceive because the hysteria is repressed out of
consciousness. Nevertheless, their unconscious anxiety has reached
such a pitch that neurotic Nines must stay in flight both from
themselves and from reality. They have nowhere to go, either into
the world to find refuge or inward to seek their own comfort and
counsel. The only way out is to push dissociation one final step in
the direction of self-abandonment. In flight both from anxiety and
reality, neurotic Nines dissociate themselves from themselves as
completely as possible.

THE SELF-ABANDONING PERSON

If something pushes them over the edge (if, for example, reality puts
pressures on them from which they cannot flee), neurotic Nines
may well split into multiple personalities. They disintegrate as persons, into the most extreme state of dissociation from who they are.
As we have seen, their receptive orientation to life has facilitated

their flight from self-awareness. Now, breaking up into parts, they completely flee from themselves.

Neurotic Nines unconsciously abandon themselves as whole persons, reinvesting consciousness into various fragments of themselves, each of which may represent an aspect of the self which has been repressed and denied and undeveloped. Nines can then respond to the environment under the guise of one of their multiple personalities, some of which are probably more capable of dealing with reality than the whole self was.

To abandon themselves as persons and live as one of their separate selves is a "solution" of sorts, because then it is not really they who live, but someone else through whom they can live. We have seen that average Nines live through the other; now we see that they live through the other-self, the fragment of the self which has become like an "other." The core self has been so traumatized that it is as though in a dream without a dreamer. This can hardly be called living. Furthermore, because one of the subpersonalities can do harm to other people or to itself, this is neither a safe nor truly adaptive way to live.

Fragmenting into multiple personalities is an ironically appropriate outcome for neurotic Nines because they have never shown much interest in themselves as individuals. Now they are truly not individuals: they are many different "people" — and no one.

The Dynamics of the Nine

THE DIRECTION OF DISINTEGRATION: THE NINE GOES TO SIX

It is difficult to know whether those Nines who deteriorate into multiple personalities go to Six, or what precisely it would mean if one or more of the multiples should deteriorate further. Most probably, after the fragmentation into multiple personalities, some form of schizophrenia (probably paranoid schizophrenia, which can be interpreted as a move to Six) would likely result. In any event, it is possible for a less unhealthy Nine to go to Six, and since this is more typical, it is what we will concern ourselves with here.

When unhealthy dissociated Nines go to Six, anxiety finally breaks through their massive repression. All the feelings and realizations they have been warding off come crashing down upon them. The person who was once so easygoing becomes an overreacting hysteric, anxiety-ridden, fearful, agitated, apprehensive, tearful, panicked. More than ever, deteriorated Nines need someone else to take care of them and to save them from whatever threatening situation they have gotten into. To elicit help from others, they may become abjectly self-abasing ("morbidly dependent" in Horney's phrase) and masochistically self-destructive so that others will have to care for them.

Deteriorated Nines at Six may well also do something self-defeating and humiliating, putting themselves in worse positions than ever before. The motive behind this is twofold: self-punishment to expiate the intense guilt they feel for letting down others and making them suffer; and self-abasement to repair the separation from others by drawing people back to them.

These psychological tactics do not work, however, because besides anxiety, deteriorated Nines have also unwittingly let loose aggression toward themselves and others from the Pandora's box of the unconscious. No longer able to repress aggressive feelings, they become self-punishing and full of self-hatred. They also become intensely hostile toward others, lashing out at anyone who increases their anxiety rather than immediately relieving it. If others do not magically restore peace, they become "the enemy."

Unfortunately, deteriorated Nines have no defenses with which to handle anxiety or aggression. They can no longer repress the particularly acute anxiety of being rejected by those who have been significant to them. They will likely turn to alcohol and drugs to control their hysteria or will resort to suicide if they cannot find some kind of peace again.

THE DIRECTION OF INTEGRATION: THE NINE GOES TO THREE

When healthy Nines integrate to Three, they become self-assured and interested in developing themselves and their talents to the fullest extent possible. They move from self-possession to making something more of themselves, from a just-being-born presence in the world to an active, inner-directed force. Because they are already healthy and extremely balanced, they no longer live through someone else, nor do they need to conform to conventional roles as sources of self-esteem and identity. Instead, integrating Nines create themselves by asserting themselves properly. They no longer fear change, becoming more flexible and adaptable, entirely capable of dealing with reality as persons in their own right.

Integrating Nines have connected with their vitality. In Freudian terms, they get in touch with the id, the aggressive and instinctual side of themselves. Nines have always feared their aggressive impulses, and now they realize that they no longer have to, since these impulses are not necessarily destructive, but rather can lead to self-development.

Their peace becomes less fragile because Nines discover that they can assert themselves without being aggressive toward others, and hence without jeopardizing their relationships. As their self-esteem increases, their relationships become more mature and satisfying. Integrating Nines find that they no longer have to be self-effacing to find someone with whom they can have a relationship. By being (and becoming) themselves, they attract others who find integrating Nines more interesting and desirable than ever before. It may surprise them, but others may even begin to identify with them, to seek them out, to accommodate themselves to them. While integrating Nines will likely discourage others from being dependent on them, it will please them nonetheless, as well it should.

The Major Subtypes of the Nine

THE NINE WITH AN EIGHT-WING

The traits of the Nine and those of an Eight-wing conflict with each other: Nines are passive and desire harmony with others, while Eights are aggressive, asserting themselves and following their self-interest. Since Nine is the basic personality type, people of this subtype tend to be fundamentally oriented to others, receptive, unselfconscious, passive, and so forth, while some part of them asserts itself strongly, at least at times. This is one of the most difficult subtypes to understand because the component types are in such diametrical opposition to each other. Noteworthy examples of this subtype include Dwight Eisenhower, Gerald Ford, Ingrid Bergman, Bing Crosby, Perry Como, George Shultz, Walter Cronkite, Hugh Downs, Lady Bird Johnson, and Marc Chagall.

In healthy persons of this subtype, the Eight-wing adds an element of inner strength and will power, as well as an expansive, passionate quality to the overall style of the personality. Despite their unselfconsciousness, healthy people of this subtype are able to assert themselves effectively; despite their graciousness and concern for others, they can be quite strong and forceful; despite their ability to subordinate themselves to others and to common goals, they can be courageously independent; despite an easygoing manner, they can have formidable tempers, although these are rarely resorted to. Thus, healthy persons of this subtype give the impression of strength and good nature, sensuality and power.

Average people of this subtype compartmentalize their emotions completely. While their self-image is one of peacefulness, they may occasionally be quite aggressive without realizing the extent of it. They can be complacent, even lazy, about achieving success in some areas of their lives, while being extremely competitive in others. If they are not intellectually gifted, they may seem slightly slow-witted — good-natured, but thick-headed — because neither the Nine nor the Eight is a particularly intellectual or thinking component. These people have strong elemental drives for psychological and sexual union with the other. Their self-interest is bound up with material comfort. When their protective instincts are aroused, they do not wish to hurt others so much as protect themselves and their property. Average persons of this subtype can become belligerent and confrontational toward others, but with little long-lasting personal animosity. Their greatest ire is aroused against those who attack their families, their beliefs, or their way of life. But once the crisis has past, they are apt to sue for peace, making allies of their former enemies.

Unhealthy Nines with an Eight-wing are capable of violence with little concern about the consequences of their actions. Aggressions and id impulses are strong in people of this subtype, and there is little superego or conscience to regulate these forces. Their aggressions may be particularly aroused by sexual jealousy of their spouses. Separation from a loved one through the alienation of affections is devastating to the Nine's sense of self and inflames the Eight's rage out of wounded pride. As a result, Nines with an Eight-wing can be physically dangerous, striking out impulsively. They may retaliate against those with whom they have come into conflict while dissociating themselves emotionally from the harm they do.

THE NINE WITH A ONE-WING

The traits of the Nine and those of the One-wing tend to reinforce each other. Nines repress their emotions to maintain their peace, while Ones repress their emotions to maintain self-control. In this subtype we see people who are more emotionally controlled and cooler than those in the other subtype, although they may well display moments of anger and moral indignation. Noteworthy examples of this subtype include Ronald Reagan, Corazon Aquino, Abraham Lincoln, Queen Elizabeth II, Rosalynn Carter, Cyrus Vance, Henry Fonda, Gary Cooper, Jimmy Stewart, David Hartman, Princess Grace of Monaco, Rose Kennedy, Jim Henson, Walt Disney, Norman Rockwell, Dame Joan Sutherland, Ralph Waldo Emerson, Desdemona, Edith Bunker, and Mary Hartman.

Healthy persons of this subtype possess enormous integrity and are extremely principled. Their great common sense helps them be wise in their judgments, particularly about others. They are alert to issues of fairness and objectivity when they are called on to act or to judge situations. The One-wing adds a thinking component to this subtype, balancing the Nine's unselfconscious, receptive orientation. Healthy people here are interested in sharing what they know and appreciate the ideas and discoveries of others. They enjoy teaching and may be moral leaders, teaching most effectively by their example. The Nine's openness is combined with the One's objectivity; the result is simplicity and guilelessness toward others, peacefulness and moderation toward themselves.

Average persons of this subtype may be crusaders of some sort because they have an idealistic streak which makes them want to improve the world in whatever ways they can. They are sure of their opinions and usually have fixed conventional and conservative ideas about everything that touches on their basic beliefs. People of this subtype tend to be orderly and self-controlled, particularly more emotionally controlled and less openly passionate than Nines with an Eight-wing. They can also be quite busy organizing the environment or planning its organization by others, while maintaining the emotional disconnectedness characteristic of average Nines. Complacent and disengaged, they want to avoid all personal conflicts and antagonisms, but may be easily moved to anger since there is a testiness and edginess in this subtype. They may rationalize, moralize, or appeal to political, class, or religious ideologies to bolster their arguments. They can also be surprisingly impersonal and callous in their disregard for others, since average persons of this subtype abstract from the real world a great deal in favor of their idealistic notions.

Unhealthy persons of this subtype can be punitive toward others. They can become extremely angry, although in a highly compartmentalized way, acting impulsively, as if out of the blue. They are more resentful than Nines with an Eight-wing, stewing over wrongs and injustices. If they act, unhealthy Nines with a One-wing can become quite arbitrary, contradicting their more ordinary behavior. Obsessive-compulsive tendencies are among their neurotic traits, and unhealthy persons of this subtype may become obsessive about their apparent troubles while dissociating themselves from either their compulsive actions or their real problems. They may, for example, decide to forget what has just been the focus of their obsession as if nothing had happened. Because defense mechanisms are less global than in the other subtype, neurotics here will tend to feel their conflicts more and will therefore be more likely to have severe emotional problems or breakdowns if they become very unhealthy.

Some Final Thoughts

Looking back at the deterioration of Nines, we can see that average to unhealthy Nines have brought about the very thing they most fear, the fear of separation. Now that they are fragmented personalities, they are not only separated from others, they are separated from themselves. They are profoundly alienated from and terrified of themselves. Only with the greatest difficulty will the core personality which remains be able to begin to reclaim the self.

It seems that relatively few Nines deteriorate to this state of neurosis. Probably what happens in most cases is that they deteriorate into unhealthy states (denial, dissociation) after a crisis, but are able to bounce back to some degree of normal functioning. Their defenses are very powerful because they are so all-encompassing, and for better or worse, Nines are able to repress most traumas and go on living. Nevertheless, their ability to endure is always purchased at the price of leading an emotionally and personally impoverished life.

From this perspective, we can also see that their central problem has been how to awaken to themselves and how to maintain self-possession once they have attained it. The answer is that Nines must learn to accept suffering, especially the suffering involved with anxiety. Suffering, consciously accepted, has the ability to catalyze people, shocking them into awareness. Suffering also compels us to choose what meaning it has for us. When we choose a meaning for our experiences, we create ourselves. When Nines actively use suffering as a positive force in their lives, they not only give meaning to their lives, they sustain their awareness of themselves. The person who is able to give meaning to his or her suffering is both the self who suffers and the one who transcends it. In that moment, the self is possessed.

Chapter 12

Type One: The Reformer

The One in Profile

Healthy: Becomes wise, discerning, and tolerant. Profoundly realistic and balanced in his or her judgments. Rational, conscientious, moderate. Highly principled, always trying to be fair and objective. Very ethical: truth and justice mean a great deal. Personal integrity: moral teacher.

Average: The high-minded idealist, striving for excellence in everything: the reformer, advocate, crusader. Orderly and efficient, but impersonal, too emotionally controlled. Gets very critical, judgmental, and highly opinionated: the perfectionist and workaholic. Moralizing, scolding, indignantly angry, and abrasive toward others.

Unhealthy: Can be self-righteous, intolerant, dogmatic, and inflexible. Severe in judgments and cannot stand being proved wrong. Obsessive thoughts and compulsive, contradictory actions, hypocritically doing the opposite of what he preaches. Cruel and condemnatory, punitive toward others. Nervous breakdown and sudden, severe depression likely.

Key Motivations: Wants to be right, to strive higher and improve others, to justify his or her own position, to be beyond criticism so as not to be condemned by anyone.

Examples: Pope John Paul II, Margaret Thatcher, Elie Wiesel, Barbara Jordan, Eric Sevareid, Ralph Nader, Sandra Day O'Connor, William F. Buckley, Anita Bryant, and Mr. Spock.

An Overview of the One

Voicing the common theme of evangelical consciousness of the self before regeneration, John Greene, a New England Puritan of the mid-seventeenth century, acknowledged that God had let him "see much of the wretchedness" of his heart, and he "thought none so vile as I none so evil an heart so proud so stubborn so rebellious and I thought God would never show mercy to so vile a miserable wretch as I was." This vision of the inward self, a vision experienced in greater and lesser degree by most evangelicals, was the source of the despair and hopelessness that so often preceded conversions. . . . Not until individuals could bring themselves, or be brought by God, to reject their very selves as worthless, sinful, and justly damned creatures, could they ever hope to be born again. (Philip Greven, *The Protestant Temperament,* 75.)

The Puritans' desire for self-regeneration by striving after ideals is an expression of the personality type One. Not content to be as they are, Ones and Puritans alike feel the obligation to be better. They must somehow rise higher, beyond human nature into the realm of the Absolute.

To this personality type, the advice of "Desiderata" sounds foolish and dangerous: "Beyond a wholesome discipline, be gentle with yourself. You are a child of the universe, no less than the trees and the stars; you have a right to be here. And whether or not it is clear to you, no doubt the universe is unfolding as it should." As far as average to unhealthy Ones can tell, the universe is emphatically *not* unfolding as it should. People are not trying hard enough to improve either the universe or themselves.

What Ones typically do not see is that, given their fundamental premises, they are locked in conflicts between opposing forces that cannot be reconciled either in themselves or in the universe. They keenly feel the struggle between good and evil, the flesh and the spirit, the ideal and the real. For Ones, the battle lines are sharply drawn between the chaotic, irrational side of their natures and the clarity of their rational minds, between their dark libidinous impulses and their self-control, between their metaphysical aspirations and their human needs — between their heads and their hearts.

IN THE RELATING TRIAD

Ones appear to be very sure of themselves, although their self-confidence lies less in themselves than in the rightness of their ideals. Despite appearances, Ones relate to the world by seeing themselves as "less than" an ideal toward which they strive. They subordinate themselves to an abstraction — usually an intangible, universal value such as truth or justice — striving to be as perfect as it is. Unlike Nines, who see themselves in union with another, Ones know that the ideal is not actually a part of themselves. The ideal is, by definition, something they must work toward but can never fully attain. Nevertheless, as we shall see, average to unhealthy Ones certainly feel uplifted from the run of ordinary mortals by the attempt to do so.

This is where Ones begin to have problems. As they deteriorate toward neurosis, average Ones begin to identify with the ideal so completely that unhealthy Ones think that they have attained it — and that everyone who has not should be condemned. On one level of awareness, even unhealthy Ones know they are not perfect, yet on another level they think and act as if they were already perfect to avoid being condemned either by their consciences or by anyone else. Average to unhealthy Ones are convinced that the more zealously they strive for perfection, the more they are made righteous by the attempt. They think that by aligning themselves with the ideal, they will always be in the right, no matter how badly they fail. The mere act of identifying themselves with the ideal makes them feel that they are better than the rest of the world. They are among the saved because they know the right way, the way everything ought to be.

PROBLEMS WITH REPRESSION AND AGGRESSION

Like the other two personality types in the Relating Triad, Ones have a problem with the repression of some part of their psyches. Ones repress their emotions, attempting to sublimate them in a quest for perfection. Their emotions gradually become more and more repressed as Ones are caught in conflicts between striving after ideals and implementing them in the real world. The picture is further complicated, however, because Ones relate to the world dualistically: they see themselves as less than the ideal, while giving the impression that they are also greater than the environment, which they are obligated to improve. They constantly measure not only the distance between themselves and the ideal, but also the distance between their present perfection and their past imperfection.

Actually, there is a double dichotomy in Ones. The first is the external dichotomy we have just seen: the pressure of living up to an ideal versus the conviction of already being more perfect than others. The second is an internal dichotomy, which is less obvious: a split between the coolly controlled, rational side of themselves which they present to the world versus their repressed feelings. Even though Ones are not what anyone would call emotional or passionate, they are nevertheless keenly aware of their emotions, particularly their aggressive and sexual impulses. Although they attempt to keep their feelings in check as much as possible, they are never as successful in this as they would like.

Because of these dichotomies, average to unhealthy Ones always feel caught in conflicts: between the perfection of their ideal and their own imperfections; between feeling virtuous and feeling sinful; between their actions and their consciences; between their desire for order and the disorder they see everywhere; between good and evil; between God and the devil.

The personality type One corresponds to the extroverted thinking type in the Jungian typology; it is one of Jung's clearest descriptions.

> This type of man elevates objective reality, or an objectively oriented intellectual formula, into the ruling principle not only for himself but for his whole environment. By this formula good and

evil are measured, and beauty and ugliness determined. Everything that agrees with this formula is right, everything that con-
tradicts it is wrong. . . . Because this formula seems to embody
the entire meaning of life, it is made into a universal law which
must be put into effect everywhere all the time, both individually
and collectively. Just as the extraverted thinking type subordinates himself to his formula, so, for their own good, everybody
round him must obey it too, for whoever refuses to obey it is
wrong — he is resisting the universal law, and is therefore unreasonable, immoral, and without a conscience. His moral code for-
bids him to tolerate exceptions; his ideal must under all
circumstances be realized. . . . This is not from any great love of
his neighbor, but from the higher standpoint of justice and
truth. . . . "Oughts" and "musts" bulk large in this programme. If
the formula is broad enough, this type may play a very useful role
in social life as a reformer or public prosecutor or purifier of
conscience. . . . But the more rigid the formula, the more he develops into a martinet, a quibbler, and a prig, who would like to
force himself and others into one mould. Here we have the two
extremes between which the majority of these types move. (C. G.
Jung, *Psychological Types*, 347.)

From our point of view, we can see that Jung is describing various
points along the Continuum of the One's traits: average Ones are
reformers and public prosecutors, whereas unhealthy Ones intoler-
antly try to force others into their mold, and so forth. As we will
see, the full spectrum of the One's traits encompasses some of the
most noble and least admirable aspects of human nature. When
they are healthy, Ones can be the most objective, principled, and
wise of all the personality types. As much as humanly possible,
they try not to let their personal feelings get in the way of dealing
fairly with others. They are deeply concerned with justice, not
merely for themselves but for everyone.

But to contrast this, when they are unhealthy their lives are a
relentless application of their ideals to every conceivable situation.
Unhealthy Ones become extremely intolerant of anyone who disagrees with them, and since they are convinced that they alone
know the TRUTH (writ large, in capital letters), everything follows
from that. What does not is condemned and severely punished. The
problem is, however, that human nature keeps cropping up: unhealthy Ones find that they cannot control themselves as perfectly

as they feel they must. Their impulses can be repressed for only so long. The flesh will have its day.

CHILDHOOD ORIGINS

Ones develop as they do because as children they identified negatively with their fathers or with a father substitute. Their negative orientation to their fathers, and what their fathers symbolized, was of central importance to the development of their superegos: these children learned to fear condemnation and to avoid it by always attempting to be blameless.

The principal message they received from their fathers was "You are not acceptable as you are; you must be better, always better." Their own wishes and feelings were rarely if ever countenanced; instead, these children always had to toe the line to avoid being criticized or condemned. As a result, their emotions and other impulses were repressed by forces symbolized by a punishing father. (Freudians see toilet training as the arena in which the anal traits of the obsessive-compulsive type which correspond to the One were learned. While the Freudian anal traits of orderliness, parsimony, and obstinacy are seen in Ones, especially those with a Nine-wing, we do not have to restrict ourselves to toilet issues alone to understand the origins of this personality type.)

These children may have been negative toward their fathers for any number of reasons. The father may have been absent from the family or been abusive or have treated the child unfairly. Or as a result of a stern moral and religious upbringing and the threat of eternal punishment, the child may have feared offending God the Father and being condemned. The child may have feared being sent to hell for being impulsive, pleasure seeking, selfish, or for other actions which were, after all, merely the natural behavior of a child. In a sense, Ones were not allowed to be children but were forced to become little adults before their time. Because of such situations, they decided not to be like their fathers. To avoid being condemned, they would have to be better than their fathers.

It is also worth noting that they did not rebel against strictures on themselves; rather, they internalized control in their consciences by feeling guilty for their transgressions. Nevertheless, they also felt angry that the burden of perfection was placed on them, and more angry still when they saw others who were not subject to the same control of their feelings and impulses. The freedom of others (to Ones, the license which others grant themselves) antagonizes them and makes them chafe under the weight of their own prohibitions.

PROBLEMS WITH ANGER AND PERFECTION

Ironically, Ones vent their anger most unfairly at others when they are angry primarily with themselves for not being perfect. Instead of resolving their own disordered feelings, average to unhealthy Ones find fault everywhere else. Their self-righteous anger makes Ones aggressive; however, the One is not an aggressive personality type as such. Actually, Ones are compliant to their ideals, since the ideal is the yardstick by which they measure everything, including themselves. The aggression in their personalities is an expression of anger at themselves and others for not complying perfectly to the ideal.

Moreover, their anger signals the fact that they put too great a load upon themselves and others: perfection is a burden that human nature cannot bear. What is difficult for Ones to accept is the interdependence of flesh and spirit which is the natural state of man. Of its nature, the irrational part of themselves cannot be perfected or controlled in the same way that the rational part of themselves can be. Nevertheless, they try to do so, denying all that is base, that is, human, in themselves so that they will be more like the ideal. Ultimately, Ones feel guilty for being human. They fear being condemned because they are not angels.

When Ones are healthy, however, their objective orientation to life allows them to remain firmly in touch with human realities, including their own. They are the most discerning, moral, and reasonable of all the personality types, tolerant of others and of themselves. They recognize that their ideals may not apply equally to everyone in all circumstances. But when they are unhealthy, their behavior is a twisted caricature of their virtues because their humanity has become perverted. Unhealthy Ones punish others for their least faults while absolving themselves of their greater sins. They are completely without mercy because they have lost contact with humanity. If ideals do not serve human beings, what purpose do they serve?

Analyzing the Healthy One

THE WISE REALIST

Very healthy Ones permit their humanity to surface, discovering that their impulses are not as chaotic or threatening as they feared. They do not repress their feelings, except to the degree necessary for healthy functioning, just as everyone must. Thus, their feelings come into balance with the rest of their psyches and are integrated into their total personalities. Their subjective side comes into alignment with objective reality, and they become exceptionally realistic and tolerant, even of themselves.

Because they are so realistic about themselves, very healthy Ones are unusually mature and well-balanced. Still attracted to ideals, very healthy Ones do not see them as unilateral, stifling commands but as something which they personally find fulfilling. They do not feel the need either to make everything perfect or to become absolutely perfect themselves: it is a hopeless enterprise, and therefore not a proper moral imperative. Becoming a full human being is sufficiently challenging. Paradoxically, by becoming full human beings, Ones will come as close to perfection as is humanly possible. When they are this healthy, Ones are "a little less than the angels," embodying great nobility of spirit.

Very healthy Ones are the wisest of the personality types because of the extraordinary accuracy of their judgment. Their judgment is superb because Ones are grounded in the real rather than the ideal. They go beyond logical reasoning to discern the best thing to do in whatever circumstance they are in. Just as very healthy Fives have the most penetrating understanding of the physical world, very healthy Ones have the clearest vision of the moral world, prompting others to seek them out for guidance.

Just as they are tolerant of themselves, very healthy Ones are also tolerant of others. When most people use the word *tolerant*, they usually mean *permissive*, that people should be allowed to do whatever they like. However, tolerance of others is not the same as permissiveness. True tolerance is the ability to respect the differences of opinion well-informed people of good will have arrived at. The tolerant One who is a Protestant allows the Jew and the Catholic, the Muslim and the Hindu the same freedom to worship God which he himself enjoys. This does not necessarily mean that tolerant Ones think that the religious beliefs of others are correct, or that religious differences do not matter, but that Ones allow others the freedom to discover the truth on their own, in their own way. They understand other points of view without endorsing them and without imposing their own views on anyone else.

They are able to be this tolerant because very healthy Ones keep ultimate values before their minds. By keeping the transcendental, spiritual realm in view, healthy Ones attain a larger perspective on reality, which endows them with the ability to see everything in its proper context. The depth of their discernment is such that healthy Ones are able to focus on what is truly most important in any situation. They know virtually at a glance what "the greater good" is. (And if they do not know, their ignorance does not cause healthy Ones alarm because they are able to wait until reality presents them with an answer.)

They are so convinced of the reality of truth and the objectivity of transcendent values that they recognize the right of others to be wrong. The faith which very healthy Ones have in the moral order is so deep that they allow others, in their view, to be wrong all of their lives because they believe that error will not ultimately prevail over truth. They believe that what is true will always prevail because truth is of the nature of reality itself. This is why to be completely realistic is to be wise. Wisdom goes beyond reason, encompassing the irrational, taking it into account. It is to see the real order of things, and hence always to know what is right and good.

Thus, very healthy Ones are transcendental realists because they have transcended their own personal understanding of reality to see that, on some profound level which cannot be comprehended or expressed, all is well — "the universe is unfolding as it should."

THE REASONABLE PERSON

Unfortunately, healthy Ones are not always this healthy. They may succumb to the fear of being condemned for being wrong and compensate for this fear by desiring to be right in everything. They want to have right relations with the world, with others, and with themselves. Their sense of self is based on being reasonable and rational at all times.

Healthy Ones are indeed the soul of reason. They are extremely sensible and prudent, exemplars of rational good sense. And even though healthy Ones are somewhat less healthy than at the previous stage, they still possess exceptionally good judgment, enabling them to know what is more or less important in virtually every circumstance. They are able to sort out issues clearly (moral issues in particular) because they can see the consequences of whatever decisions are being made. They are also not afraid to make judgments, to say "This is right or wrong," "That is good or bad," and to take responsibility for their judgments and for the actions that follow from them. To describe their judgment this way makes it sound more logical than it actually is. Good judgment comes naturally to healthy Ones because they see the world objectively.

Healthy Ones are so objective that they can stand aside from themselves and judge their own actions, attitudes, and feelings. They do not want to be in error and are glad to admit their mistakes as soon as they are aware of them. They feel that nothing is to be gained by clinging to mistaken notions. Righteousness and truthfulness are important to them, not holding erroneous opinions out of pride.

Ones know right from wrong and good from bad because they have strong consciences and a strong sense of moral obligation. Their consciences motivate them to do what is right. Healthy Ones abhor whatever selfishness, pettiness, and wayward passions they find in themselves, and they feel obliged to root out these sources of disorder. They are at peace with themselves when they are virtuous and, of course, feel guilty when they fail.

Understanding how valuable reason, moderation, temperance, and impartiality are in their lives, healthy Ones do not feel that the restraints they have internalized limit them in any way. Indeed, they believe that without constraints of conscience, human society would not be possible. Many of the most worthwhile gains of civilization result from their willingness to delay personal rewards for higher goals.

Nor do Ones feel that whatever virtue they possess, or even the fact that they desire to be good, spares them from evil and suffering in life. They have not made a pact with God to bless them for being virtuous; they do not feel exempt from the conditions of life because of their attraction to the good. For example, healthy Ones do not see anything happening to others which could not also happen to them. Instead of asking "Why me?" when suffering strikes, they are as likely to ask "Why not me?" They do not expect that life will be easy or carefree, but on the other hand, healthy Ones are not pessimists. They are simply being realistic.

THE PRINCIPLED TEACHER

Having a conscience enables healthy Ones to lead outstandingly moral and useful lives because they not only want to be right, they want to do what is right. They want to put objective values into practice and to be unswayed by their passions, so that, as much as is humanly possible, they can do what is objectively right.

Whereas righteousness was the primary virtue at the previous stage, truth and justice now enter the picture. Thus, healthy Ones are extremely concerned that others be treated fairly. They hate injustice wherever they find it, whether it is their friends, total strangers, or they themselves who are harmed by injustice. Healthy Ones are on fire for justice and righteousness — these are not arid principles, they are their passions. More than those of any other personality type, healthy Ones willingly put themselves on the line for their moral beliefs and would rather suffer injustice themselves than act unjustly toward anyone else.

Healthy Ones have enormous integrity and are extremely ethical: to lie or to cheat someone is virtually unthinkable. They are extremely principled, having personal standards from which they will not deviate, making decisions based on what they see as objective, rational foundations, doing things regardless of their immediate self-interest. In civic life, for example, they vote their consciences rather than their pocketbooks. As parents, they decide issues on the basis of what they believe is right rather than what will favor their own children. As religious persons, they act on their religious principles, even if it means disobeying civil authorities. Healthy Ones can be extremely courageous in this regard, subordinating themselves, their possessions, their reputations, even their lives for their principles. They do not want to sacrifice their principles because to do so would corrupt their integrity, and by violating their integrity, they would ruin something essential, their capacity for goodness and virtue, sources of deep satisfaction to them.

Ones at this stage stand up for what is right, appealing to the consciences, good will, and fairness of others, fearlessly expressing their beliefs, no matter whom they please or displease. Thus, not the least good that healthy Ones do for society is to be moral teachers and "witnesses to the truth," communicating their principles and moral vision to others. This is perhaps the highest form of teaching, not limited to merely passing on a body of knowledge but communicating a vision of the proper way to live. Without a clear notion of right and wrong, and of the consequences of acting rightly or wrongly, human beings would have no direction in life, and no means of finding one.

But even so, their consciences speak primarily to *them* — they are not obligations laid on the whole world. Healthy Ones teach by personal example, not by preaching to others. They are confident that, whether or not others listen to them, the truth will ultimately be heard because the truth speaks to the soul in a voice which cannot be ignored.

Analyzing the Average One

THE IDEALISTIC REFORMER

Guided by their consciences, Ones are always subject to guilt and anxiety when they disobey. If for some reason they fear that they are not fulfilling their moral principles as perfectly as they ought, they begin to strive after an extremely high standard of excellence in everything. They want to make everything better. They become idealists, reformers, and crusaders, people with a mission, exhorting themselves and others toward perpetual improvement.

The difference between healthy Ones and average Ones is that average Ones want to improve the world according to *their* particular interpretation of the ideal. Personal conscience has shifted to the feeling of obligation to strive after the ideal in everything. Thus, average Ones begin to relate to the world from a position of moral superiority, as if they were saying, "I know the way things ought to be, so you should listen to me." They are elitists, possessing a sense of noblesse oblige by virtue of the loftiness of their ideals and their other claims to excellence.

What average Ones personally define as the ideal becomes the norm for everyone else. They are convinced that they know the way everything ought to be. The weight of moral "shoulds" and "oughts" makes itself felt: not only should Ones do or not do this or that, but so should everyone else. They feel it is up to them to right wrongs, educate the unlettered, guide the aimless, and instruct others of the "correct" view. The problem is that they do not trust other people to do the right thing. ("If I don't do it, who will?")

Average Ones take an Olympian view of human nature, presenting themselves as the lawgivers and legislators of humanity, making rules which everyone must follow. Nothing is too small or too personal to escape their notice or their value judgments. Smoking, drinking, seat belts, the quality of television, pornography, and rock music are just a few of the subjects about which average Ones proselytize. (Of course, they may well be right in their opinions, but they do not allow people to find out for themselves.)

They are ever mindful of how they are approximating their ideals, so progress is an important concept for them: they very much want to measure — at least by their moral yardstick — their improvement in whatever spheres concern them. Thus, they are extremely purposeful, always having a higher goal in view. They should never watch television for entertainment but only for education since they should always be improving themselves and doing something worthwhile. This is also why average Ones associate themselves with, and often lead, high-minded causes, whether picketing for migrant workers, organizing the neighborhood for a political party, or rallying for environmental concerns.

As reformers and crusaders, average Ones know precisely where they stand on every issue, and they argue for their positions with the zeal of a missionary. Usually quite articulate, they love to debate and are able to propound their views effectively. And because they truly believe that their cause is right, they have an enormous amount of self-confidence, taking on the world like sculptors eager to get their hands on a shapeless mass of clay. Of course, therein lies the beginning of their real difficulties — and the difficulties of others with them. The world and particularly other people are not lumps of clay to be molded according to their reforming impulses. Reality already has its own shape, although average Ones want to give it another.

THE ORDERLY PERSON

Since by this stage Ones have taken public positions as reformers of some sort, if only among family or friends, they do not want there to be any inconsistency between their private feelings and their official idealistic positions. They want to have control over every area of their lives, particularly over their emotions.

Their healthy self-discipline has deteriorated into brisk efficiency and orderliness. Average Ones want the rational mind to rule everything. Reason is pitted against emotion, revealing the dualistic nature of their psyches. They see everything as black or white, right or wrong, good or bad, done correctly or incorrectly. There is and can be no room for subjective preferences, which they view as mere self-indulgence. Impersonal logic and order become the principal ways in which average Ones attempt to control themselves, others, and the environment.

Meticulous and thorough, they attempt to organize the world into neat categories (as strictly as they control, or would like to control, their emotions). They are sticklers for detail, planning and working out every conceivable contingency so that "everything will be under control," a favorite phrase. (Flow charts are virtually symbolic of their approach to reality.) Orderly everywhere, they make lists and plan their schedules carefully so they will not waste time. Time is extremely important to them, and average Ones are always able to account for their use of it. They are always on time and insist that others be equally punctual. No other personality type so personifies the Protestant work ethic, the person who feels that life is serious business. There can be no vacation from ideals, never a moment during which they feel they can relax and do whatever they want.

The way they think is highly orderly, too. Slightly pedantic and always precise, they are adept at making logical distinctions. Average Ones have hierarchical minds, judging everything and automatically assigning a ranking or evaluation to it, as if to say, "This is better than that" — as if they were schoolteachers on holiday who cannot stop grading everything.

In sum, average Ones at this stage are the classifiers, accountants, and taxonomists of reality — Freud's anal type. Everything should be tidy, clean, and neat; nothing should be out of place, and there should be no loose ends. Clocklike precision is their goal. Of course, the orderliness of Ones has many positive effects, especially for the organizations in which they work and for society as a whole. Everything runs more smoothly if things are organized, from business meetings to railroad schedules to wrapping Christmas gifts. Very little would get done if people could not count on a certain amount of order in the world and on those who provide it.

However, as with anything else, orderliness is a matter of appropriateness and degree. It would be good for Ones to relax. They do not allow themselves to be spontaneous, but if they do, there is a stiff, forced quality about it, as if they had decided that it was time to be spontaneous. In interpersonal relationships, they tend to be proper and schoolmarmish in a slightly stuffy, correct way, relying on propriety and etiquette to express themselves. Having proper manners allows average Ones to function socially without reference to their personal feelings.

Since self-control is their desire, average Ones take sides against their impulses, doing the opposite of what they would like to do, as if their personal inclinations were somehow always suspect. If Ones want to do something, like going to a movie, they will give it up, just because they want it and feel that they must control their desires. On the other hand, if they do not want to do something, like working on the weekend, they will force themselves to do it, again, to discipline themselves. The irony is that average Ones begin to be more controlled than ever by their impulses because of their constant awareness of them.

Although much depends on which wing they have, there is, in general, an ascetic, austere, antiseptic quality about average Ones, especially in matters pertaining to sex, pleasure, and the flesh. Sexual impulses are particularly threatening, since these impulses are not only irrational but may be of a "forbidden" nature, contrary to their consciences. Their musculature is frequently tight: lips pursed, teeth clenched, neck and face stiff. *Tense, taut, stiff,* and *rigid* are words that can be applied to much of their behavior, as well as their emotional world, at this stage.

Although they are self-controlled, they do not see themselves that way. Average Ones are very much aware that they have irrational impulses and sexual desires. From their point of view, they are doing the world a favor by being orderly and efficient. But not only that, they are protecting the world from their passions — which would wreak havoc if they ever let them loose. They fear that if they ever allowed themselves to do as they please, their emotions would get out of control and they would be swept away by their wildest impulses, inevitably falling into the darkest sins of the heart. Who knows what lives in the unconscious? Ones think it wise not to tamper.

This stage is a turning point in their deterioration along the Continuum because life is not as orderly as Ones would have it, and they are not as orderly as they would like to be. Their restrained impulses keep breaking through the barricades of repression. From this stage onward, Ones attempt to control themselves and the environment ever more tightly so that their prohibitions will keep their darker impulses in place. Not lessening their desire for internal and external order, they begin to become obsessed with rooting out disorder everywhere.

THE JUDGMENTAL PERFECTIONIST

The more tightly they try to control their impulses, the more average Ones feel that they cannot let go. At this stage, they fear relaxing self-control so much that they strive yet higher. Mere order is not enough: perfection is required.

Ones become extremely threatened if the orderliness and self-control they desire for themselves and the environment do not materialize. Although it is difficult to perceive, Ones at this stage are as hard on themselves as they are on others. Their superegos have become demanding, and their overall attitude can be summarized as "nothing is ever good enough," an echo of what their fathers once told them. They constantly pick at things, not able to let well enough alone, and overcompensating for the fear of being judged by others, they become "judges" themselves. The one emotion they regularly allow themselves is anger in its many forms, criticism, irritation, resentment, and indignation.

Highly critical of everything, they interfere with others, brusquely interrupting them, constantly telling them what to do, pointing out their mistakes, preaching about how they can improve themselves. "I told you so" and "If you had only listened to me, this would not have happened" are often heard from judgmental Ones. They are critical of everything — didactic, pontificating, lecturing, and scolding. They lose their tempers easily over trivialities and are stern disciplinarians, impatient and faultfinding, quick to slap a wrist, literally or figuratively. They have an opinion about everything which they present as the Truth, not merely as a personal opinion. It does not occur to judgmental Ones that they could be wrong. (Out of politeness or false modesty, they may occasionally allow that it is possible they could be wrong, but at this stage Ones really do not believe their disclaimers of infallibility.)

Moreover, they almost never change their opinions because their opinions are based on their ideals, and their ideals are fixed, like compass points enabling them to know where right lies in any matter. Life thus becomes a never-ending application of the ideal to particulars, the constant fixing of mistakes, the unending redoing of what was first done badly by someone else.

They become indignant and resentful about the errors and lack of perfection of others, as if they were personally injured by everyone's behavior. It is a personal affront if someone litters the street or if someone they know does not pay taxes or is having an affair. Even if they are right in their criticisms of others, their manner is so abrasive and irritating that it practically invites defiance or disobedience. From impersonal politeness they have deteriorated into acerbic dogmatism. But no matter: critical Ones are concerned not with pleasing others, but with making them do what is right.

In their own lives, they are workaholics, feeling guilty if they are not being productive all the time. But perfectionistic Ones are so concerned with minutiae that, ironically, their efficiency is often reduced and they frequently accomplish less than their less driven counterparts. They constantly make specious improvements, not because something really needs it, but because they have to improve things to justify their existence. Of course, their perfectionism also drives others crazy, making Ones difficult to work for (never "with"). They are very thin skinned, and cannot be criticized. They do not delegate work and decisions to anyone because they feel that no one would do as good a job as they. They feel it would take them longer to train someone else than it would take them to do the job right in the first place.

Naturally their perfectionism takes the enjoyment out of what they do, since nothing is ever good enough. Things are never finished until they are perfect, and it takes a lot of time to make them perfect, if they can be. Thus, workaholic Ones are caught in a conflict: even though they do not enjoy working, they do not enjoy not working.

Interpersonal conflicts increase because Ones have all the answers and no one can tell them anything: Mr. Know-It-All knows better. Moreover, they get into the irritating habit of making pronouncements about things they actually know little about, highhandedly condescending to others, explaining things as if others were children who would do nothing right without guidance. They presume to tell people what they can and cannot do, putting prohibitions on them, like a priest who instructs couples about married life or a well-heeled columnist who lectures the poor about thrift.

As we saw in the Overview, Ones resent that they must be perfect. It seems unfair to them that the burden of perfection has fallen on their shoulders more than on others'. Of course, striving for perfection and having moments of feeling perfect is deeply satisfying to them because their sense of self depends upon feeling right and knowing where perfection lies. But still, something in Ones chafes over the freedom of others. Since they are not having much fun, why should anyone else?

Analyzing the Unhealthy One

THE INTOLERANT PERSON

Unhealthy Ones cannot allow themselves to be proved wrong, either by objective facts or by someone else's better arguments. They are utterly convinced that they are always right about whatever they say or do. Ideals have become sterile and forbidding absolutes, and unhealthy Ones are completely inflexible about them.

Their ideals are rigid dogmas from which they cannot deviate. They see everything and everyone in the light of absolutes — right or wrong, good or evil, saved or damned. There is no middle ground, no gray area, no possibility of exceptions being made. They refuse to consider any circumstances which would call for a compromise with absolute perfection. As they see it, the slightest imperfection ruins the whole and must therefore be mercilessly rooted out. However, living according to absolutes necessarily involves a corresponding negation of their humanity. The higher they climb, the more of humanity they leave behind. They become misanthropes who love humanity but hate individuals.

The difference between perfectionistic average Ones and intolerant unhealthy Ones is that the former, at least occasionally, include themselves in their own criticism and feel guilty when they fail to attain perfection. This is no longer the case with unhealthy Ones, who exclude themselves from condemnation. Unhealthy Ones are supremely self-righteous, feeling that their adherence to the strictest ideals of perfection justifies them, whether or not they put the ideal into practice. ("I am right, therefore everything I say and do is right.")

Anger remains their most prominent, perhaps only, emotion. Unhealthy Ones would like to think that they are completely impersonal about administering justice to wrongdoers, but an unmistakable element of vindictiveness is beginning to motivate them, although they cannot admit it to themselves, much less to anyone else. Their image of themselves is too lofty for them to admit anything less than a perfect motivation.

The fact is that they are completely intolerant of the beliefs and behaviors of others, considering anyone who disagrees with them as immoral and evil. Angrily forcing their views on others, unhealthy Ones feel that others must be made to do the right thing, as defined by them, of course. Religion, justice, truth — any or all of their ideals — may be invoked to bolster their position and make others feel wrong or sinful. But in doing so, unhealthy Ones ironically get themselves into strange positions, propounding doctrines which can be defended only by sophistry. They will argue that to save a village, it may be bombed into annihilation. To convert a people to their religion, they may be sold into slavery. To protect the lives of un-born fetuses, the lives of adults may be taken. Realizing that they may be using sophistry does not deter unhealthy Ones for a mo-ment, since they are adept at rationalizing whatever they do, no matter how much their actions conflict with their stated beliefs.

However, they are so enraged at others that the irrationality of their anger disturbs even unhealthy Ones themselves, although, of course, they feel justified in being angry. Even so, they attempt to increase self-control lest their anger get out of hand. The irony is, however, that unhealthy Ones are becoming less self-controlled than ever. They are so tightly wound that their very tightness acts as a lightning rod for repressed feelings to erupt unexpectedly.

THE OBSESSIVE HYPOCRITE

Unhealthy Ones now become obsessed (neurotically preoccupied) with whatever has become the focus of their fury, but which, be-cause of their need to control themselves, they cannot act upon directly. As a result, they act compulsively, controlled more than ever by their irrational impulses.

At this stage, the double dichotomy, noted in the Overview, be-comes more apparent. On the one hand, there is a split between their impulses and the strength of the forces necessary to maintain the repression of those impulses. On the other hand, there is a split between their need to control themselves and moments when their control breaks down. Obsessions and compulsions are both attempts to control their irrational thoughts and actions, respectively, and symptoms of the fact that the control they seek is crumbling.

Obsessive thoughts go repeatedly through their minds. Obses-sions are extremely threatening to their consciously held beliefs, since they may be obscene, sacrilegious, or violent. The intensity of their obsessions may be so troubling to neurotic Ones that they may feel possessed by demons. In a certain sense neurotic Ones are "possessed," although their demons are the repressed feelings and impulses they have not allowed themselves to deal with. Moreover, neurotic Ones are unable to resolve their obsessive thoughts because they are unable to acknowledge what is really disturbing them: their hatred of others. As a result, they spend a great deal of time trying to control their thoughts so that even more upsetting ones do not overwhelm them.

To focus their thoughts on something other than their real problems, neurotic Ones may become obsessed with cleanliness or rooting out other kinds of "dirt" and disorder associated with impulses and feelings they have repressed. Obsessions about sexual feelings and control of the body may be displaced onto food, possibly resulting in anorexia or bulimia. Or they may throw themselves into obsessive-compulsive cleaning or counting, the compulsive nature of their actions ironically contradicting their normal orderliness and self-control.

Obsessions are strangely adaptive, however, because neurotic Ones neither completely admit into consciousness nor wholly act on their impulses. On the other hand, their obsessions profoundly disturb them, and they act out just enough of them to become compulsive, and thus arbitrary, contradictory, and hypocritical.

When neurotic Ones are unconsciously controlled by their erupting impulses, they may act contrary to their stated beliefs, for example, preaching the virtues of absolute sexual purity while falling into the grip of compulsive sexual activity. They do precisely what they condemn, like a censor who is "forced" to watch pornography, or a sex researcher who must hear the lurid stories of rapists, or a judge who is a shoplifter. Compulsive Ones may even put themselves in the way of temptation to prove that their moral strength is so solid that it can withstand testing. Thus, they can have it both ways: they can flirt with, and occasionally succumb to, vice in the name of virtue.

Corruption of any sort is always more shocking in the Lord High Protector of Public Morals than it is in the ordinary person. Neurotic Ones get into perversity because, having repressed their feelings so thoroughly, they have denied and twisted their emotions until they have become deformed. The deformity of their emotional lives is what makes neurotic Ones and their impulses dangerous, not necessarily the original impulses themselves.

THE PUNITIVE AVENGER

Someone or something has stirred up such unacceptable feelings that neurotic Ones cannot deal with them directly. Neurotic Ones are now no longer even remotely motivated by ideals, but by their overriding need to restore self-control before their obsessions and compulsions get completely out of hand. But they cannot resolve obsessions by being obsessive, or compulsions by being compulsive. They therefore "solve" their neurotic conflicts by attempting to do away with the apparent cause of their disturbances, whipping themselves into a fury over what they see as the evildoing of others, although what is really at stake is their own sanity.

Their hypocrisies are so deep, their obsessions so intense, and their compulsions so threatening, that neurotic Ones cannot back down. The possibility that they may have been wrong is too much for their pride to bear. More than ever, they must justify themselves. Not only must others be proved wrong, they must be punished. And since others are hideous sinners, they can be condemned and destroyed without guilt.

No love, no mercy, no human sympathy can be shown to those who have become the focus of their righteous retribution. Neurotic Ones become inhumanly cruel and, with whatever power they have, they make sure that others suffer. "They are only getting what they deserve!" is the rallying cry, and since the end justifies the means, any means can be used.

Completely unmerciful and unforgiving, they set in motion injustices and atrocities, while trying to portray them as the work of an impersonal agent. Neurotic Ones act as if justice itself were responsible for their sadistic punishment of others. Because their twisted morality now sanctions it, they are capable of having others thrown into prison, tortured, or burned at the stake.

The personality type which fears being condemned condemns others mercilessly. The personality type which once may have been so concerned with justice has become the perpetrator of gross injustices. The personality type which was once the soul of reason is now completely unreasonable.

The Dynamics of the One

THE DIRECTION OF DISINTEGRATION: THE ONE GOES TO FOUR

When neurotic Ones go to Four, their last moorings break loose. The hideousness of their punitive attitudes and actions crashes down upon them. They see their own corruption and are rightly horrified. ("Oh my God, what have I done?") They fear that they have transgressed so grievously that they cannot be forgiven.

Ones at Four come under the spell of their unconscious processes, although they are completely unprepared to be plunged into the maelstrom of the unconscious. They are strangers to that territory, and what they discover about themselves fills them with horror, disgust, and self-loathing. With appalling clarity, they suddenly see the extent of their emotional chaos and the evil they have done. The ideals by which they have lived and controlled themselves are no longer of any help.

Their convictions now convict them. But while deteriorated Ones rightly condemn themselves for their hatred, intolerance, and cruelty, they go overboard and condemn themselves as harshly as they have condemned others. From a position of finding nothing good in others, they now find nothing good in themselves.

They become profoundly depressed, hopeless, and emotionally disturbed. Deteriorated Ones are prey to extreme guilt, self-hatred, and emotional torment from which it is difficult to reemerge. There seems to be nothing worthwhile outside themselves to which they can reattach, no ideals with which they feel worthy of associating. It finally becomes clear to them that they themselves are the real cause of their problems — their hypocrisies and hatreds, their contradictions and twisted passions. Now the only way to resolve what is tearing them apart is to do away with the self. An incapacitating breakdown and suicide become very real possibilities.

THE DIRECTION OF INTEGRATION: THE ONE GOES TO SEVEN

As we have seen, Ones exercise too much control over their feelings and impulses. The essence of the move to Seven is that integrating Ones relax and learn to take delight in life. They learn to trust themselves and reality, becoming life-affirming rather than controlled and constricted. They discover that life is not always grim and serious: happiness is a legitimate response to existence. Pleasure can be taken without sinking into the morass of sensuality; people can please and fulfill themselves without becoming irresponsible or selfish.

Integrating Ones no longer feel that they must make everything perfect. Thus, they progress from obligation to enthusiasm, from constraint to freedom of action. They are more relaxed and productive and are able to express their feelings spontaneously. Integrating Ones are more responsive to the world, more playful, and much happier.

A great burden has been lifted from them, the burden of unnecessary perfection. They realize that they can enjoy what is good in life without constantly feeling obligated to improve it, especially in those areas in which perfection is not an issue. Things do not have to be perfect to be good. ("This is good, but so is that.") They realize that much in life is already very good, even wonderful. Integrating Ones marvel at nature, the beauty of the arts, or the extraordinary accomplishments of others who, like they, are imperfect, yet have been able to make valuable contributions.

Moreover, they discover that it is frequently possible for them to be flexible without compromising genuine values. The old adage "The good is not the enemy of the better" becomes meaningful. They stop preaching from the abstract and experience life as it is. Integrating Ones have come down from Olympus to join the human race.

The Major Subtypes of the One

THE ONE WITH A NINE-WING

The traits of the One and those of a Nine-wing tend to reinforce each other. Both component types tend to be removed from the environment: the One because it relates to ideals, and the Nine because it relates to idealizations of people rather than to people themselves. The result is that Ones with a Nine-wing are somewhat disconnected from others, impersonal, and emotionally cooler than Ones with a Two-wing. Noteworthy examples of this subtype include Margaret Thatcher, Ralph Nader, Sandra Day O'Connor, Katharine Hepburn, William F. Buckley, Peter Jennings, Jeane J. Kirkpatrick, Diane Feinstein, Joyce Brothers, David Stockman, Walter Lippmann, Eric Sevareid, C. S. Lewis, Elliot Richardson, Thomas Jefferson, Cotton Mather, Saint Ignatius Loyola, and Mr. Spock.

When they are healthy, people in this subtype are unusually objective and moderate in their judgments and dealings with others, since they have a special interest in remaining dispassionately involved. There is a spiritual, mystical side to people of this subtype, and an attraction to nature, art, and animals rather than humans. Since One is the main component type, they are rational, fair-minded, concerned with justice and truth. There is less personal warmth and emotional expressiveness even in healthy people of this subtype. However, they frequently make up for it by intellectual brilliance and an unselfconscious devotion to principles.

Average persons of this subtype combine the noblesse oblige of Ones with the conservatism of Nines to produce aristocratic elitists, classic preppies bred in the Establishment. Notions of class, privilege, and public responsibility are important to them. Their ideals may lead them into causes either for or against their social backgrounds. Average people of this subtype are noticeably less related to individuals than they are to abstract ideas. Moreover, the impersonalness of Ones and the disconnectedness of Nines produce people who preach to others almost entirely from abstract notions while trying to exclude anything personal in their behavior. Their emotions are subdued, and they have a tendency to be unconcerned, and even obtuse, about human motivations and human nature in general. Brilliant as individuals of this subtype may be, their mental world is compartmentalized: areas of interest and disinterest, conviction and indifference, discipline and laxity, consistency and inconsistency manifest themselves.

Unhealthy people of this subtype are almost completely dissociated from their emotions and contradictions. They resist seeing what does not fit into their world view. They tend to be inaccessible emotionally and intellectually, barricading themselves behind stubbornly held opinions. They can be very severe because their punitive tendencies are not checked by any real compassion for or identification with other human beings. Unhealthy Ones with a Nine-wing are extremely intolerant and self-righteous. They readily become obsessed with what they see as the evildoing of others, and compulsive about taking measures to rectify it, while dissociating themselves from contradictions in their own behavior. They cause others a great deal of harm because they do not understand the nature or extent of the suffering they unhesitatingly inflict on others.

THE ONE WITH A TWO-WING

The traits of the One and those of a Two-wing are in some degree of conflict with each other. Ones are rational and impersonal, while Twos are emotional and involved with people. Although One is the basic personality type, there is a noticeable degree of warmth as well as an interpersonal focus in people of this subtype compensating for the One's emotional control. Noteworthy examples of this subtype include Pope John Paul II, Mario Cuomo, Jane Fonda, Tom Brokaw, John Chancellor, Shana Alexander, Barbara Jordan, Gene Siskel, Alistair Cooke, Bill Moyers, Edwin Newman, Saint Thomas More, Anita Bryant, and Jean Harris.

The Two-wing softens the One's tendency to be overly harsh and judgmental. To the extent that thoughtfulness and love of neighbor are among their ideals, Ones with a Two-wing will attempt to be caring and personal; they try to temper the rigor of their ideals so they can take the needs of individuals into consideration. Healthy people of this subtype mix tolerance with compassion, integrity with concern about others, objectivity with empathy. They can be generous, helpful, kind, and rather good-humored, markedly offsetting the One's cooler demeanor. They are often found in many of the helping professions (such as teaching and nursing), since their idealism is much more effective when it has an interpersonal focus.

Average people of this subtype are well intentioned and proselytize others both from a feeling of idealistic obligation and a desire to exert a personal influence over them. They are convinced not only that they are right, but that they are well-meaning. They are frequently involved in idealistic public causes and reforms of one sort or another out of a sense of personal responsibility for the welfare of others. Average Ones want to control themselves, while average Twos want to control others: these motives reinforce each other, making it difficult for those around Ones with a Two-wing to break away from their influence. People of this subtype allow themselves clearly defined emotional outlets as a reaction to their self-control. Tendencies to perfectionism, a strict conscience, self-satisfaction with their own goodness and self-importance are also possibilities here. They tend to lecture and scold people more than Ones with a Nine-wing do, since other people, rather than abstractions, are the focus of their attention. They are prone to anger and resentment when others do not follow their "suggestions." But they are thin skinned and do not like their ideals, their motives, or their lives to be questioned.

Unhealthy Ones with a Two-wing may be intolerant of and condescending to those who disagree with them. They may attempt to manipulate others emotionally, making them feel guilty for being less perfect than they should be. These people have a tendency toward self-deception about their own motives and self-righteousness when their motives or actions are questioned. They can be high-handed and hypocritical, guilty of the very faults they condemn in others. Self-deception and feelings of entitlement make their defenses particularly difficult to break. There is a tremendous amount of covert aggression in persons of this subtype, both from the repressed aggression of the One and the indirect aggression of the Two. Unhealthy Ones with a Two-wing may have physical problems (conversion reactions), compulsive habits, or nervous breakdowns as the result of the anxiety generated by their contradictions.

Some Final Thoughts

Looking back on their deterioration, we can see that neurotic Ones have brought about the very thing they most fear. They are so inhumanly cruel that they are certain to be condemned by others — and condemned even by their own consciences. They have done something so contrary to their principles that they can no longer rationalize their actions. Justice now works against them rather than for them.

We can also see that many of the propositions which average to unhealthy Ones preached as objective truths were at least partially personal predilections. The truth of many of their dogmas is not usually as self-evident as Ones think it is. This does not mean that they should not act on what they believe, but that they should recognize the role which the subjective and the irrational play in their lives. After all, reason is not the only faculty human beings possess, and once Ones pit reason against their feelings, they begin to get into trouble. Reason alone is a trap which leads to unreasonable behavior, because it does not take other parts of human nature into account.

Unless they are very healthy, Ones are motivated by an underlying fear that unless they constantly adhere to the strictest ideals, they will precipitously and calamitously fall into the depths of depravity. Life to them is like walking a tightrope over a chasm: one slip, and they are doomed. There is so little joy in this view of life that Ones should not be surprised if others do not follow them more readily. If their ideals were genuine, and the way they lived their ideals healthy, their ideals would be attractive to others without Ones having to cajole people into submitting to them. Real ideals do not need badgering advocates. Their rightness is the source of their attraction.

PART III

Chapter 13

Advanced Guidelines

IN THIS CHAPTER, I hope to answer whatever remaining questions you may have about how the Enneagram works. I will go into more detail about most of the topics already covered in the Guidelines. Now that you have read at least some of the descriptions, you probably have a good working sense of the Enneagram, so refinements will be more meaningful to you. We will examine three major areas in some detail: the Directions of Integration and Disintegration, the Wings, and the Continuum of Traits.

The Directions of Integration and Disintegration

As you know from the descriptions, each personality type has a Direction of Integration and a Direction of Disintegration, as indicated on the Enneagram below. Each type's *wing* also has a Direction of Integration and Disintegration. The wing's directions follow the same patterns we have seen. For example, in a Nine with a One-wing, the Direction of Integration for the One-wing is to Seven, and its Direction of Disintegration is to Four. Likewise for all the wings of all the subtypes.

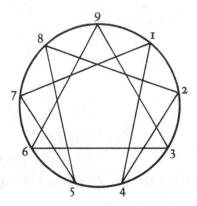

The Direction of Integration

1–7–5–8–2–4–1

9–3–6–9

The Direction of Disintegration

1–4–2–8–5–7–1

9–6–3–9

One point of confusion sometimes arises about four subtypes in particular — the One with a Two-wing, the Two with a One-wing, the Seven with an Eight-wing, and the Eight with a Seven-wing — because the same type seems to be the Direction of both Integration and Disintegration for that subtype. For example, it is unhealthy for a person who is a One with a Two-wing to move to Four. However, Four is also the Two-wing's Direction of Integration. So it seems to be contradictory that someone would be going to Four in both integration and disintegration.

The confusion arises because Four represents unhealthy tendencies in the One, while Four also represents healthy tendencies in the One's Two-wing. The solution to this apparent contradiction lies in remembering that if a person is healthy, his or her unhealthy tendencies are not active. So while Four represents a One's unhealthy direction, a healthy One who is integrating will move to Seven, and only the Two-wing will integrate to Four.

Remember that the basic personality type and the wing both move in their respective Directions of Integration and Disintegration. To return to the example, the One would integrate to Seven, and the Two-wing would integrate to Four. If the person is unhealthy, the One would disintegrate to Four, and the Two-wing to Eight.

If you reflect on yourself, you will see that your wing actually does integrate or disintegrate just as your basic type does. However, it is not feasible to give a description for the development or deterioration of the wing for all the personality types, since there are too many possible states in which this happens. Once you have gotten used to seeing how your basic personality type integrates or disintegrates, you will be able to recognize the movement of your wing as well.

It is important to realize that the personality type in the Direction of Disintegration is not unhealthy in any absolute sense since it is, after all, another personality type — and no type is fundamentally unhealthy. The type lying in the Direction of Disintegration is considered "unhealthy" only because it embodies what we most need for our personal development, but for a reason inherent in the character structure of our basic type, we cannot yet deal with. Therefore, the type which lies in the Direction of Disintegration is only *relatively* unhealthy because we cannot immediately integrate into ourselves the psychological capacities it symbolizes. The unhealthy type represents those aspects of ourselves which are the most difficult for us to come to terms with.

Eight, for example, lies in the Direction of Disintegration for Two. There is nothing inherently unhealthy about Eight, although going to Eight immediately is unhealthy for Twos because they must first resolve their aggressions. The move to Eight symbolizes the eruption of dangerously aggressive impulses into a neurotic Two's behavior.

Similarly, for the remainder of the personality types, we can see why it is unhealthy to move in the Direction of Disintegration. In brief, Threes most need to deal with dissociating from their feelings, symbolized by Nine. Fours most need to deal with their feelings of entitlement, symbolized by Two. Fives most need to deal with impulsiveness, symbolized by Seven. Sixes most need to deal with hostility toward those whom they fear, symbolized by Three. Sevens most need to deal with obsessiveness, symbolized by One. Eights most need to deal with their denied fear of others (paranoia), symbolized by Five. Nines most need to deal with denied anxiety (hysteria), symbolized by Six. And Ones most need to deal with self-inhibitions, symbolized by Four.

We are often tempted to move in our Direction of Disintegration because the normal and neurotic conflicts we get into impel us to find a quick solution to our emotional needs. The type which is in the Direction of Disintegration seems to hold out the promise of being just such a solution, although it never is. To return to the above example for a moment, a move to Eight is tempting because, as Twos become increasingly unhealthy, they become more resentful toward those they feel have been ungrateful to them and have ignored their needs. A "solution" to their aggressive feelings toward others is to lash out at people, coercing a response through openly aggressive behavior. But if unhealthy Twos succumb to the temptation to go to Eight, their anger is certain to do more harm than good, driving away the very people whose love they want by destroying the relationship. A move to the Direction of Disintegration never solves anything; it only makes everything worse.

Let us consider another refinement about the Directions of Integration and Disintegration.

You may have noticed that Threes, Sixes, and Nines have to move only two places in their Direction of Integration before returning to their basic type. The remaining types have to move six places in the Direction of Integration before returning to their basic type. It may seem unfair that six types have twice as far to go on the Enneagram as the Three, Six, and Nine.

I have already used the terms "primary" and "secondary" types in the descriptions. The primary personality types — Three, Six, and Nine — are most seriously affected by — most out of touch with — the characteristic problem of their Triads. As you recall, Three is the primary type of the Feeling Triad, Six of the Doing Triad, and Nine of the Relating Triad. The secondary types are the six remaining personality types — One, Four, Two, Eight, Five, and Seven. They are less affected by the corresponding problems of their Triads. They either overfeel or underfeel, or overdo or underdo, or overrelate or underrelate, depending on their Triad.

It may seem that there is an advantage to being one of the primary types, since there is less distance to go to integrate around the Enneagram. A Three, for example, has to integrate only to Six and then to Nine before it returns to Three. But because the goal of psychological development is to become a fully functioning person, being a primary or a secondary type is neither an advantage nor a disadvantage. The psychological agenda for both the primary and secondary types comes to the same thing — developing all their potentials in a balanced way.

There is nevertheless an important difference between the primary and the secondary personality types: the primary types have a more difficult time integrating because they are more seriously blocked by the root problem of their respective Triads. The primary types, although they do not have as far to go, find it more difficult to overcome their characteristic problems. But when they do, their development is revolutionary — they make an abrupt change for the better. The development of the secondary types is more gradual, or evolutionary, as they move around the Enneagram. The secondary types have farther to go, but they change less abruptly as they integrate from type to type in their Direction of Integration.

So, from one point of view, there is an advantage to being one of the primary types, since they can potentially become integrated more quickly than the secondary types. But from another point of view, there is an advantage to being a secondary type, because integration is more gradual and therefore less daunting. However, no matter how you look at it, there is no absolute advantage to being either a primary or secondary type since the goal for everyone is the same: to integrate all their healthy potentials. It does not matter where on the Enneagram you begin this process.

The process of integration is never ending: the Enneagram is as open ended as human nature itself. We are able to grow constantly in an upward spiral of self-transformation without ever reaching a final point of perfection or complete wholeness, something which this interpretation of the Enneagram certainly does not promise. Perfection and wholeness are ideals which beckon us onward; they are not states we can ever fully attain.

On the other hand, while we can continue to integrate as long as we live, it seems that no one goes through all the stages of deterioration in the Direction of Disintegration. Before an individual could do so, he or she would have had such a complete breakdown that a profound psychotic break with reality, or death, would probably have occurred first. In other words, deterioration is self-limiting because when people disintegrate psychologically, and usually physically as well, they simply cannot go on endlessly getting worse. Schizophrenics finally burn out, exhausting themselves mentally and physically; depressives may well commit suicide; hysterics may have serious accidents. In different ways and for different reasons they all reach dead ends, and if they do not get the help they need, they either languish in the vacuum of psychosis or die.

The potential for healthy development is not so limited: as long as we live we can become more integrated persons. While we will never become totally free from the limitations of human nature, we can become less oppressed by them.

The Wing

We have seen that no one is a pure personality type. Everyone is a mixture of two types — the basic type and the wing — which are adjacent on the circumference of the Enneagram. The wing's influence accounts for a great deal of the variety we see in daily life among different people.

You may also recall that the wing is only *one* of the two types on either side of your basic personality type. For example, a Five has either a Six-wing or a Four-wing, but not both. A Three has either a Four-wing or a Two-wing, but, again, not both. Once you have determined your basic personality type (or that of someone else), the next step is to determine which wing you have. You can do this by the process of elimination: one of the two possible wings will be a better fit than the other.

There are several refinements we can now make about the wing. The wing is one of the two personality types *adjacent* to the main type — the wing does not lie somewhere else on the Enneagram. A person cannot be a Nine with a Four-wing or a Seven with a Two-wing. In real life people are not an arbitrary combination of psychological components. If they were, there would be no overall pattern to their personalities. They would be like characters in a badly written novel whose traits conflict in nonsensical ways. (Traits can be, and are, in conflict with each other, but they cannot be mutually exclusive, like being an honest man and a thief at the same time.) For instance, a combination of the traits of a Seven and a Three in the same person is contradictory, like simultaneously having sight and being blind. Such random mixtures of traits and types do not occur in human beings, so they do not occur in the personality types of the Enneagram.

Our basic personality type and wing result from our orientation to our parents and represent various possible identifications with the mother, the father, or both parents. These combinations cannot be contradictory, which they would be if the basic type and the wing were an arbitrary combination of types on the Enneagram. For example, no one can be a Seven with a Three-wing because such a combination would have contradictory attitudes toward the mother. The Seven is negative to the mother; the Three is positive to the mother. Their basic motivations are different: Sevens want to achieve happiness by having a wide range of possessions and experiences. Sevens are not fundamentally oriented to people. Threes, on the other hand, are oriented to people and want their value to be affirmed by others. You simply do not find someone who is both related and not related to people in the same person. Moreover, the whole spectrum of traits of Sevens and Threes is quite different, and a description of this combination cannot be found in the psychiatric literature. Nor can any such person be found in daily life because the mixture of the traits of the Seven and the Three does not exist in real people. On the other hand, this is not true of a Seven with a Six-wing or a Seven with an Eight-wing. The materialistic Seven may have a secondary motivation of wanting to be secure (the Six-wing) or a desire for power and independence (the Eight-wing). Sevens with a Six-wing are negative toward their mothers and positive toward their fathers; Sevens with an Eight-wing are negative toward their mothers and ambivalent toward their fathers — orientations which are consistent with each other.

Since a complete explanation of the parental orientations for all eighteen subtypes is extremely complicated, we will go no further into them here. On this point alone, however, the Enneagram indicates the main patterns of personality by categorizing people as they really are. The structure of the Enneagram itself, the nine personality types, and the interrelationships of the personality types are not arbitrary. They are unified in a system of amazing complexity and simplicity.

Another point about the wings is worth discussing in some detail. Close observation indicates that among persons *of the same basic type and wing*, the proportion of the wing to the basic type varies significantly. In analyzing someone, it is necessary to identify the wing and to estimate the proportion of the wing to the basic type. For example, two individuals who are Eights with a Nine-wing will have similar personalities, but there will still be noticeable differences between them. These differences are partially attributable to the "amount" of Nine which each of the Eights has in his or her overall personality. One of the Eights with a Nine-wing may have virtually a 51 percent to 49 percent split (speaking in crude numerical terms) between Eight and Nine, which means that the person has a very high proportion of wing to the basic type. The other Eight may have very little Nine-wing, say 85 percent to 15 percent, in which case, the Nine component, while discernible, is not a very significant part of the overall personality.

The exact proportion of the wing to the basic type is probably impossible to measure objectively. It is possible, nevertheless, to make gross estimates of the proportion of the wing to the basic type along the following lines: if an individual has a high proportion of wing to basic type, we can say that he or she has a "heavy" wing. If the wing is discernible but the basic type markedly dominates the overall personality, we can say that the person has a "moderate" wing. And if the basic type so dominates the overall personality that the wing is negligible, we can say that the person has a "light" wing. Note that in every case, the basic type must, by definition, make up at least 51 percent of the overall personality. One of the two types *always* dominates the personality as a whole. There is no such thing in personalities as a true fifty-fifty split between the wing and the basic type, since then there would be no way of telling which was the basic type.

It is worth making these sorts of distinctions about the wing because when you look at the eighteen major subtypes of the

Enneagram — the nine basic types with two wings per type — you can see that we are actually no longer talking about eighteen subtypes, but about fifty-four subtypes when we consider heavy, moderate, and light wing proportions to the basic type. And if you were to take the wing's precise influence into consideration — 99 percent to 1 percent, 98 percent to 2 percent, 97 percent to 3 percent, and so forth — you can see that the Enneagram can account for literally hundreds of subtypes, far more than in any other typology.

Theoretically, the most accurate way to describe the personality types would be to describe each major subtype as a discrete category. Instead of nine descriptive chapters in this book there would be eighteen, because there is no such thing as, for example, a pure One. There are only Ones with a Two-wing and Ones with a Nine-wing, and so forth. But because the proportion of the wing to the basic type can vary so widely, describing all the subtypes would be nearly impossible. No book can take every variation into account. This is why it is so important for you to personalize the descriptions yourself.

The Continuum of Traits

As noted in the Guidelines and the descriptions, there is an overall structure to each personality type. The analysis of each type began with a description of its healthy traits, then moved to its average traits, and then its unhealthy traits. That structure is the Continuum of Traits which forms each type. The great fluidity of human nature — the way people change from day to day and even from moment to moment — can, at least in part, be attributed to the fact that we constantly move along the Continuum of our personality traits.

Although psychologists have thought that personality traits could be arranged along a Continuum of some sort, since the basic personality types themselves were not clear, it was impossible to know where to assign most of the traits. With the help of the Enneagram, we are now in a position to do so with some accuracy. We will now make a few refinements about the Continuum.

You will recall that the Continuum for each of the basic personality types looks like this:

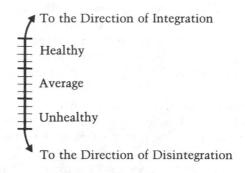

To the Direction of Integration

Healthy

Average

Unhealthy

To the Direction of Disintegration

The Continuum of Traits

The nine different Levels are unnumbered in the descriptions, but if you go back to those chapters, you will see that they are clearly marked and that they serve as signposts for what is happening to the personality type as it deteriorates along the Continuum. If you count from the beginning of the analysis, you will find nine Levels of Development, namely, Levels 1 to 3 in the healthy part of the analysis, Levels 4 to 6 in the average part, and Levels 7 to 9 in the unhealthy part. The ability to specify which Level someone is at is helpful for a number of reasons.

First, the precision it is possible to achieve with the Levels of Development enables us to distinguish further subtypes within each personality type. People of the same personality type (and wing and proportion of wing) can still be quite different because they are at different Levels. For example, a contentious, reductionistic Five (the Five at Level 6) is quite different from the healthy, perceptive Five (at Level 2). Or a domineering Two (at Level 8) is quite different from the nurturing Two (at Level 3).

Each of the nine Levels of Development produces nine distinct subtypes which are closely interrelated since they comprise the personality type as a whole. As we will see in the Theory chapter, other personality typologies describe many of the same personality subtypes as those of the Enneagram. But because of similarities among the different subtypes, other theorists have often confused them. For example, Karen Horney describes one personality type as a "resigned type" and another as the "well-adjusted automaton." From the point of view of the Enneagram, we can see that these are not actually two distinct personality types, but two subtypes of personality type Nine — the "well-adjusted automaton" is the average Nine ("the passively disengaged person" at Level 5), while the "resigned type" is also the average Nine ("the resigned fatalist" at Level 6). Many of the categories used by psychologists are really descriptions of one or two Levels of a personality type rather than the type as a whole. Thus, for example, the "depressive personality disorder" is really the Four at Levels 7 and 8, "the alienated depressive" and "the emotionally tormented person."

Second, keeping the Continuum in mind helps us to understand and describe people more accurately. People are constantly shifting along the Continuum. Different things happen at each of the Levels of Development; different traits and defense mechanisms emerge and combine with already existing traits. Each personality type is constantly changing as it spirals down the Continuum toward neurosis or moves upward toward health and further integration. And, as you might expect, there is an internal symmetry among the traits of each type. Each personality type is not an arbitrary collection of traits but a dynamic whole having an internal structure with many interrelated parts.

For example, in healthy Fours self-awareness emerges at Level 2. But by Level 5, self-awareness has deteriorated into self-absorption, and by Level 8, self-absorption has deteriorated into self-hatred. Or, to give another example from Fours, we can trace their healthy sensitivity into the vulnerability of average Fours and finally to the emotional torment of neurotic Fours. These are but two of many traits in Fours which we can follow down the Continuum, tracking them as they deteriorate into related but different forms. And, of course, we can do this for all the personality types.

It is important to understand that the personality types are not made up of a static group of arbitrary traits. There is an enormous amount of internal coherence within each type, and that coherence is provided by the fact that traits metamorphose into each other as the person shifts up and down the Levels of Development in response to fears and desires, anxiety, and defense mechanisms.

Moreover, there are so many interrelationships within each type, as well as symmetries and interrelationships among the nine personality types themselves, that it would be impossible to provide an adequate commentary on them here. However, to give you a better idea of some of the most important activities at each Level, I have included the following short explanation. If you review any of the analytic sections of the descriptions, you will see how they fit the following patterns.

In the **Healthy** Levels

At Level 1: The type at its healthiest, a state of psychological balance, freedom, and the emergence of special spiritual capacities or virtues. The ideal state for the type prior to going to the Direction of Integration.

At Level 2: The type is still healthy, but the ego and its defenses begin to emerge in response to basic anxieties from childhood. Deepest fears and desires emerge, the result of relationships with parents. Sense of self and the type's cognitive style as a whole manifest themselves.

At Level 3: Still healthy, but less so. The ego is more active, producing a characteristic persona. The healthy social characteristics which the type brings to others and society appear.

In the **Average** Levels

At Level 4: The type has begun to become subtly imbalanced by drawing on its characteristic source of psychic energy, which is different for each type. Each type's unwitting psychological dead end emerges, which, if followed, will create increasing intrapsychic and interpersonal conflicts.

At Level 5: The ego inflates as the type tries to control the environment in characteristic ways. Defense mechanisms become more serious. A marked turning point in the deterioration of the type; traits noticeably less healthy, more negative. Conflicts with others increase.

At Level 6: The person begins to overcompensate for conflicts and increasing anxieties. Characteristic forms of self-centeredness emerge. Conflicts with others inevitable as various forms of self-ishness are acted upon.

In the **Unhealthy** Levels

At Level 7: The person employs an unhealthy survival tactic, different for each type, in a desperate attempt to bolster the ego, which is assailed by increasing anxiety. Serious interpersonal conflicts now.

At Level 8: Serious intrapsychic conflicts and resulting delusional defenses employed. Attempts to remake reality rather than succumb to it and anxiety. A neurotic state: person getting out of touch with reality in some way, different for each type.

At Level 9: A fully neurotic state. Person out of touch with reality, willing to destroy self and others to save illusions and spare self from the anxiety of realizing what he or she has done. Different forms of immediate or remote self-destructiveness manifest themselves, resulting in serious violence, breakdown, or death.

This short description of what happens at each of the nine Levels of Development does not begin to do justice to them. We might take one example from the personality types to illustrate how the type flows from Level to Level. If you review personality type Eight, you will see that the Eight at its best is the magnanimous hero, then becomes the self-confident person, the constructive leader, the enterprising adventurer, the dominating power broker, the confrontational adversary, the ruthless tyrant, the omnipotent megalomaniac, and finally the violent destroyer. You can see how self-confidence deteriorates into the drive for power and then into delusional megalomania. You can also see that, at its best, the Eight has an enormously positive effect on a large number of people and that, when the Eight is unhealthy, it has just the reverse effect. These and many other interrelationships are discernible when you review the descriptions with these sorts of structural ideas in mind.

It can be absolutely riveting to follow each personality type from its healthiest Level downward as it succumbs to the infuence of its fears and desires, conflicts and defenses, spiraling into the grip of neurosis. Like a morality play, the dissolution of each type has a certain inevitability about it. If each type is not both wise and fortunate, it knowingly and unknowingly falls into the hands of its fears and illusions until it ends in disaster. Thus, the Continuum helps us to have a clarity about human nature which we do not always have in life. The accuracy of its predictions is nonetheless something we can all recognize from our own experience.

The Levels of Development are among the most significant aspects of the personality types. The more you appreciate the fluidity and movement within and between each of the types, the more you will have a sense of the Enneagram as a dynamic symbol and as a reflection of human nature itself.

It is also necessary to take the Levels of Development into consideration because by doing so we can appreciate just how sophisticated and nuanced the Enneagram is as a typology. As you recall, we are able to delineate 18 subtypes from the nine basic personality types and two wings. Adding the three degrees of wing proportion — heavy, medium, and light — to those subtypes gives us 54 subtypes (18 x 3). When we add the nine Levels of Development, it is clear that the Enneagram can account for 486 subtypes (the nine pure types times two wings times heavy, moderate, and light wing proportions times nine Levels of Development). The differences among the 486 subtypes are probably too subtle to describe precisely, although they exist. You will be able to sense them intuitively as you recognize the vast combinations of traits which make up these subtypes.

As you can see, the Enneagram is a unified whole. Each of its parts — the nine personality types — modifies and balances the others in highly complex ways. The view of human nature presented here is not static. Human beings are infinitely variable, and the Enneagram takes this fact into account as much as any intellectual system can.

Experience has shown that ... personalities ... may be grouped into various major categories, and for purposes of studying them this is a helpful device. Classifications must never be taken too seriously — they ruin much thinking — but the fear to use them has prevented much more thinking.

— Karl A. Menninger, *The Human Mind*

Chapter 14

The Theory of the Enneagram

THE ENNEAGRAM is by no means the first personality typology. The search for an accurate typology has gone on for thousands of years, beginning with the Greek philosophers, if not earlier. Galen (130? — 200?) is credited with popularizing Hippocrates' theory of the four bodily humors: the melancholic, choleric, phlegmatic, and sanguine temperaments, depending on the predominance of one of the major fluids of the body, black bile, yellow bile, phlegm, and blood, respectively. The theory of the four temperaments was used for fifteen hundred years, until the scientific inquiries of the Enlightenment gradually discredited it. Nevertheless, this ancient system continues to play a role in our language and culture because it conveys a useful insight into human nature.

Popular intuition and an informal consensus among psychologists have always maintained that personality types exist in some form. The problem for psychologists has been to find the proper categories for each fundamental type, however many there may be, so that each is discrete, meaningful, useful, and comprehensive.

Traits from one type should not overlap with traits from another, yet there are obviously similarities between types which must be accounted for. Each basic personality type must describe people in ways meaningful to them, or at least meaningful to specialists, and where possible, it should be scientifically verifiable. A useful personality typology would be one which laymen as well as professionals could use in daily life and in therapeutic situations. A comprehensive typology would account for as much of the variety in human personality as possible, from healthy, to average, to neurotic, and to psychotic states.

The Enneagram's remarkable properties suggest that this symbol presents us with discrete, meaningful, useful, and comprehensive fundamental categories. The Enneagram seems to divide personality types into the categories we find in daily life. It is so comprehensive that it can act as a framework for other typologies, in many cases completing them. The fundamentals of the Enneagram as a system are easy to grasp and meaningful: people see themselves and their friends in it. And the Enneagram is useful because it helps deepen our self-understanding and our understanding of others.

In short, the Enneagram rings true. The more accurate a typology is, the more we are justified in feeling that the categories it employs are not artificially imposed on human nature but reflect something real in human nature itself. We feel that the categories have been discovered rather than invented.

If this is so, what explanation do we have for the Enneagram? How can we account for its accuracy? Is it really the typology psychology has been searching for? Because the answers to these questions are abstract and complex, I have waited until now to examine the theory of the Enneagram in some detail.

We will look at the theory of the Enneagram in two parts: first, to compare the Enneagram with other typologies, and second, to examine the abstract reasons why the Enneagram works as it does.

The Enneagram and Other Typologies

The Enneagram's many remarkable properties will become even more evident when we compare it with the typologies of Karen Horney, Sigmund Freud, Carl Jung, and the pathological categories employed in psychiatry. Although these comparisons are necessarily brief, I hope to indicate that the Enneagram is not only consistent with modern psychological systems, but suggests ways to clarify some of the obscurities in those systems.

KAREN HORNEY AND THE ENNEAGRAM

On the basis of her clinical observations, the psychoanalyst Karen Horney (1885–1952) suggested that there are three general neurotic "solutions": "moving away from people" (the *withdrawn* types), "moving against people" (the *aggressive* types), and "moving toward people" (the *compliant* types). These general neurotic solutions are a helpful way of categorizing personality types in a very broad, yet accurate way.*

We have seen that the Triads are dialectically related to each other as problem areas of feeling, doing, and relating. Another dialectical relationship exists at the level of analysis introduced by Horney's interpersonal concepts. We can correlate her three solutions with the nine personality types of the Enneagram. If we place her three designations on the Enneagram, we see that each Triad is a mixed group of personality types. Each Triad is a "mixed Triad," with each Triad having one of Horney's three solutions represented in it. Each Triad is composed of an aggressive type (that is, it "moves against others"), a compliant type (that is, it "moves toward oth-

* See Karen Horney, *Our Inner Conflicts*, 14–18. Horney devotes one chapter to each solution. I also highly recommend her *Neurosis and Human Growth*, in which she develops these three styles under the headings "the expansive solutions" (corresponding to the "moving against" or aggressive types); "the self-effacing solution" (corresponding to the "moving toward" or compliant types); and "resignation" (corresponding to the "moving away from" or withdrawn types).

ers"), and a withdrawn type (that is, it "moves away from others"), as illustrated below.

In each Triad, we can interpret these designations as follows:

In the Feeling Triad
Twos are compliant to their self-image of being all-good.
Threes are aggressive (i.e., competitive) toward other people.
Fours are withdrawn, not expressing their feelings directly.

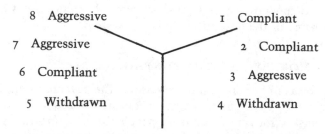

9 Withdrawn

8 Aggressive   1 Compliant

7 Aggressive   2 Compliant

6 Compliant   3 Aggressive

5 Withdrawn   4 Withdrawn

Horney's Neurotic Solutions and the Enneagram

In the Doing Triad
Fives are withdrawn, away from action, into the world of thought.
Sixes are compliant to (i.e., dependent on) an authority figure.
Sevens are aggressive about satisfying their appetites.

In the Relating Triad
Eights are aggressively forceful about getting their way.
Nines are withdrawn (i.e., self-effacing) about self-development.
Ones are compliant to the ideals after which they strive.

In looking at the nine Enneagram personality types, we can see that three are *withdrawn*: Fours, Fives, and Nines. Three are *compliant*: Ones, Twos, and Sixes. And three are *aggressive*: Threes, Sevens, and Eights. Grouping the nine personality types this way reveals *a new set of symmetries*, new groups of three, which have properties in common. What is significant about this is that the Triads of Feeling, Doing, and Relating are not the only "triadic" relationships in the Enneagram. There are others, which we will begin to discover, as illustrated below.

We will see these new groups later in this chapter in different contexts. It is worth noting in passing that while Horney did not work out nine personality types herself, her clinical observations brought her to the brink of doing so. She briefly described the three subtypes in the "expansive solution" (the aggressive types which "move against" others and the environment) as the "narcissistic," the "perfectionistic," and the "arrogant-vindictive" types.*

Horney did not work out the subtypes of the "self-effacing" solution (the compliant types which "move toward" others, essentially searching for love). Nevertheless, her discussion includes elements of what we would consider to be Enneagram types Two, Six, and Nine. While I agree that the Two and Six are compliant types, the Nine is more accurately conceived of as a withdrawn, rather than as a compliant, type, although there are superficial elements of apparent compliance to others in the Nine, as my description of this type indicates.

Horney also attempted to work out the subtypes of the "resigned" solution (the withdrawn types which "move away from" others in a search for inner freedom). She discusses what we would consider to be the personality type Nine (the "persistently resigned" subtype), the Five ("the rebellious group"), and the Four (the "shallow living" group). This last group she subdivides further into three other forms: one with "the emphasis on fun" (corresponding to Enneagram type Seven), one where "the emphasis is on prestige or opportunistic success" (which corresponds to Enneagram type Three), and a third form called "the well-adapted automaton" (which corresponds to the average to unhealthy Nine).†

It would take a much longer analysis to compare and contrast Horney's types with those of the Enneagram thoroughly. Since space does not allow this, I will only repeat my belief that Horney was independently on the way to discovering a three-times-three personality typology. Unfortunately, she was inconsistent about the

---

* See Horney, *Neurosis and Human Growth*, 193 ff. These three types correspond to the Enneagram Three, One, and Eight, respectively. I differ with Horney's listing of the "perfectionistic" type (the One) as aggressive. While the perfectionistic type has aggressive elements, its compliance to ideals forms the basis of its motivation, not the aggrandizement of its ego or its aggressive behavior as such.

† See ibid., 281 ff.

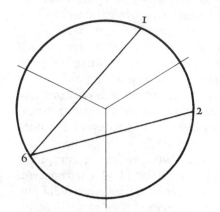

The Compliant Types
One, Two, and Six

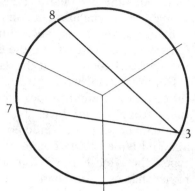

The Aggressive Types
Three, Seven, and Eight

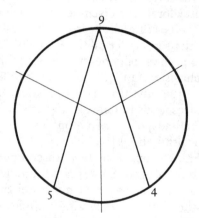

The Withdrawn Types
Four, Five and Nine

Other Triadic Relationships

number of subcategories she employed, and she created separate categories for what is really the same personality type at different Levels of Development. Nevertheless, I believe that the correspondence between the Enneagram types and her "withdrawn," "compliant," and "aggressive" types is very much worth noting since it reveals useful insights.

FREUD AND THE ENNEAGRAM

The nine personality types of the Enneagram correlate to Freudian categories and to character types based on Freudian concepts. Naturally, a full discussion of Freud's ideas, and those of his many followers, is beyond the scope of this book. Nevertheless, two approaches to the Enneagram based on Freudian concepts are worth exploring in some detail, since Freud is so important to psychology and psychiatry.

Freud theorized that there are three areas of fixation for libido — psychic energy of a specifically sexual nature — during our childhood development, which he called the three "psychosexual" stages. He maintained that libido could be fixated around the mouth (the "oral" stage), around the anus during toilet training (the "anal" stage), or around the genitals (the "phallic" stage). What happens at these stages has not been fully worked out, and the language used to describe each resulting "character type" varies from writer to writer. There is also some inconsistency in the basic categories themselves. Some authorities give only two subtypes at the oral stage, while others describe three subtypes at the anal and phallic stages. Some talk of the "oral-dependent" type for those who are fixated with sucking and the "oral-sadistic" type for those at the oral-biting stage. Thus, we are given dependent and sadistic oral types, but no anal-dependent or anal-sadistic types. Among the anal types, there are the "anal-expulsive" and the "anal-retentive" types — but no "anal-receptive" type, and so forth. It becomes very confusing.

The problem is that while Freud and others agreed upon three psychosexual stages (oral, anal, and phallic), they were inconsistent about the other variables involved. There was no consistency about whether the oral, anal, or phallic fixation points were modified by dependent, retentive, expulsive, receptive, or sadistic traits. Perhaps the Freudian categories may be clarified as follows. In Freudian terms, there are three general dispositions of psychic energy at each of the libidinal stages: receptive, retentive, and expulsive — that is, we can think of them as a dialectic of three dispositions of energy. The oral, anal, and phallic points of libidinal fixation also form a dialectic among themselves. Thus, we have two dialectical groups of three, producing nine "Freudian" character types. Had they been worked out in this manner, these neo-Freudian psychosexual dialectics would consist of the categories shown in Table 14.1.

Oral		Receptive
Anal	×	Retentive
Phallic		Expulsive

Table 14.1. **Neo-Freudian Psychosexual Categories**

If we go through the permutations, the resulting nine personality types are the oral-receptive (corresponding to the Nine), the oral-retentive (corresponding to the Four), the oral-expulsive (corresponding to the Five); the anal-receptive (corresponding to the Six), the anal-retentive (corresponding to the One), and the anal-expulsive (corresponding to the Two); the phallic-receptive (corresponding to the Three), the phallic-retentive (corresponding to the Seven), and the phallic expulsive (corresponding to the Eight). If we arrange them in the order of the Enneagram, as below, we can see the patterns which emerge.

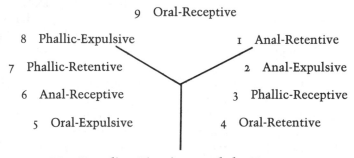

9 Oral-Receptive

8 Phallic-Expulsive   1 Anal-Retentive

7 Phallic-Retentive   2 Anal-Expulsive

6 Anal-Receptive   3 Phallic-Receptive

5 Oral-Expulsive   4 Oral-Retentive

Neo-Freudian Fixations and the Enneagram

It is difficult to see how these designations can be taken as more than vaguely symbolic language for psychological processes and not as literal fixations of libido around the mouth, anus, or penis. Nevertheless, many orthodox Freudians take these designations literally, which may be why they have so much trouble applying them to real life. If, however, we take these designations as *metaphors*, they do hold clues to the traits of the personality types involved. Furthermore, if we consider the Freudian terminology metaphorically, we do not get into the problem of applying phallic terminology to women, nor do we have to find a literal meaning for a peculiar designation such as the phallic-receptive type.

To give a few examples, my so-called phallic-receptive type actually corresponds to a character type (the urethral character*) proposed by Ernest Jones, a close associate of Freud, as well as to the Enneagram personality type Three. This type of male narcissistically invites admiration of his body (phallus) from others, and is often sexually exhibitionistic. It is clearly preferable to use the Enneagram designation, personality type Three, rather than the phallic-receptive type or even the urethral character for women or for anyone whose problems involve narcissism rather than a fixation of libido around the genitals. Is narcissism better understood as the unconscious desire to have one's genitals admired, or to have one's self admired? Even if a strictly Freudian interpretation could be shown to be the ultimate truth, such an interpretation is usually so far out of the range of normal awareness and behavior as to be all but meaningless. It seems better to work on overcoming one's inflated self-love, for example, than to reduce narcissism to the desire to have one's genitals admired.

The classic Freudian anal type (or more properly, the anal-retentive type) is characterized by frugality, obstinacy, and orderliness, which aptly describe elements of the personality type One, although they are more accurately traits of a One with a Nine-wing. However, certain elements of frugality are also found in the Six — another anal type — resulting from its caution and insecurity. The Six is also obstinate — negativistic and passive-aggressively blocking others — although, in a different way, so is the Nine — stubbornly refusing to deal with reality. Thus, there are a

* Otto Fenichel, *The Psychoanalytic Theory of Neurosis,* 492.

number of personality types in which the classic anal traits can be distinguished.

To give one last example, the oral-receptive type corresponds to the Nine, the type which optimistically believes that the environment will provide its needs like milk flowing from its mother's breast without much effort on its part. Freudians call this the oral-dependent type, although Nines are so self-effacing and accommodating to others that, more than "depend" on others, they virtually live through them — so "receptive" is a more accurate designation.

These and other subtle but useful distinctions can be helpful to clarify the Freudian categories so commonly used in psychology and psychiatry. Other useful meanings can be worked out if you think of the Freudian psychosexual designations as a symbolic shorthand for the overall style of the personality types rather than as categories which result from libidinal fixation points occurring during early childhood. If you review the descriptions of the personality types with this in mind, you will see how my reworking of the Freudian psychosexual designations applies to the other types of the Enneagram.

You will also note that the new triadic relationships I pointed out among Horney's types correlate to my neo-Freudian libidinal types. The three oral types (the Enneagram Four, Five, and Nine) in my neo-Freudian system are the withdrawn types according to my modification of Horney's typology. The anal types (the Enneagram One, Two, and Six) in my neo-Freudian system are the compliant types in Horney's typology, and the phallic types (the Enneagram Three, Seven, and Eight) in Freud's system are the aggressive types in Horney's typology.

FREUDIAN STRUCTURAL CONCEPTS

Freudian "structural" terminology can also be applied to the Enneagram types, depending on whether the ego, id, or superego in each of the nine basic personality types is the focus of its problem area. I have added Horney's terms to the Freudian structural terms in the illustration below.

Notice that the types whose principal imbalance is in their egos also correspond to Horney's withdrawn types, that the types whose imbalances are in their ids are the aggressive types, and that the types whose imbalances are in their superegos are the compliant types. These designations are meaningful even from a commonsense

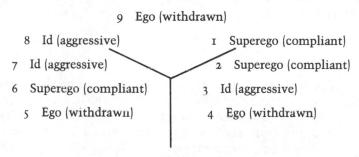

9   Ego (withdrawn)

8   Id (aggressive)   1   Superego (compliant)

7   Id (aggressive)   2   Superego (compliant)

6   Superego (compliant)   3   Id (aggressive)

5   Ego (withdrawn)   4   Ego (withdrawn)

Structural Concepts and the Enneagram

point of view. For example, aggressive people are dominated in some way by the instinctual energies of the id. These interrelationships can be further interpreted as follows.

Fours, Fives, and Nines are all *withdrawn* from the direct expression of their egos, compensating in characteristic ways: Fours by dissociating from reality through their imaginations, Fives by dissociating from reality through their all-engrossing thought processes, and Nines by dissociating from reality through an intense identification with another.

Ones, Twos, and Sixes are all *compliant* to an internalization of someone or something in their superegos which exerts a dominant influence in their behavior. Ones are compliant to their idealistic obligations which are impressed on them by their superegos. Twos are compliant to the demand of their superegos that they always be loving; and Sixes are compliant to an authority figure they have internalized through their superegos.

Threes, Sevens, and Eights are all *aggressive*, that is, their ids are aggressively oriented to various aspects of their environments. Threes are aggressive (competitive) toward other people to whom they seek to compare themselves favorably. Sevens are aggressive (acquisitive) toward their environment, from which they try to obtain more satisfactions for themselves; and Eights are aggressive (self-assertive) toward their environment, constantly trying to project themselves in the environment so that it will become a reflection of them.

We will see these Freudian structural concepts (ego, id, superego) in the next section of this chapter when we analyze why the Enneagram works.

JUNG AND THE ENNEAGRAM

The nine personality types of the Enneagram can also be correlated to the eight "psychological types" of the Jungian typology. In the descriptions of each personality type, I correlated a Jungian type to the Enneagram type and gave a relevant quotation from Jung.

To review Jung's system for a moment, Jung posited that there are two general psychological *attitudes* (extroversion and introversion) and four psychological *functions* (thinking, feeling, intuition, and sensation). This two-times-four scheme produces eight psychological types — the extroverted thinking type, the introverted thinking type, the extroverted feeling type, the introverted feeling type, and so forth.

As you can see, the problem with correlating the eight Jungian types to the nine types of the Enneagram is that the Enneagram has one more personality type than the Jungian typology, so a one-to-one equivalence might not exist between the two systems. However, a careful reading of Jung's descriptions indicates that these two systems correspond, some very closely, some only in part. In the broadest terms:

The One corresponds to the extroverted thinking type.
The Two corresponds to the extroverted feeling type.
The Three does not correspond to any Jungian type.
The Four corresponds to the introverted intuitive type.
The Five corresponds to the introverted thinking type.
The Six corresponds to the introverted feeling type.
The Seven corresponds to the extroverted sensation type.
The Eight corresponds to the extroverted intuitive type.
The Nine corresponds to the introverted sensation type.

Table 14.2. **The Jungian Correlations**

If you consult Jung's *Psychological Types*, you will see how his eight types correspond to my descriptions of the Enneagram types, except for the Three. A close reading of Jung will reveal, however, that sections of the descriptions of several of his types do in fact correspond to Enneagram type Three. While Jung did not have a separate category for the Three, he must have been aware of this personality type from his clinical and personal experience. In a sense then, Jung inadvertently described some elements of the Three without considering this type as a separate psychological entity, something which would have thrown off the symmetry of his two-times-four theoretical framework.

There is also a certain poetic appropriateness to the fact that the Three (whose personality is so unfixed and changeable) does not correspond to one of the Jungian types. As the most adaptable of the personality types, the Three is treated in several of the Jungian types without having a category of its own.

Besides its not being comprehensive enough, there are several other problems with Jung's descriptions, which I can only mention briefly here. Unfortunately, not all of Jung's descriptions are equally insightful, and it is not always easy to understand what he is trying to describe. It is something of a paradoxical truism to say that once you understand what Jung means, you know what he means. You have to get "inside" each of his descriptions to know what he is talking about. Here again the Enneagram can help.

From the point of view of the Enneagram, we can see that Jung usually describes some of the traits of the average person of each psychological type, freely ranging around what we would consider to be the Levels of Development. He intuitively shifts to the Direction of Disintegration at the end of each of his descriptions when he mentions neurotic and psychotic developments. Occasionally, however, he confuses traits of one type with those of another, as when, for example, he describes elements of Enneagram type Nine as if they belong to the introverted feeling type (Enneagram type Six). There are also confusions between other types, for example, between elements of the extroverted and introverted thinking types (Enneagram types One and Five, respectively). There are other confusions as well.

These are fine points, but they are significant. While people have sensed that Jung's descriptions point to something true, they have also found it difficult to translate his descriptions into fuller accounts of each type, which is not surprising because Jung was unclear about several of them himself.

PSYCHIATRIC DESIGNATIONS AND THE ENNEAGRAM

The Enneagram personality types also correlate with the personality disorders of the third edition of the *Diagnostic and Statistical Manual of Mental Disorders*, informally referred to as DSM-III. This highly technical book is considered the primary reference work for psychiatrists and others in the mental health field, bringing together the current state of the art about personality syndromes from the clinical point of view. As you would expect, the terminology adopted in the DSM-III is pathologically oriented and, as you might *not* expect, it sometimes seems rather arbitrary. There has been a lot of disagreement within the psychiatric community about the DSM-III categories for the personality disorders, although there is little agreement about how they can be revised. Perhaps the Enneagram can throw light on the psychiatric personality disorders by sorting out the basic personality types, which, after all, are what become disordered when people become neurotic.

One of the main problems with the DSM-III is that its compilers erroneously, albeit understandably, combine traits from one personality type with another, with the result that the brief schematic descriptions they offer are sometimes confusing. For example, the DSM-III designates a "histrionic" type to get away from the older designation of the "hysterical" type. However, the description the DSM-III offers of the "histrionic" personality disorder combines elements of Enneagram personality types Two and Seven, both of which are clearly histrionic, although in different ways and for different reasons. The Two may best be thought of as histrionic in the ordinary sense of the word because it displays its emotions theatrically. If neurotic, the Two deteriorates into hysterical conversion reactions in which anxiety is translated directly into physical symptoms and illnesses. On the other hand, the Seven is histrionic in the sense that it is flamboyant and impulsive, acting out its emotions rather than controlling them. The Seven also becomes hysterical, but as the result of panic reactions to anxiety attacks. Thus, while there are genuine similarities between these two types, a review of the descriptions of them in this book indicates that they are two distinct personality types. Their traits should not be lumped together into the single histrionic type of the DSM-III.

Space limitations prevent me from going into a full comparison between the official DSM-III psychiatric types and the Enneagram personality types. For the sake of completeness, however, and to indicate from yet another viewpoint how the Enneagram personality types are not only reinforced by modern psychiatry, but how the Enneagram can help psychiatry, I will simply list the general correspondences between the personality disorders in the DSM-III and the personality types of the Enneagram. The following should be taken only as the roughest of approximations, since a great many distinctions would have to be made to sort out the correspondences in any clear-cut way.

Type One corresponds to the Compulsive Personality Disorder.

Type Two partly corresponds to the Histrionic Personality Disorder.

Type Three corresponds to the Narcissistic Personality Disorder.

Type Four corresponds to the Avoidant Personality Disorder.

Type Five corresponds partly to the Paranoid Personality Disorder and partly to the Schizotypal Personality Disorder.

Type Six corresponds partly to the Passive-Aggressive Personality Disorder and partly to the Dependent Personality Disorder.

Type Seven corresponds partly to the Manic-Depressive Personality Disorder and partly to the Histrionic Personality Disorder.

Type Eight corresponds to the Antisocial Personality Disorder.

Type Nine corresponds partly to the Dependent Personality Disorder and partly to the Passive-Aggressive Personality Disorder.

Table 14.3. **The DSM-III Correlations**

Analyzing the Enneagram

What, then, is the theoretical basis for the Enneagram as a psychological system? Why, for example, are there nine basic personality types and not eight, ten, twelve, or some other number? What is the basis for each of the individual personality types? Is the Enneagram an ancient typology which is a precursor to essentially Freudian ideas? Or is it really a Jungian typology or one which foreshadows the ideas of Karen Horney or some other psychologist? A complete discussion of these questions is so complex and abstract that I can offer only some preliminary answers.

Let me give you my conclusion first. Even though I will present several explanations of the Enneagram, it seems that, in the final analysis, there is no single theoretical explanation why the Enneagram works as it does. No one underlying theory is the sole basis for the Enneagram. It cannot be reduced solely to Freudian, Jungian, or Hornevian concepts. If you approach the Enneagram from a Freudian point of view, you will find that it can accommodate Freudian ideas. If you look at the Enneagram from a Jungian or a Hornevian viewpoint, you will find that it can be used to represent those ideas as well. This in itself suggests that the Enneagram is a universal psychological symbol, one which can accommodate many different interpretations while retaining its unique character.

True, not everything in other psychological systems can be placed on the Enneagram, and some aspects of modern psychological systems contradict each other and cannot be reconciled. Nevertheless, the Enneagram is able to organize many common discoveries because it operates at a number of levels of abstraction while allowing a great deal of specificity. We can approach the Enneagram on many different levels, and each approach we make to it yields some new insight.

Human beings can be analyzed from a broad spectrum of viewpoints, each revealing and illuminating one facet of the whole. Human beings can be interpreted biologically, psychologically, sociologically, historically, as physical objects by physicists, and as spiritual beings by theologians. But just as there is no one all-encompassing explanation for human nature, there is no one all-encompassing explanation for the Enneagram. We cannot say that the Enneagram is a Freudian system, because it accounts for more than Freudian ideas. Nor is it a Jungian or a Hornevian system or a system belonging to any other school of thought. It is itself: a comprehensive, dynamic symbol of the human psyche.

Since we cannot reduce the Enneagram to any single psychological explanation, we will look at several different approaches by which we can understand it better. I will interpret the Enneagram from a dialectical approach, a developmental approach, and a Freudian dynamic approach.

A DIALECTICAL APPROACH

The reason why there are nine personality types in the Enneagram is that its structure is the result of a three-times-three arrangement, or two dialectically related groups of three. No matter which level of analysis we may wish to take toward the Enneagram, we find that the dialectically related factors produce nine distinct personality categories.

If there is a single explanation of why the Enneagram works as it does, and why it is such a comprehensive system, it is because the Enneagram is a dialectical system, and as such it can be used to analyze different aspects of human nature dialectically.

On this, the most basic level of analysis — one which has been seen in the Guidelines and throughout the descriptions — the Enneagram can be thought of as an arrangement of three Triads containing three different personality types. Each Triad is a dialectic of the problem of that Triad. In each Triad, one type has overdeveloped the characteristic faculty of the Triad, another has underdeveloped the faculty, and a third is most out of touch with the faculty.

When we apply this pattern to the types in the Feeling Triad, we see that Twos overdevelop their feelings, expressing only their positive emotions while repressing their negative ones. Threes are most out of touch with their feelings, projecting an image to others as a substitute. Fours underdevelop the expression of their feelings, revealing themselves through some form of art or aesthetic living.

In the Doing Triad, Fives underdevelop their ability to do. They substitute thinking for doing. Sixes are the most out of touch with their ability to act on their own without the approval of an authority of some sort. Sevens overdevelop their ability to do, becoming hyperactive and increasingly manic.

In the Relating Triad, Eights overdevelop their ability to see themselves in relation to their environment. They view themselves as bigger than everyone and everything else. Nines are the most out of touch with their ability to relate to their environment since they identify with another person, living through the other rather than developing themselves. Ones underdevelop their ability to relate to the environment in the sense that they feel less than an ideal which they constantly strive to attain.

When we consider dialectic patterns (of thesis, antithesis, and synthesis), we are always considering interrelated groups of three. In the comparison of the Enneagram types with those of Horney and Freud, we saw several different dialectical groups: Horney's withdrawn, compliant, and aggressive types, Freud's ego, id, and superego, and his oral, anal, and phallic types. It seems that the nature of the dialectic pattern reflects something in the patterns of the mind itself. If there is a single reason why the Enneagram works, this is it.

A DEVELOPMENTAL APPROACH

We can understand why there are nine basic personality types in the Enneagram if we consider them from yet another point of view, that of a child's relations with its parents.

From a developmental point of view, the Enneagram is a universal typology that applies to all people at all times and in all cultures because it delineates the nine possible relationships which everyone can have with his or her parents. Everyone, without exception, has two parents, whether those parents are living or dead, present or absent, good or bad. There are nine basic personality types because there are only nine fundamental orientations which every child can take to his or her parents. Because of the sum total of childhood experiences, including genetic predispositions and environmental factors, everyone eventually adopts one of the following nine general orientations and therefore develops into one of the nine basic personality types.

Everyone's basic personality type is the result of having had a primary orientation to his or her *mother*, or a primary orientation to his or her *father*, or a primary orientation equally to his or her *mother and father*. (Note that this set of three orientations forms a dialectic.) Second, the primary orientation may have been essentially *positive, negative,* or *ambivalent.* (Note that this set of three attitudes is yet another dialectic.) Nine discrete personality types are generated, depending on which parent the child relates to and the quality of that orientation.

Taking this developmental approach, we have another three-times-three pattern which results in nine basic personality types. For example, one child may have had a positive orientation to his mother, while another child may have had an ambivalent relationship to his mother, and a third child may have had a negative orientation to his mother (who, of course, may be the same person in all three instances). The first child would develop into a personality type Three, the second into an Eight, and the third into a Seven. These relationships can be seen more clearly in Table 14.4.

Parent	Kind of Orientation		
	Positive	Ambivalent	Negative
Mother-oriented types	3	8	7
Father-oriented types	6	2	1
Mother-and-father-oriented types	9	5	4

Table 14.4. **Childhood Origins**

As it turns out, this grouping of the personality types is extremely revealing. Reading the table horizontally, you will notice similarities with Horney's system, which we have already seen. The Three-Eight-Seven group (the mother-oriented types) are the personality types which defend themselves aggressively (Horney's "moving against" types). It is very suggestive to reflect on the cultural ramifications of this finding — namely, that the most aggressive members of society are those who related primarily to their mothers during their childhoods. One reason for the rise of violence in our culture may be traced to the high divorce rate and the rearing of many children by their mothers. This and other cultural factors lead to a rise in the number of aggressive personality types in society — narcissistic psychopaths (unhealthy Threes), manic-depressive materialists (unhealthy Sevens), and belligerent antisocial thugs (unhealthy Eights). All three types are infantile in different ways and have active ids in Freudian terms.

Moreover, the Six-Two-One group (the father-oriented types) are the personality types which defend themselves by being compliant

(Horney's "moving toward" types). In general, these are the law-and-order personality types. While compliance dominates the overall picture, they are in fact a mixture of aggressive and compliant tendencies. Under pressure either from others or from anxiety, the law-and-order types tend to explode in destructive behavior. The influence of the father and of internalized prohibitions symbolized by the father create the suspicious, authoritarian personality (the unhealthy Six), the self-righteous punitive character (the unhealthy One), and the guilt-instilling, manipulative type (the unhealthy Two). All three types take the role of authority figures in different ways, since they have internalized the mores of society; in Freudian terms, they also have very active superegos.

Last, the Nine-Five-Four group (the mother-and-father-oriented types) are the personality types which defend themselves by withdrawing (Horney's "moving away" types). They are the loners, intellectuals, and dreamers of society. Because their childhoods produced an orientation to both parents, they have problems interacting with others, since they tend to be overwhelmed by forces either inside or outside themselves. We see the emotionally tormented, self-hating type (the unhealthy Four), the isolated paranoiac (the unhealthy Five), and the traumatized, dissociating person (the unhealthy Nine). All three types tend to dissociate themselves from reality in different ways. In Freudian terms, they have problems with their egos.

It cannot be surprising that a child's orientation to his or her parents is one of the major determinants of personality and that personality types ultimately influence cultural changes, which, in turn, influence how parents raise their children, thus perpetuating the cycle. The person, the family, and the culture are interdependent: there cannot be one without the others. Freudian schools and interpersonal schools may not be so far apart regarding the interrelationship between the individual and society: they simply operate at different levels of analysis.

A DYNAMIC FREUDIAN APPROACH

Freud represented the dynamics of the mind as the interaction of the id, the ego, and the superego. This has been called his "structural hypothesis," which was illustrated on page 329. These character types were never fully described either by Freud or his followers, perhaps for the following reason.

It would be advantageous if psychoanalytic charactcrology were to give us a dynamic classification. However, none of the attempts made hitherto seems to have been successful. Choosing one aspect as the criterion of the division neccssarily neglects other aspects.

The most important of these attempts were instituted by Freud himself. After having subdivided the mind into the categories of id, ego, and superego, he asked whether it would not be possible to distinguish types of human characters according to which of thcsc three authorities is dominant. There may he "erotic" types whose lives are governed by the instinctual demands of their id; "narcissistic" types who feel so dominated by their sense of ego that neither other persons nor demands from the id or the superego can touch them much; and there may be "compulsive" types whose entire lives are regulated by a strict superego that dominates the personality. Freud also described "mixed" types in which a combination of two forces outweigh the third one. . . .

Besides the question whether Freud's descriptions of an "erotic" and a "narcissistic" type correspond to persons whose id or ego is accentuated, there is a more important objection to his suggested typology: Psychoanalysis is essentially a *dynamic* discipline. It evaluates given phenomena as a result of conflicts. . . . A categorization of "id persons," "ego persons," and "superego persons" is not a dynamic concept. What would be characteristic for dynamic types would not be either id or ego or superego but the various interrelationships of id, ego, and superego. That is why Freud's typology has not been used much for the comprehension of neurotic character disordcrs. (Fenichel, *The Psychoanalytic Theory of Neurosis,* 525–526.)

But this is precisely why the Enneagram is able to represent the full range of character, or personality, types. The Enneagram types represent a dynamic interrelationship of the id, ego, and superego.

In each of the resulting nine types, all three of the Freudian functions of the mind interact with each other. It is not necessary to choose "one aspect as the criterion of the division," as Fenichel points out, to the neglect of other aspects. All three aspects of the mind are simultaneously taken into account in each personality type and in the Enneagram as a whole.

Each Triad is dominated by one of the three Freudian categories of the mind, which is why the Triads are characterized as having problems with feeling (id-dominated types), doing (superego-dominated types), or relating (ego-dominated types). In other words, there is a core problem in each Triad: the types of the Feeling Triad have common problems stemming from their ids, the types of the Doing Triad have common problems stemming from their superegos, and the types of the Relating Triad have common problems stemming from their egos. The Freudian designations are shown at the center of the illustration below, within their respective Triads.

In addition to a core problem in each Triad, we discover that each personality type is dominated by one of the Freudian functions of the mind which is in conflict with the core problem of the Triad. For example, the personality type Two is dominated by its superego. If you will recall, the Two's self-esteem was conditional to feeling that it was loved by others for its good works and good intentions. The Two feels guilty when it is unloving, selfish, or aggressive, and so forth. Its superego dominates its mental life, and its id (its aggressive, sexual drives) is also an important part of the picture.

So, to interpret the Freudian dynamics, we would say that the Two's superego and id are in some sort of potential conflict with each other. The Two needs to bring its ego into balance with its superego and id by going to Four (where "ego" is on the circumference of the illustration. On the other hand, if the Two becomes neurotic, and moves to its Direction of Disintegration, it goes to Eight, adding more id forces to its already strong id, with the result that its aggressive impulses become overwhelming and destructive.

Putting these relationships on the Enneagram illustrates them more clearly.

Several other brief examples might help to clarify the usefulness of this interpretation. The Five's ego is in conflict with its superego and needs to go to Eight to bring its psyche into balance with the aid

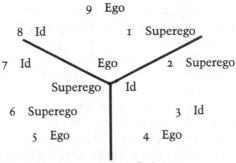

The Freudian Dynamics of the Enneagram

of the id. But, of course, if the Five goes to Seven, it also comes in contact with the id — so there appears to be a problem with id forces in both the Directions of Integration and Disintegration for the Five. This is accurate because the id is precisely what the Five needs to get under control. When a healthy Five integrates to Eight, its id comes into balance with its ego and superego, principally by becoming sublimated (transformed) into genuinely productive work. But when the Five deteriorates and goes to Seven, it becomes increasingly aggressive and impulsive until it virtually flies to pieces. This analysis points out that the id is what the Five most needs to work on in either direction on the Enneagram.

Last, you can see that the particular problem in each Triad is reinforced for the Three, Six, and Nine. These primary types have the most problems with feeling, doing, or relating, and therefore with the id, superego, or ego, respectively. For example, the Three can be characterized as having some sort of special problem with its id, the Six with its superego, and the Nine with its ego. For example, the Three's id problems result in its being most out of touch with its feelings, becoming maliciously hostile when unhealthy. The Six's superego problems result from internalizing the aggressions of authority figures, turning them both outward toward others in belligerence and inward toward itself in masochism. The Nine's ego problems result in its being most out of touch with itself as an individual, eventually becoming inadequate and dissociated from reality.

Let us look at the Three more closely. As you know, the Three is the personality type in the Feeling Triad which is "most out of touch" with its feelings. The Three needs to go first to Six and then to Nine to bring its psyche into balance with the aid of the superego (at Six) and the ego (at Nine). The Three's ego tends to be overdeveloped (narcissistic and exhibitionistic), so a move to Nine would compound this. Clearly, the Three needs to activate its superego (and develop its conscience) first, before it can bring its ego into balance with the rest of its psyche.

This interpretation of the Enneagram accounts for several things: why each type is different, why the Directions of Integration and Disintegration are as they are, and why the Enneagram as a whole is a symbol of each of us. The Enneagram is a universal symbol because our fundamental problems can be thought of as id-related problems, ego-related problems, and superego-related problems. All human beings are affected by all three problem areas, whether we call them by their Freudian names or by the Enneagram names of feeling, relating, and doing.

There is much more to say about all of this — more about the descriptions and more about the theory. Nevertheless, even with this brief exposition, you can see that we can approach the Enneagram types from a number of different avenues.

The reason the Enneagram encompasses so many different psychological viewpoints is that it operates at various levels of abstraction simultaneously — psychosexual stages of fixation, structural areas within the psyche, object relations theory, developmental origins, interpersonal styles, and so forth. There seems to be no one theoretical explanation for why the Enneagram works as it does. It comprehends them all.

The Enneagram is an extraordinary framework for understanding more about ourselves. No matter from which point of view we approach it, we discover fresh conjunctions of new and old ideas. As I mentioned at the beginning of this chapter, this is highly suggestive that the Enneagram is a universal psychological symbol, something discovered rather than invented. What Mendeleyev's periodic table is to physics, the Enneagram may be to psychology — a way of organizing vast complexities in more understandable ways.

Just as the interrelationships between the families of atoms are too complex to have been designed by anyone, the Enneagram is too complex to have been designed by the human mind. Its immense intricacies and suggestiveness — and its paradoxical simplicity — could not have been engineered from a checklist of elements needed for a typology. Rather, the Enneagram seems to be a symbol which reflects the symmetries and irregularities of the mind itself.

Chapter 15

Afterword: A Personal Note

To FACE THE WORLD and the terrifying insecurity of human existence naked and defenseless is an overwhelming situation for anyone to be in. Each of the personality types attempts to buffer itself
from the full realization of the insecurity of its existence in different ways. Each type adopts different strategies for inflating the ego
as a defense against being insecure and alone.

The paradox is that we cannot do otherwise but defend ourselves
from the full awareness of our existence. Human beings are in danger from the mystery of their existence whether they affirm it in
hope or recoil from it in despair. And yet, as we have seen in the
descriptions, if each of the personality types inflates its ego and
pushes its defenses to an extreme, it brings destruction upon itself.
Too much openness to life and we run the risk of being immolated;
too little, and we destroy ourselves from within. Too much freedom
is as threatening as no freedom at all. When all is said and done,
existential anxiety may be the proper response for beings who are
aware of their own mortality. Like Moses before the burning bush,
we quake with terror in the realization that we ultimately stand
before the abyss of being.

There seems to be only one way out of the conundrum: to hope to find a meaning for our lives, a meaning that connects with something real beyond ourselves.

However, we are in the insoluble position of trying to find a meaning for our lives without being able to know our lives as a whole. There is no way to know with certainty what that meaning is without being able to step outside of our life to find its ultimate context. But to step outside of our existence can happen only in the moment of death, when this life has come to an end. In that moment we will either be annihilated or we will realize that we still exist. If we still exist, we will know whether our life has had meaning — and what that meaning is. So much of the mystery and tragedy of existence comes about because we cannot possibly know with certainty what our life means before that decisive moment.

Although the ultimate meaning of life is mysterious, it affects every moment that we live. What we believe about the meaning of life influences what we value and every choice we make. In considering these realities, we move from the psychological to the metaphysical, where the human context ultimately will or will not have meaning. It may be that human existence is absurd because there is no ultimate personal context, only the endless recycling of matter and energy in an impersonal universe. Or it may be that the ultimate context of human life is personal, that there is a God whose existence is the reason for our own. This either is or is not so, and there is no way of knowing which is true while we are still alive. This is why the meaning of life always involves "faith," whether we call it that or not.

We cannot live without some kind of beliefs. If we do not have faith in God, we must have faith in something else. Because we cannot live without meaning, without reference to something outside ourselves, we inevitably create idols as substitutes for faith in the transcendent and the meaning which it supplies. Of course, the supreme and universal idol is pride, the ego inflating itself, attempting to be the cause of its own being, attempting to find its own meaning within its own resources. Each of the personality types is tempted toward a particular form of pride as a way of defending itself against the anxieties involved in its existence. The Nine's temptation is to believe that its tranquillity is an ultimate value, the Eight's is to believe in its own power, the Seven's is to believe that it will find fulfillment in material possessions, the Six's is to believe in the security provided by other people, the Five's is to believe in knowledge as an end in itself, the Four's is to believe in its freedom to do as it pleases, the Three's is to believe in its own excellence, the Two's is to believe in its own importance, and the One's temptation is to believe in its own righteousness. While these temptations are characteristic of each of the personality types, they are all our own temptations, too.

If there is a theme in this book, or a lesson to be learned by studying the personality types, it is that while we legitimately look for happiness by seeking our personal fulfillment, we often seek it wrongly. Every personality type creates a self-fulfilling prophecy, bringing about the very thing it most fears while losing what it most desires as it looks for happiness. If, when we search for happiness, we inflate our ego at the expense of deeper values, we may be sure of failing in our search. The inflation of the ego at the expense of what is genuinely good is folly, leading us into a maze of apparent goods, false goods, and idols. Each personality type contains within itself a source of self-deception which, if played into, invariably leads us away from the direction of our real fulfillment and deepest happiness. This is an irrevocable law of the psyche, something of which we must become convinced if we are to have the courage to look for happiness in the right place and in the right way.

Looking at each of the personality types as a whole teaches us what we can expect if we inflate our ego at the expense of other values. By coercing others to love them, Twos end by being hated. By aggrandizing themselves, Threes end by being rejected. By exclusively following their feelings, Fours end by wasting their lives. By imposing their ideas on reality, Fives end by being out of touch with reality. By being too dependent on others, Sixes end by being abandoned. By living for pleasure, Sevens end by being frustrated and unsatisfied. By dominating others to get what they want, Eights end by destroying everything. By accommodating themselves to others too much, Nines end as undeveloped, fragmented shells. By attempting to be perfect without humanity, Ones end by perverting their humanity. The way out of these inexorable conclusions is to become convinced that only by transcending the ego can we hope to find happiness. As wisdom has always recognized, it is only by dying to ourselves that we find life.

Thus, a related lesson can be drawn from these pages, one which I call the law of psychic retribution. We do not have to expect punishment from the hands of a wrathful God for our wrongdoing. On the contrary, because of the nature of the psyche we bring some kind of punishment on ourselves because we inevitably pay a price for every choice we make. The price we pay may well not be immediately apparent, which is why we so easily fool ourselves into thinking that there will be no consequences for our actions. But the cost to ourselves is always paid in the kind of person we become. By our choices we create ourselves and shape our future, whether that future is ultimately one of happiness or unhappiness.

How, then, can we go about transcending the ego? What would motivate us to do so? How can we know what will really make us happy?

People always seek what they think will be good for them, even if they turn out to have been mistaken in their choice. Some seek wealth, others fame, others security, as each desires to possess that which he or she thinks will bring happiness. But unless we find what is truly good by seeking what we really need, we will be sidetracked into the pursuit of what we desire until we are distracted by merely superficial goods. If people settle for superficialities, they turn the objects of their desires into idols which cannot satisfy. Then they suffer and wonder why.

The strange thing is that, as with our search for the meaning of life, we are in the difficult position of searching for what is truly good for us without having a clear understanding of what it is. Each of the personality types tends to seek what it thinks will be good for it in the wrong places, or in the wrong ways, or both. The Two thinks that it will be happy if it is loved (or worshipped) by others; the Three if it is admired by others; the Four if it can be totally free to be itself; the Five if it can have intellectual certitude; the Six if it has absolute security; the Seven if it can possess all that it wants; the Eight if it can get its way; the Nine if it can merge with someone else; and the One if it is perfect. All these strategies fail because they are only partial goods which have been raised to the status of the prime good in life.

How, then, can the Enneagram help us know what is really good for us? The answer is simple: by pointing out that what each personality type genuinely needs lies in its Direction of Integration.

The difficulty is that before we can move in the Direction of Integration we must first be able to transcend ourselves. We must be willing and able to go beyond ego to reach out to something more, to some value outside ourselves.

Self-transcendence is difficult and fearful because it entails going into unknown territory, feeling, doing, and relating in ways foreign to our personality, contrary to our past habits, at odds with our old attitudes and identity, having begun to overcome the handicaps of our childhood. In a sense, it is a kind of rebirth, the coming into being of a new person who is learning to leave the old ways behind and strike out into a new world.

Yet this is precisely what each personality type must do if it is ever to find real happiness. The Two needs to overcome its tendency toward self-deception by moving toward the self-understanding of the healthy Four. The Three needs to overcome its malicious envy of others by moving toward the loyalty and commitment of the healthy Six. The Four needs to overcome its self-destructive subjectivity by moving toward the objectivity and self-discipline of the healthy One. The Five needs to overcome its nihilism by moving toward the courage of the healthy Eight. The Six needs to overcome its suspicion of others by moving toward the receptivity of the healthy Nine. The Seven needs to overcome its impulsiveness by moving toward the involvement of the healthy Five. The Eight needs to overcome its egocentricity by moving toward the concern for others of the healthy Two. The Nine needs to overcome its complacency by moving toward the ambition of the healthy Three. And the One needs to overcome its inflexibility by moving toward the productivity of the healthy Seven.

In the last analysis, learning how to transcend the ego is nothing less than learning how to love. Only love has the power to save us from ourselves. Until we learn to truly love ourselves and others, there can be no hope of lasting happiness or peace or redemption. It is because we do not love ourselves properly that we lose ourselves so easily in the many illusions ego sets before us.

This is what psychology must take into account if it is to become less sterile. After all, Freud's own goal of therapy was to help a person "to work and to love." Modern psychology seems to have lost sight of how to accomplish this because it has abjured the transcendent, stopped considering values, taken no position on right and wrong, and despaired of teaching others how to live. Unless acquiring the ability to work (and hence to re-create the world) and to love (and hence to re-create the self) becomes one of the main goals of psychology, it will ultimately be a vain enterprise. Therapeutic techniques can do little lasting good unless they help us toward a recognition of where human fulfillment really lies. About that, the testimony of the greatest human beings who have ever lived bears witness that fulfillment lies in seeking the good beyond oneself.

This is as easy to say as it is difficult to practice. It seems to be part of the human condition for us to learn the most valuable lessons in life the hard way. However, only by suffering from our mistakes does knowledge become our own. Who would believe that happiness lies in the direction of self-transcendence unless he found this out for himself? We seem to need to forget what we require for happiness until we discover the truth for ourselves.

> According to the proverb, the longest way round is the shortest way home. It seems to be necessary to try to discover the secret by going somewhere in order to learn that [you already possess it]. The path always takes you round in a circle, back to the place where you stand. (Alan Watts, *The Meaning of Happiness,* 119–120.)

To put this in terms of the Enneagram, the movement we make in the Direction of Integration brings us full circle back to ourselves — "the longest way round is the shortest way home." Our fulfillment does not lie in the direction of a jealously guarded self but in the direction of self-transcendence as we learn to make room in ourselves for the other. Alan Watts expands on this. He says that even after we have applied all the psychological techniques at our disposal, we are still left unsatisfied because we have been looking in the wrong place for happiness.

> There is always something it [psychological technique] leaves unsolved, for there remains a subtle, indefinable and elusive inner discontent. . . .
> This is truly a "divine discontent" for I believe it to be what the mystics describe as the yearning of the soul for God; as St. Augustine says, "Thou hast made us for Thyself, therefore we

may not rest anywhere save in Thee." By a hundred different techniques we can adjust the details of our lives and make ourselves happy in the superficial sense of having nothing specific to be unhappy about. But techniques can only deal with details, with separate parts; something different is required to transform one's attitude to life as a whole, and to transform the whole of one's life. Without this transformation the real unhappiness remains, expressing itself in all manner of disguises, finding innumerable substitutes for God which do not work because they are always *partial* things. They are, as it were, the parts of God, but not the whole of Him. Techniques can find these parts; it can find acceptance, wealth, pleasure, experience, knowledge, and all the . . . unknown realms of the soul. But even when all these many parts are brought together, there is still something which no technical trick or device can discover, and this is the whole which is greater than the sum of its parts. (Ibid, 120–121.)

Psychology, self-help books, and the Enneagram cannot save us. They cannot make us genuinely happy or, at any rate, happy for very long, because they present partial views of human nature, each groping toward the truth in its own limited way. Of course, psychological insights can help us be more perceptive about what we are afraid of and the regular sources of our unhappiness. Psychology can help us sort out how we behave, what we typically desire, and how much of what we desire leads us into wasteful conflicts and illusions.

Although they are complicated and subtle, the personality types delineated by the Enneagram remain but crude reflections of human nature. While it is valuable to reflect on them to understand ourselves more objectively, using the Enneagram cannot provide us with any ultimate answers about ourselves, since that belongs to another realm. It cannot work magic, nor can it transform us into perfectly realized beings.

But by helping us to understand ourselves as we are, at our best and at our worst, from yet another tradition, the Enneagram reaffirms some age-old insights into human nature. In the end, however, the Enneagram is merely a tool, something useful up to a certain point, whereupon it should be put aside in favor of what cannot be expressed about human nature.

Bibliography
Credits
Index

Bibliography

Because of the unique historical transmission of the Enneagram and the nature of the personality types, there were very few sources to which I could go for material for this book. Because I wanted to ground the Enneagram personality types in modern psychology, I consulted books on psychoanalytic psychology and psychiatry. In many ways, this body of literature has been the most helpful, since it is based not only on theory but on clinical observations.

I have also consulted popular self-help books to see how other writers have approached the problem of describing personality types from different points of view. Rather than being an exhaustive bibliography of all these sources, what follows is a selected list of books I have found of interest. I recommend them to any reader who would like to know more about personality types and related areas. To one degree or another, I am indebted to them all.

Becker, Ernest. *The Denial of Death.* New York: Free Press, 1973.

Beesing, Maria, O.P., Robert J. Nogosek, C.S.C., and Patrick H. O'Leary, S.J. *The Enneagram: A Journey of Self-Discovery.* Denville, N.J.: Dimension Books, 1984.

Bennett, J. G. *Enneagram Studies.* York Beach, Me.: Samuel Weiser, 1983.

————. *Gurdjieff: Making a New World.* New York: Harper and Row, Colophon Books, 1973.

Cameron, Norman. *Personality Development and Psychopathology.* Boston: Houghton Mifflin, 1963.

De Christopher, Dorothy. Reprinted from *The Movement Newspaper* (May 1981) in *Interviews with Oscar Ichazo.* New York: Arica Institute Press, 1982.

Diagnostic and Statistical Manual of Mental Disorders, 3d ed. Washington, D.C.: American Psychiatric Association, 1980.

Feldman, Silvia. Review of Barbet Schroeder's movie *General Idi Amin Dada. Psychology Today* (December 1976).

Fenichel, Otto. *The Psychoanalytic Theory of Neurosis.* New York: W. W. Norton, 1945.

Fine, Reuben. *A History of Psychoanalysis.* New York: Columbia University Press, 1979.

Freud, Sigmund. *Character and Culture.* New York: Collier Books, 1963. Collection of articles originally published between 1907 and 1937.

————. *The Ego and the Id.* New York: W. W. Norton, 1960. Originally published in 1923.

————. *A General Introduction to Psychoanalysis.* New York: Washington Square Press, 1952. Originally published between 1915 and 1917.

————. *The Interpretation of Dreams.* New York: Avon Books, 1965. Originally published in 1900.

Fromm, Erich. *Man for Himself.* New York: Fawcett, 1965. Originally published in 1947.

Galbraith, John Kenneth. *The Anatomy of Power.* Boston: Houghton Mifflin, 1983.

Goldenson, Robert M. *The Encyclopedia of Human Behavior.* New York: Dell, 1970.

Greenberg, Jay R., and Stephen A. Mitchell. *Object Relations and Psychoanalytic Theory.* Cambridge: Harvard University Press, 1983.

Greven, Philip. *The Protestant Temperament.* New York: New American Library, 1977.

Hinsie, Leland E., and Robert J. Campbell. *Psychiatric Dictionary,* 4th ed. New York: Oxford University Press, 1970.

Horney, Karen. *Neurosis and Human Growth.* New York: W. W. Norton, 1950.

————. *The Neurotic Personality of Our Time.* New York: W. W. Norton, 1937.

———. *Our Inner Conflicts.* New York: W. W. Norton, 1945.

Jung, Carl. *Psychological Types.* Princeton: Princeton University Press, 1971. Originally published in 1921.

Keen, Sam. Reprinted from *Psychology Today* (July 1973) in *Interviews with Oscar Ichazo.* New York: Arica Institute Press, 1982.

Keirsey, David, and Marilyn Bates. *Please Understand Me.* Del Mar, Calif.: Prometheus Nemesis Books, 1978.

Kernberg, Otto. *Borderline Conditions and Pathological Narcissism.* New York: Jason Aronson, 1975.

Korda, Michael. *Power!* New York: Random House, 1975.

Leary, Timothy. *Interpersonal Diagnosis of Personality.* New York: Ronald Press, 1957.

Lilly, John C. *The Center of the Cyclone.* New York: Bantam Books, 1972.

Lilly, John C., and Joseph E. Hart. "The Arica Training," in *Transpersonal Psychologies,* ed. Charles T. Tart. New York: Harper and Row, 1975.

Lowen, Alexander. *Narcissism.* New York: Macmillan, 1983.

Maccoby, Michael. *The Gamesman.* New York: Simon and Schuster, 1976.

Maddi, Salvatore R. *Personality Theories.* Homewood, Ill.: Dorsey Press, 1968.

Malone, Michael. *Psychetypes.* New York: E. P. Dutton, 1977.

Meisser, W. W. *The Borderline Spectrum.* New York: Jason Aronson, 1984.

Metzner, Ralph. *Know Your Type.* New York: Doubleday, 1979.

Millon, Theodore. *Disorders of Personality.* New York: John Wiley, 1981.

Mullen, John Douglas. *Kierkegaard's Philosophy.* New York: New American Library, 1981.

Myers, Isabel Briggs, and Peter B. Myers. *Gifts Differing.* Palo Alto: Consulting Psychologists Press, 1980.

Nicholi, Armand M., ed. *The Harvard Guide to Modern Psychiatry.* Cambridge: Harvard University Press, 1978.

Nicoll, Maurice. *Psychological Commentaries on the Teaching of Gurdjieff and Ouspensky,* vol. 2. Boulder: Shambala, 1952.

Offit, Avodah. *The Sexual Self.* New York: Lippincott, 1977.

Ouspensky, P. D. *In Search of the Miraculous.* New York: Harcourt, Brace and World, 1949.

Rycroft, Charles. *A Critical Dictionary of Psychoanalysis.* Harmondsworth: Penguin Books, 1972.

Shapiro, David. *Neurotic Styles.* New York: Basic Books, 1965.

Speeth, Kathleen Riordan. *The Gurdjieff Work*. Berkeley: And/Or Press, 1976.

Speeth, Kathleen Riordan, and Ira Friedlander. *Gurdjieff, Seeker of the Truth*. New York: Harper and Row, 1980.

Stone, Michael H. *The Borderline Syndromes*. New York: McGraw-Hill, 1980.

Storr, Anthony. *The Art of Psychotherapy*. New York: Methuen, 1979.

———. *The Dynamics of Creation*. New York: Atheneum, 1985.

Tart, Charles, ed. *Transpersonal Psychologies*. New York: Harper and Row, 1975.

Waldberg, Michel. *Gurdjieff, An Approach to His Ideas*. London: Routledge and Kegan Paul, 1981.

Watts, Alan. *The Meaning of Happiness: The Quest for Freedom of the Spirit in Modern Psychology and the Wisdom of the East*. New York: Harper and Row, 1979.

Webb, James. *The Harmonious Circle: The Lives and Work of G. I. Gurdjieff, P. D. Ouspensky, and Their Followers*. New York: G. P. Putnam, 1980.

Credits

Index

Index 365